THE
TREK
UNIVERSAL
INDEX

Other Trek titles available from Boxtree

THE NEXT GENERATION TECHNICAL MANUAL

EXPLORING DEEP SPACE AND BEYOND

CAPTAINS' LOGS – THE COMPLETE TREK VOYAGES

CAPTAIN'S LOG SUPPLEMENT – THE NEXT GENERATION 6TH

SEASON GUIDEBOOK

THE DEEP SPACE LOGBOOK – A FIRST SEASON COMPANION

And Coming Soon . . .

CAPTAIN'S LOGS SUPPLEMENT II – THE NEXT GENERATION 7TH

SEASON GUIDEBOOK

THE LAW OF TREK

GREAT BIRDS OF THE GALAXY

THE MAKING OF THE TREK FILMS

THE TREK
UNIVERSAL
INDEX

THOMAS MAXWELL

BXTREE

First published in the UK in 1994 by
BOXTREE LIMITED
Broadwall House
21 Broadwall
London SE1 9PL

10 9 8 7 6 5 4 3 2 1

Front cover photos:
(top and left) ©G. Trindl/Shooting Star
(right) ©Timothy White/Onyx
Back cover photos:
(left and middle) ©G. Trindl/Shooting Star
(right) ©David Strick/Onyx

ISBN 1 85283 398 X

Cover designed by Paul Nicosea
Text designed by Design 23

Printed and bound by Redwood Books,
Trowbridge, England

A catalogue record for this book is available from
The British Library

CONTENTS

THE TREK UNIVERSAL INDEX
· · · · · · · · ·
AN INTRODUCTION

Over the past three decades, *Star Trek* has arisen from its own ashes so often that it would give the Phoenix a run for its money.

It began with "The Cage", a 1964 television pilot created by Gene Roddenberry that was rejected by NBC as being too cerebral for the television audience. The network nonetheless gave the green light for a second pilot, an unprecedented move at that time.

"Where No Man Has Gone Before", which followed a year later, provided the necessary action-adventure quota with a few solid ideas thrown in for good measure, and *Star Trek* was scheduled for the 1966 television season – which almost became its last. The show, while somewhat embraced by critics, was low rated and NBC discussed the possibility of cancellation, but a letter-writing campaign stayed the execution. The ratings remained the same during the second season, however, and cancellation was imminent until an even stronger campaign gave the network no choice but to renew it for a third – and ultimately final – year.

Star Trek went off the air in 1969, but refused to die. The reruns grew more popular, fans began holding conventions to celebrate the show and NBC okayed a 1973 Saturday morning animated spin-off that lasted two years. That *should* have been the end of the show, but the phenomenon continued to grow. Finally, in 1979, Paramount Pictures premiered *Star Trek: The Motion Picture*, a $44-million disappointment that was dismissed by critics and the fans.

Again, this should have been the death knell for the final frontier, but the studio, taking account of the sheer number of people who had gone to see the film, decided to bankroll a more modestly budgeted sequel, *Star Trek II: The Wrath of Khan* which, in turn, begat entries three through six, *The Search For Spock*, *The Voyage Home*, *The Final Frontier* and *The Undiscovered Country*.

Realizing that there was a finite number of films that could be produced starring the classic cast, Paramount decided to syndicate a television series featuring an all-new crew. Gone were Captain James T. Kirk, Mr. Spock, Dr. Leonard "Bones" McCoy and their comrades, and in their place was a bald English-Frenchman named Captain Jean Luc Picard, an android named Data, a blind navigator (figure that one out) and a female doctor. No one expected it to last a year.

Surprisingly, *Star Trek: The Next Generation*, which has wrapped its seventh and last season, brought new life to the phenomenon, expanding the mythos and paving the way for a new series of films (the first, *Star Trek: Generations*, will be released Christmas 1994) as well as the spin-off series *Star Trek: Deep Space Nine* and *Star Trek: Voyager*.

During the past 30 years, audiences – with the help of the starships *Enterprise* and the DS9 space station – have explored innumerable strange new worlds, and sought out a wide variety of new lives and new civilizations. The *Trek Universal Index* is a guide to that ever-expanding universe.

Broken into five sections, the A-Z encyclopedia-like listings provide a detailed look at *Star Trek's* "Aliens", "Characters", "Planets & places", "Spaceships", and "Artifacts, Plants, Plauges, Phrases, Procedures, Substances, Beliefs, Designations & Devices".

For those wishing to gain a fuller understanding of the Star Trek mythos, *The Trek Universal Index* is an indispensable guidebook.

THOMAS MAXWELL
FEBRUARY 1994

Key
Entries in bold lettering = 24th Century
All other entries = 23rd Century

PLANETS AND PLACES

ACAMAR THREE: Ruled by the Sovereign Marouk whom Picard visits when the Federation wants to reunite the Acamarians with the Gatherers. (see "The Vengeance Factor")

ACHRADY SEVEN: Referred to in "Captain's Holiday" by Troi as a planet Lwaxana was visiting.

ACTOS FOUR: An oligarchy where youths have something similar to the Betazoid grace ritual. (See "Manhunt")

ALCYONE: A planet whose residents were believed to have killed the last of the Terellian plague carriers, until a ship of them is encountered by the Enterprise. (See "Haven")

ALDEA: A legendary planet long hidden from the Federation. Located in the Epsilon Mynos system, this planet is inhabited by a race protected by a Custodian computer. The Custodian cloaks the planet from the outside universe, but this drains its ozone layer and subjects the people to radiation which makes them sterile. They make themselves known to the Enterprise because their race is dying out and they need children to populate their race since they are now apparently sterile. They kidnap some Enterprise children but the matter is eventually solved when it is shown that the Aldeans sterility results from radiation poisoning caused by their depletion of their world's ozone layer. (See "When The Bough Breaks")

ALDEBARAN COLONY: The planet where the Enterprise picks up Dr. Elizabeth Dehner. (See "Where No Man Has Gone Before")

ALDRON FOUR: The Enterprise heads here after departing Relva. (See "Coming Of Age")

ALPHA 177: A freezing cold planet where a landing team nearly meets its doom during a transporter problem. (See "The Enemy Within")

ALPHA CARINAE II: The world which is to serve as the test of the M-5 computer's judgment capacities. (See "The Ultimate Computer")

ALPHA CARINAE V: The world where the Enterprise encounters the Drella. (See "Wolf In The Fold")

ALPHA CENTAURI: A star system; location of Zefrem Cochrane's home world. (See "Metamorphosis")

ALPHA CYGNUS NINE: The location of a planet where Sarek negotiated a treaty, as mentioned in "Sarek."

ALPHA LEONIS: A planet the Enterprise takes medical supplies to. (See "The Vengeance Factor")

ALPHA PROXIMA II: One of the planets visited by the Jack-the-Ripper entity before its encounter with Scotty and the Enterprise crew. (See "Wolf In The Fold")

ALTAIR III: A planet visited by Riker when he served on the U.S.S. Hood. He would not allow his captain to join an Away Team. (See "Encounter At Farpoint")

ALTAIR VI: The Enterprise's destination until Spock's attack of Pon Farr diverts them to Vulcan. (See "Amok Time")

ALTERNATIVE WARP: The passageway between our universe and the anti-matter universe. (See "The Alternative Factor")

AMARGOSA DIASPORA: A star region which the Enterprise is sent to map. (See "Schisms")

ANDROMEDA: A galaxy, home of the ancient race that built the androids of Planet Mudd, as well as the home of the Kelvans, who plan on moving out due to slowly (very slowly) increasing radiation levels. (See "By Any Other Name")

ANGEL ONE: A planet run by a matriarchy. Men are considered second-class citizens, as Riker learns much to his dismay there. When an escape pod from the Federation ship *Odin* lands on that world, the leaders consider these men a threat to their way of life and intend to execute them. (See "Angel One")

ANGOSIA: Ruled by Prime Minister Nayrok, the Angosians have dedicated themselves to developing their intellect, but following the Tarsian War they force their genetically enhanced veterans to live apart from normal society, which creates civil unrest. (See "The Hunted")

ANTEDE THREE: The homeworld of the Antedians, an aquatic race. They hate spaceflight and travel in a catatonic state. (See "The Hunted")

ANTICA: A planet whose people are wolf-like humanoids, at war with the reptilians of nearby Selay, located in the Beta Renner system. (See "Lonely Among Us")

ANTOS IV: A peaceful planet whose inhabitants taught their techniques of shapeshifting to Garth of Izar in order to save his life — only to have him turn against them when he decides to take over the known universe. (See "Whom Gods Destroy")

APNEX SEA: Located on Romulus. Jarok's home overlooks the Apnex Sea. (See "The Defector")

ARCHER FOUR: In the alternate timeline, when the Federation and the Klingon Empire were at war, the Klingons suffered a major defeat on this world. When time resumes its normal course, Picard orders the *Enterprise* to set its destination towards this world. (see "Yesterday's Enterprise")

ARDANA: The planet which is the only source of Zienite. (See "The Cloud Minders")

ARGELIUS II: A peaceful planet invaded by the Jack-the-Ripper entity. There are still punitive laws there which remain unrevoked because there have been no crimes for centuries — no one has had to think about the laws for so long. When Scotty is framed as the killer while on Argelius (a popular vacation world), ancient psychic techniques must be used to discover the truth and save him from the old,

and potentially brutal, laws. (See "Wolf In The Fold")

ARGOLIS CLUSTER: The *Enterprise* is en route to this region of space when it picks up a new crew member, Amanda Rogers. (See "True Q")

ARGUS X: The planet where Kirk is destined to encounter his old foe, the vampiric cloud creature. (See "Obsession")

ARIANNUS: A planet saved from a deadly bacterial plague by the *Enterprise*. (See "Let That Be Your Last Battlefield")

ARKARIA BASE: A Federation outpost above which the Remmler Array hangs in orbit. (See "Starship Mine")

ARLOPH NINE: When the *U.S.S. Charleston* is called here, the *Enterprise* must take the revived 20th Century humans back to Earth itself. (See "The Neutral Zone")

ARMUS IX: Preparing for his diplomatic activities on Angel One, Riker recalls a visit to Armus IX, where he wore feathers to appease the local authorities. (See "Angel One")

ARNEB: A star visible from 'aucdet Nine. (See "The Child")

ARRET: The world where only three survivors — Henoch, Sargon, and Thalassa — remain in a subterranean vault, to be found many millennia after their world's destruction by Kirk and crew. (See "Return To Tomorrow")

ASPHIA: The *U.S.S. Odin* was wrecked here; some crew members escape to Angel One. (See "Angel One")

ASTRAL-FIVE ANNEX: When the thousand-year-old-Promellian battlecruiser *Cleponji* is discovered, Picard tells Data to inform the annex about it. (See "Booby Trap")

'AUCDET NINE: A site where strains of a plasma plague are kept in storage. It is a Federation Medical Collection Station supervised by Lt. Commander Hester Dealt. (See "The Child")

AVEDA THREE: A planet whose colonists included Beverly Crusher when she was a child. She survived a major disaster there, and learned herbal healing skills from her grandmother — the first step on her road to the study of medicine. (See "Arsenal Of Freedom")

BABEL: A neutral world where interplanetary conferences are held. (See "Journey To Babel")

BARZAN II: The planet near which the Barzan Wormhole is discovered. It appears to be the first stable wormhole ever discovered, but this turns out not to be the case. (See "The Price")

BARZAN WORMHOLE: A transdimensional gateway to another point in the galaxy. Initially this is believed to be the first stable wormhole ever found. It opens every 233 minutes due to radiation building up in the accretion disk. At first it is a shortcut to the Gamma Quadrant to a point which would otherwise have taken 100 years to reach at warp 9, thus opening up whole new vistas of commerce and exploration. But after a time the wormhole abruptly changes the location of its exit point, making it valueless and unreliable. (See "The Price")

BELTANE IX: Where Jake Kurland intended to escape with his stolen shuttlecraft. (See "Coming Of Age")

BENECIA COLONY: The planet where Janice Lester plans to abandon her body after she's trapped James Kirk's mind in it, and taken over his place. (See "Turnabout Intruder")

BENZAR: The homeworld of the Benzites. This is an odd race whose primary concern is an attempt to impress people. (See "A Matter Of Honor")

BERSALLIS THREE: A planet plagued with firestorms. When a Federation outpost is threatened by a greater than normal flareup of the firestorms, the *Enterprise* must rescue them. (See "Lessons")

BETA AGNI TWO: The site of a Federation colony where the water is contaminated with tricyanate so that it must be treated with hytritium. The contamination was purposely done by Kivas Fajo in order to lure the *Enterprise* there so he could kidnap Data. (See "The Most Toys")

BETA CASSIUS SYSTEM: Location of the planet known as Haven. (See "Haven")

BETA GERMINORIUM: A star in the system where the *Enterprise* encounters Apollo. (See "Who Mourns For Adonais?")

BETA KUPSIK: The next stop of the *Enterprise* after it leaves Starbase Montgomery. (See "The Icarus Factor")

BETA MAGELLAN SYSTEM: Location of the planet Bynaeus, home of the Bynars. (See "11001001")

BETA NIOBE: The star about to blow up and destroy the planet Sarpeidon; mistaken for Sarpeids, Kirk, Spock and McCoy are sent back in time. (See "All Our Yesterdays")

BETA PORTALAN: A system ravaged by flying parasites that resemble fried eggs. (See "Operation: Annihilate")

BETA RENNER SYSTEM: Location of the warring worlds of Selay and Antica. (See "Lonely Among Us")

BETA SIX: Where the Enterprise is headed when Trelane gums up the works. (See "Squire Of Gothos")

BETA STROMGREN: A star claimed by the Romulans where the life form Tin Man is discovered. (See "Tin Man")

BETA XIIA: The planet where the *U.S.S. Archon* went down a hundred years before Kirk's arrival. (See "Return Of The Archons")

BETA ZED: Home planet of the Betazoid race, and a member of the Federation. (See "Haven")

BILAR: An inhabitant of Beta XIIA, who attacks Tula. (See "Return Of The Archons")

BLACK CLUSTER: A region of space where the wreckage of the Vico is found. The cluster is capable of generating graviton wave front feedback in response to the presence of a starship's shields. (See "Hero Worship")

BLACK STAR: The super-dense stellar body that throws the *Enterprise* back into the 20th Century. (See "Tomorrow Is Yesterday")

BLUE PARROT CAFÉ: A galaxy-famous bar on Sarona Eight. (See "We'll Always Have Paris")

BOKARA SIX: While Deanna Troi was attending a neuro-psychology seminar there, she was abducted and surgically altered to look like a Romulan. (See "Face Of The Enemy")

BONESTELL RECREATION FACILITY: This facility at Starbase Earhart once attracted galactic riffraff such as Nausicaans. (See "The Samaritan Snare") It is an outpost where Jean-Luc Picard almost loses his life when he gets into a fight with three Nausicaans. (See "Tapestry")

BORATIS SYSTEM: Of the thirteen colonies in the area, the first was established on Boratis III. (See "The Emissary")

BORETH: A world in the Klingon Empire where the followers of Kahless study the history of this legendary Klingon warrior and await his return. As it turns out, Kahless does return to life on this very world. (See "Rightful Heir")

BOURBON STREET: A famous street in New Orleans, on Earth; Riker is diverted by the Bynars with a holodeck simulation of a Bourbon Street bar. (See "11001001")

BRASLOTA SYSTEM: In the Oneamisu sector, the Starfleet Battle Simulation between the *U.S.S. Hathaway* and the *Enterprise* took place here. (See "Peak Performance")

BRE'EL FOUR: This planet was threatened by the falling of its moon from orbit. The *Enterprise* attempted unsuccessfully to intervene. Finally Q used his omnipotent powers to restore the asteroidal moon to its proper stable orbit. (See "Deja Q")

BREKKA: Located in the Delos system, this planet's people manufacture Felicium. This drug was originally useful in dealing with a plague on the nearby world of Ornara; but the Ornaran plague is long gone, and the drug is now sold merely because the Ornarans are all addicted. The Brekkans know this and take advantage without guilt. (See "Symbiosis")

BROWDER FOUR: The destination of the *Enterprise* when it leaves Cor Caroli Five until the ship is sidetracked by an imitation Picard. (See "Allegiance")

BYNAEUS: The world of the Bynars, who are paired for life and coexist as part of a worldwide organic computer. (See "11001001")

CAFÉ DES ARTISTES: The Parisian establishment where Jean-Luc Picard missed his date with Janice Mannheim; years later he made the date, thanks to the holodeck. (See "We'll Always Have Paris")

CAMUS II: The site of Janet Lester's final archaeological researches prior to her attempt to steal James Kirk's body. (See "Turnabout Intruder")

CAPELLA IV: A planet with rich mining potential, closely regarded by the Klingons and the Federation alike. (See "The Cloud Minders")

CARRAYA SYSTEM: The area of space where the Romulans have a secret prison planet where the survivors of the Khitomer Massacre (and their offspring) have lived for many years. (See "Birthright")

CELTRIS THREE: The Federation believes that a secret lab exists on this planet and Captain Picard leads an infiltration team to investigate the matter. (See "Chain Of Command")

CENTERPLACE: Lutan's luxurious home as Primary of Ligon II; he probably loses it after he is deposed, since it probably belongs to his ex-wife. (See "Code Of Honor")

CERBERUS II: A planet where a near-mythical means of rejuvenation has become a reality. To work properly, the cure for aging must be taken according to a long-term schedule; but when Admiral Jameson obtains the drugs, he takes them all at once to accelerate the process, which ultimately has disastrous results. (See "Too Short A Season")

CESTUS III: Location of the Federation settlement destroyed by the Gorn advance. (See "Arena")

CETI ALPHA V: The planet where James Kirk left Khan and his followers, as well as Lieutenant McGivers. When the *Reliant*, under Captain Clark Terrell and Mr. Chekov stop over there, mistaking it for Ceti Alpha VI, Khan kidnaps them and hijacks their vessel in order to escape and seek his vengeance against James T. Kirk. (See "Space Seed" and "Star Trek II: The Wrath Of Khan")

CHALNA: Picard visited this world when he was

Captain of the *Stargazer*. This is the homeworld of Esoqq and the Chalnoth people. (See "Allegiance")

CHAMRA VORTEX: An asteroid in this region is where Croden has hidden his daughter. He tricks Odo into taking him there by claiming that he knows that a race of metamorphs lives there. (See "Vortex")

CHANDRA FIVE: Tam Elbrun was the sole Federation delegate assigned to this world. It is the homeworld of the Chandrans. (See "Tin Man")

CHERON: Homeworld of Bele and Lokai, destroyed ages ago by insane social beliefs; these two members of their extinct race survive to battle it out on their dead world. (See "Let That Be Your Last Battlefield")

CHERON: A battle was fought here which was a Federation victory over the Romulan Empire, apparently in the old Romulan war referred to in "Balance Of Terror." But this defeat was so humiliating that the modern Romulans still remember it. (See "The Defector") This is apparently not the same world as the homeworld of Bele and Lokai.

CHULA, VALLEY OF: A scenic locale to be found on the planet Romulus. (See "The Defector")

COALITION OF MADINA: The twin worlds of Streleb and Atlek located in the system Omega Sagitta Twelve. (See "The Outrageous Okona")

COLONY 5: The destination of the *Enterprise* when it picks up Charles Evans, a.k.a. Charlie X. (See "Charlie X")

COLTAIR FOUR: A world subjected to an unusual temporal distortion. (See "We'll Always Have Paris")

COR CAROLI FIVE: When Picard is imprisoned with other beings, one of them reveals knowledge of the mission of the *Enterprise* to this world, a mission which the being could not possibly have known unless it were reading his mind. The *Enterprise* had successfully eradicated a phyrox plague on this planet before leaving to rendezvous with the *U.S.S. Hood*. (See "Allegiance")

CORINTH IV: Location of a Starbase. (See "Man Trap")

CORNELIAN SYSTEM: When the *Enterprise* is trapped in the mysterious void, Picard has a course set for this system. (See "Where Silence Has Lease")

COUNCIL CHAMBER: One of the two last free spaces on the overpopulated world of Gideon. (See "Mark Of Gideon")

CYGNET XIV: The planet dominated by women; their technicians gave the *Enterprise* the female voice which plagued James Kirk. (See "Tomorrow Is Yesterday")

DALED FOUR: A world upon which live shapeshifters known as Allasomorphs, one of which, named Salia, is returning there from Klavdia III after being gone for 16 years. (See "The Dauphin")

DARAN V: The planet threatened by the asteroid/spaceship Yonada. (See "For The World Is Hollow And I Have Touched The Sky")

DARWIN SCIENCE STATION: The origin of the old-age-inducing plague, brought about by some genetically-engineered children. It is under the supervision of Dr. Sara Kingsley. (See "Unnatural Selection")

DAYSTROM ANNEX: Located on Galor Four, it is an annex of the Daystrom Institute of Technology. (See "The Offspring")

DAYSTROM INSTITUTE OF TECHNOLOGY: Named after Dr. Richard Daystrom, the 23rd Century scientist who invented the computer system used on the *Enterprise-A*.

DAYSTROM INSTITUTE THEORETICAL PROPULSION GROUP: One part of the renowned Daystrom Institute Of Technology. Dr. Leah Brahms graduated from this school. (See "Booby Trap")

DEEP SPACE NINE: The designation given to the space station orbiting the planet Bajor. It was formerly occupied by the Cardassians but is now run jointly by the Federation and the Bajorans.

DE LAURE BELT: An area overwhelmed by hyperonic radiation, it is the location of Tau Cygna V. (See "The Ensigns of Command")

DELOS SYSTEM: Location of the neighboring worlds of Ornara and Brekka. (See "Symbiosis")

DELPHI ARDU: Once an outlying part of the long-dead Tkon Empire, this planet still hosts a fully functional outpost with a formidable sentry. (See "The Last Outpost")

DELTA-05: This science station was located near the Neutral Zone and was destroyed by an unknown force, later believed to have possibly been the Borg. (See "The Neutral Zone")

DELTA QUADRANT: When an *Enterprise* shuttle and a Ferengi pod travel through a wormhole, they come out here, 200 light years from their point of origin. (See "The Price")

DELTA RANA IV: The site of a Federation colony where all but two of its eleven thousand inhabitants were wiped out in an unprovoked attack. (See "The Survivors")

DELTA RANA SYSTEM: The planet Delta Rana IV is located here. (See "The Survivors")

DELTA VEGA: The site of the final battle against Gary Mitchell, a desolate mining station manned only by robots. (See "Where No Man Has Gone Before")

DENEB: A planet Harry Mudd had best avoid: he faces several death penalties on this world, after selling rights he had no right to sell. (See "Mudd's Women")

DENEB IV: The planet inhabited by the Bandi. It is also called Farpoint. The Bandi captured a powerful alien and made it construct Farpoint Station. (See "Encounter At Farpoint")

DENEUS THREE: An archeological site here marks the discovery of Iconian relics. (See "Contagion")

DENEVA: Home of a million colonists, it is attacked by flying parasites which kill many colonists — including James Kirk's brother, Sam Kirk. This colony is a key link in Federation commerce routes. (See "Operation: Annihilate")

DENKIRI ARM: A Barzan probe wound up in this section of the Gamma Quadrant. (See "The Price")

DENORIOS BELT: The region of space near Bajor where the Bajoran wormhole is located.

DENUBIAN ALPS: An alien mountain range, suitable for skiing; Wesley does just that on a holodeck simulation of the region. (See "Angel One")

DEVIDIA TWO: The planet where a time portal is located which leads to 19th Century Earth and poses a threat to the people of that era. (See "Time's Arrow")

DEVIDIAN TIME PORTAL: A portal leading to 19th Century Earth which the Devidians use to prey on the life force of human beings. (See "Time's Arrow")

DONATU V: A region contested by the Federation and the Klingons, where a battle once took place. (See "The Trouble With Tribbles")

DREMA FOUR: Located in the Selcundi Drema system, it is the site of the single largest dilithium deposit ever discovered. These dilithium crystals have formed lattices resulting in geological instabilities. The *Enterprise* is able to relieve the problems which have been causing these disturbances as earthquakes threatened the primitive civilization on Drema Four.

DYSON SPHERE: An immense sphere built around a star approximately 90 million miles away so that the sphere is 180 million miles in diameter. (See "Relics")

DYTALIX-B: An isolated mining planet located in the Mira System. Picard is briefed here by officers concerned about a conspiracy in Starfleet; he thinks they're paranoid, but discovers that they are not. (See "Conspiracy")

EARTH: Home world of humanity, located in the Sol System. Jean-Luc Picard is from France. Starfleet is headquartered in San Francisco. Starfleet Academy is based on Earth as well. (See "Conspiracy", "The Best of Both Worlds", "Family", "The First Duty")

EDEN: A legendary planet which is found in Romulan space by Dr. Sevrin and his band of seekers; although truly beautiful and Eden-like, its fruits are utterly poisonous, killing in an instant and making Sevrin's quest a truly tragic one. (See "The Way To Eden")

EKOS: The world, in the M43 Alpha system, where historian John Gill violates the Prime Directive and creates a culture based on the Third Reich. (See "Patterns Of Force")

ELAS: Located in the Tellan planetary system, this is

the home of Elaan and her race, a fairly unsophisticated, mean-spirited people looked down upon by neighboring planets. (See "Elaan Of Troyius")

ELBA II: Its deadly atmosphere is poisonous to all life forms, but underneath a force field this harsh world is home to the insane and the criminal too dangerous for most modern treatments. (See "Whom Gods Destroy")

EMILA TWO: Destination of the *Enterprise* following the incident in the Tanugan system. (See "A Matter Of Perspective")

EMINIAR VII: Located in the star system NGC 321, this planet has been involved in a computerized war with the neighboring world Vendikar for centuries. (See "A Taste Of Armageddon")

ENDICOR SYSTEM: The *Enterprise* is three days away from this system when a time vortex nearly destroys the vessel. (See "Time Squared")

ENNAN SIX: When Dr. Pulaski attends Will Riker's dinner party, she brings along some ale which is the type made on Ennan Six. (See "Time Squared")

EPSILON INDI: Star system containing the world of Triacus. (See "And The Children Shall Lead") The planet Andor is located in this star system. (See "The Child")

EPSILON MYNOS SYSTEM: Location of the planet Aldea. (See "Where The Bough Breaks")

EPSILON NINE: The space station destroyed by V'ger as it moves through space on a direct heading to Earth. Epsilon Nine is the station which detects the destruction of three Klingon ships by V'ger and transmits the pictures back to Starfleet Operations. (See "Star Trek: The Motion Picture")

EPSILON NINE SECTOR: The *Enterprise* is slated to conduct an astronomical survey here of a newly discovered pulsar cluster. (See "Samaritan Snare")

EXCALBIA: The world occupied by rock-like creatures, a carbon-based life form. (See "The Savage Curtain")

EXO III: Site of Dr. Roger Korby's discovery of an ancient dead race and their deadly android technology. He himself builds an android body and spends his last days in it. Exo III has a dangerously

frigid atmosphere, but Korby lives underground and is thus protected. (See "What Are Little Girls Made Of?")

FABRINA: Before its nova, this star supported eight orbiting planets. (See "For The World Is Hollow And I Have Touched The Sky")

FAIRMONT HOTEL: When Dixon Hill's secretary sees Picard in his Starfleet costume, she thinks that Hill has been working as a bellboy at this hotel. (See "The Big Goodbye")

FARPOINT STATION: The first stop of the *Enterprise* after Jean-Luc Picard becomes Captain. He goes to Farpoint Station to pick up his new First Officer, Lt. William Riker. The Bandi built this establishment to impress the Federation, but by enslaving an alien being to create it they make a big mistake. (See "Encounter At Farpoint")

FARSPACE STARBASE EARHART: In the days before the Klingons joined the Federation, this was the only "frontier" outpost. It is also where the Bonestell Red Facility is located. (See "Samaritan Snare")

FICUS SECTOR: Although there is no record of any Earth colonies existing here, it turns out that there are two. The fifth planet in the system is a Class M planet. (See "Up The Long Ladder")

GAGARIN FOUR: The Darwin Genetic Research Station is located here. (See "Unnatural Selection")

GAL GA'THONG, THE FIRE FALLS OF: A place of exceeding beauty on the planet of Romulus, referred to by Jarok. (See "The Defector")

GALOR FOUR: The location of another annex of the Daystrom Institute, as well as of a Starfleet research center. The Starfleet officer, Haftel, is from there and plans to return there with Lal. (See "The Offspring")

GALORNDON CORE: A Romulan scout ship

crashes on this world. The atmosphere is filled with charged particle precipitation which interferes with the use of such devices as tricorders, communicators and even Geordi's Visor. (See "The Enemy")

GAMILON V: The gravitational field of this planet captures a 300-year-old space barge filled with radioactive wastes which threaten the population of Gamilon V. Using construction modules, the *Enterprise* attaches thrusters to the barge in order to steer it into the system's sun, but the barge begins to break up, and the *Enterprise* must tow it with a tractor beam through an asteroid belt, while radiation levels on the ship approach lethal levels. (See "Final Mission")

GAMMA CANARIS N: The small planetary body where Zefrem and Nancy Cochrane are destined to spend their final days. (See "Metamorphosis")

GAMMA 400 SYSTEM: Where Starbase 12 is located. (See "Space Seed")

GAMMA HROMI II: The Gatherer encampment led by Brull was located here. (See "The Vengeance Factor")

GAMMA HYDRA IV: An Earthlike world near Starbase 10 afflicted by the accelerated aging disease caused by radiation from the tail of a passing comet. (See "The Deadly Years")

GAMMA QUADRANT: An expanse of space 200 light years from Barzan II which was briefly reached through the Barzan wormhole. (See "The Price") This region of space became permanently accessible through the Bajoran wormhole. It is 70,000 light years from Bajor, so the wormhole opens up the Gamma Quadrant as a trading route. (See "Emissary")

GAMMA SEVEN SECTOR: This was being patrolled by the *U.S.S. Langtree* (See "Unnatural Selection")

GAMMA 7A SYSTEM: An inhabited solar system completely annihilated by the giant space amoeba. (See "The Immunity Syndrome")

GAMMA TAURI IV: Planet where some Ferengi stole a K-9 Converter, leading to their pursuit by the *Enterprise*. (See "The Last Outpost")

GAMMA TRIANGULI VI: The world whose people are ruled by the computer Vaal; a luxurious tropical haven. (See "The Apple")

GAMMA II: The unmanned station where Kirk, Uhura and Chekov are abducted by the Providers of Triskelion. (See "The Gamesters Of Triskelion")

GARON II: Ensign Ro Laren was court marshaled and sent to prison for an incident on Garon Two in which she disobeyed orders, resulting in the death of members of her Away Team. (See "Ensign Ro")

GAULT: The world where Worf was raised by his human foster parents after he survived the massacre at Khitomer; a farming world. (See "Heart Of Glory")

GEMARIS FIVE: The homeworld of the Gemarians. A dispute was mediated there by Picard. (See "Captain's Holiday")

GENESIS: The name of a planet created from the material of a nebula. It is also the name of the device which, when detonated, created this unstable planet. (See "Star Trek II: The Wrath Of Khan")

GENOME BIOSPHERE: Aaron Conor, the leader of this closed society on Moab Four, believes that their biosphere can withstand quakes measuring 8.7 magnitude. But Data reveals that the stresses caused by the approaching stellar core fragment will create disturbances beyond that level. (See "The Masterpiece Society")

GHORUSDA: This is the site of the Ghorusda disaster. The Federation sent Tam Elbrun to deal with the society. (See "Tin Man")

GIDEON: The most overpopulated planet in the known universe. Practically immortal but ideologically opposed to birth control, the people of Gideon lure James Kirk to a complete replica of the *Enterprise*. Their goal, which succeeds, is to have him introduce disease organisms into their midst, a radical solution that will trim their population once the bacteria from Kirk, which he is used to, make their way through the defenseless immune systems of the people of Gideon. (See "Mark Of Gideon")

GLYRHOND: A Bajoran river whose course was diverted by the Cardassians during the occupation. As a result the course of the river was pushed 20 kilometers west of its original location, which affects the terms of the Paqu/Navot treaty wherein the border between their territories has been determined by the course of the river Glyrhond. (See "The Storyteller")

GOL: The high plateau on Vulcan where one goes to the Masters to undertake the ritual of Kolinahr. (See "Star Trek: The Motion Picture")

GOTHOS: Trelane's artificial planet, which he created solely for his own amusement. (See "Squire Of Gothos")

GRAVES WORLD: Dr. Ira Graves and Kareen Brianon, his assistant, live here. When Dr. Graves is near death, the *Enterprise* is summoned by him so that he can carry out a secret plan he has in mind. (See "The Schizoid Man")

HALL OF AUDIENCES: The location of Landru on Beta XIIA. (See "Return Of The Archons")

HANOLI SYSTEM: In the mid 23rd Century a rupture in space occurred there and when the rupture expanded the system was destroyed. A similar rupture appears near Bajor. (See "If Wishes Were Horses")

HAVEN: A planet which the *Enterprise* arrives at where Troi discovers that her marriage party is waiting for her. Located in the Beta Cassius System, this planet is, as its name suggests, a truly idyllic locale in the galaxy. Its peace seems threatened with the approach of the last Terellian plague ship. Its government in headed by one Valeda Innis, the First Electorine. (See "Haven")

H-CLASS PLANETS: The Sheliak Corporate can choose to have all humans evacuated from such worlds which are in disputed areas according to the terms of the Treaty of Armens. (See "The Ensigns Of Command")

HIGHWAY 949: The road where the alien agents 201 and 347 die in a wreck on their mission to McKinley Rocket Base. (See "Assignment: Earth")

HOLBERG 917G: The planet purchased by the immortal Flint, a.k.a. Brack, to get away from the mortality of others — only to discover his own. (See Requiem For Methuselah")

HURKOS THREE: When Ral was 19, he relocated to this non-aligned world. (See "The Price")

ICARUS 4: A comet the fleeing Romulans use in their efforts to lose the *Enterprise.* (See "Balance Of Terror")

ICONIA: Located in the Neutral Zone, this is the homeworld of the Iconians. The coordinates of the world are 227 mark 359. A dead planet whose lost civilization appears to have been bombed out 200,000 years earlier. The planet is located near the Romulan Neutral Zone. (See "Contagion")

ICOR NINE: At the Astrophysics Center on this planet a symposium was held on Rogue Star Clusters. (See "Captain's Holiday")

IDINI STAR CLUSTER: A cluster that lies in the *Enterprise*'s path on its way to Mordan IV with Admiral Jameson. (See "Too Short A Season")

IDRAN: A star in the Gamma Quadrant which is 70,000 light years from Bajor. (See "Emissary")

IGO SECTOR: The *U.S.S. Yosemite* is lost in this sector and the *Enterprise* is dispatched to search for it. The *Yosemite* may be lost in a plasma streamer it was sent to observe. (See "Realm Of Fear")

ILLICON: One of the worlds affected by a strange time distortion. (See "We'll Always Have Paris")

INDRI EIGHT: A planet which Prof. Galen was going to visit as part of a secret project he was working on. When Captain Picard has the *Enterprise* investigate that world, they find that someone has blasted it with powerful weapons so that the atmosphere is being consumed by a plasma reaction. (See "The Chase")

INGRAHAM B: A planet devastated by flying parasites two years before they reached Deneva and killed many colonists there, including Kirk's brother. (See "Operation: Annihilate")

INTERGALACTIC SPACE: A strange, surreal region which can sometimes be reached when a vessel goes beyond Warp 9.5, well beyond recommended safety margins. Humans lose control of their senses in this bizarre place; Medusans do not. (See "Is There In Truth No Beauty")

IOTIA: The planet forever altered by the accidental

leaving behind of the book *Chicago Mobs of the Twenties* (see **Intrepid, U.S.S.**), it developed a culture based on philosophies best represented by the likes of Al Capone. Kirk manages to get matters back on track by unifying the rival gangs, but is less than pleased to learn that McCoy accidentally left a communicator on Iotia — who knows what the Iotians will do with this jump in technological information? (See "A Piece Of The Action")

IRAATAN FIVE: Kivas Fajo was educated there. (See "All The Toys")

ISIS: Where the *Enterprise* heads once it has concluded its business on Mordan IV. (See "Too Short A Season")

IZAR: The planet that is the birthplace of the famed military mastermind-turned-madman, Garth. (See "Whom Gods Destroy")

JANARIAN FALLS: A beautiful natural wonder on the planet Betazed and a place where Will Riker and Deanna Troi liked to go when he was stationed on that world. (See "Second Chances")

JANUS VI: The planet where Federation miners disturbed the Horta and suffered severe casualties before the truth of the matter — that the Horta was defending her children — was uncovered by Spock. (See "Devil In The Dark")

JARADA: A reclusive and precise race of insect derivation; Picard must learn a tongue-twisting greeting in their language and deliver it perfectly in order to win their alliance with the Federation. (See "The Long Goodbye")

JERADDO: The fifth moon of Bajor. When Bajor institutes a large-scale energy transfer experiment involving the tapping of the molten core, all of the inhabitants of Jeraddo must be evacuated. (See "Progress")

JOURET FOUR: The New Providence colony, consisting of 900 inhabitants, was located there until it was destroyed by the Borg. A magnetic resonance, or trace, is found in the blasted remains. (See "The Best Of Both Worlds")

KABATRIS: Another planet where Riker dressed in accordance with local customs. (See "Angel One")

KAELON-2: A planet where an individual must commit ritual suicide when they reach the Age of the Resolution — their 60th birthday. (See "Half A Life")

KALDRA FOUR: The planet to which a group of Ullians are being taken aboard the *Enterprise*. (See "Violations")

KALEB SECTOR: Where the Romulan warbird Kahzara is ordered to go so that a secret transfer of Romulan defectors can be made. (See "Face Of The Enemy")

KATAAN: A planet with no spaceflight. When Picard is hit by a beam from a strange space probe, he awakens a thousand years in the past on this planet. All life was destroyed on this world one thousand years ago when that system's star went nova. (See "The Inner Light")

KAVIS ALPHA FOUR: When the Nanites are removed from the *Enterprise*, they are relocated to this world. (See "Evolution")

KAVIS ALPHA SECTOR: Once every 196 years a neutron star absorbs material from the red giant and then explodes. (See "Evolution")

KAZIS BINARY SYSTEM: Where the *Enterprise* finds a capsule containing cryogenically frozen 20th Century Americans; Dr. Crusher is able to revive three of them. (See "The Neutral Zone")

KELVA: Located in the Andromeda galaxy, this world faces deadly radiation millions of years in its future. Obviously a forward-looking people, the Kelvans are looking for a replacement home for their Empire. The Kelvans encountered by the *Enterprise* take on human form when they take over the ship, but are seduced at last by the experience of physical existence and give up their mission. (See "By Any Other Name")

KHITOMER: Site of a famous treacherous attack by the Romulans. It was basically a massacre, but the child Worf survived and was taken to Gault to be raised by humans. (See "Heart Of Glory")

KLAESTRON FOUR: A world on which a military hero, General Ardelon Tandro, was killed by the terrorists he gave information to in betrayal of his own people. Curzon Dax is accused of being implicated in the killing but is later cleared. (See "Dax")

KLAVDIA THREE: Salia and Anya lived on this world for 16 years before deciding to return to Daled Four. (See "The Dauphin")

KLINZAI: The home world of the Klingons. It is also called by the name "Kling." (See "Heart of Glory") A dark world ruled by the High Council, although now with its first Emperor (Kahless) for many years.

KOINONIA: A dead world containing the ruins of two civilizations which destroyed each other. The two races were the Koinonians and non-corporal aliens who shared the planet with them. (See "The Bonding")

KORA TWO: The site of a Cardassian military academy. (See "Duet")

KRIOS: A Klingon colony where a fight for independence is under way. A Klingon, Ambassador Kell, and Picard head there to investigate the planetary governor's claim that the Federation is supplying the rebels with armaments. (See "The Mind's Eye")

K-7: Designation of a Federation space station located in the vicinity of Sherman's planet. Site of the tribble crisis. (See "The Trouble With Tribbles")

LaBARRE, FRANCE: Jean-Luc Picard's home on Earth. (See "Family")

LAPPA IV: A Ferengi world. (See "Menage A Troi")

LAVINIUS V: A dead civilization, destroyed by the flying parasites two centuries before they reach Deneva. (See "Operation: Annihilate")

LEGARA FOUR: The home world of the Legarans. (See "Sarek")

LEMMA TWO: The *Enterprise* travels to this world where Picard and Riker meet with Dr. Ja'Dar, who briefs them on the Soliton Wave discovery he needs

the *Enterprise* to help him monitor. (See "New Ground")

LIGON II: A planet where the *Enterprise* stops to acquire a rare vaccine needed to fight an epidemic of Anchilles Fever on Styris IV. Matters get complicated when the Ligonian ruler kidnaps Tasha Yar to be his mate. (See "Code Of Honor")

LIGOS SEVEN: The *Enterprise* proceeds here in response to a distress call they receive from a science team. (See "Rascals")

LONKA PULSAR: A rotating neutron star of approximately 4.356 solar masses. (See "Allegiance")

LOREN THREE: A planet linked to Prof. Galen's mystery search. It is a world devoid of intelligent life but which does have simple life forms. (See "The Chase")

LORENZE CLUSTER: This is where the planet Minos is located. (See "The Arsenal Of Freedom")

LUMAR CAFE: Beverly, Data and Worf are at this cafe when a bomb planted by the Ansata goes off. One of the waiters, Katik Shaw, is identified as being a member of the Ansata. (See "The High Ground")

LUNAR FIVE: A satellite of Angosia which is used as a penal colony. (See "The Hunted")

LYA THREE: A Federation starbase is located there. (See "The Hunted")

LYSIAN CENTRAL COMMAND: The *Enterprise* is found to have orders in its computer to attack here, but when they encounter little armament or firepower as they destroy unmanned sentry pods, Captain Picard and others question whether the Federation could truly be at war with the Lysians. Riker wonders how their enemy could be one hundred years behind them in weapons technology. (See "Conundrum")

MAKUS III: The official destination of the *Enterprise* when Kirk disobeys orders to search for Spock and the crew of the downed *Galileo* shuttlecraft. (See "The Galileo Seven")

17

MALKIS NINE: On this world, which is inhabited by the Lairons, they developed the written word in advance of developing either the spoken word or sign language. (See "Loud As A Whisper")

MALKOR: A planet on the verge of the space age but which is thus far unaware of the existence of the Federation and all that it implies. (See "First Contact")

MALURIAN SYSTEM: The four worlds of the star Omega Cygni, whose inhabitants were all killed by *Nomad* because of their inferior biological nature. Casualties exceeded four billion beings. (See "The Changeling")

MANARK IV: Where the *Enterprise* crew encounters the deadly sandbats. (See "The Empath")

MARCOS XII: The planet the "Friendly Angel" Gorgon plans to use as the first step in his plan to conquer the universe, using that world's children to kill all adults and take over. (See "And The Children Shall Lead")

MARIPOSA: The Mariposans are a race of clones who are dying out for a lack of new genetic material. They attempt to steal some from *Enterprise* personnel. This is a Class M world in the Ficus Sector, half a light year from the Bringloidi system. (See "Up The Long Ladder")

MARS: Located in the Sol system, the next planet out from Earth; the Utopia Planecia shipyards, where the *Enterprise* was built, are located here.

MARTIAN COLONY THREE: The original home of Mira Romaine. (See "The Lights Of Zetar")

MAXIA ZETA: Where the *U.S.S. Stargazer,* commanded by Jean-Luc Picard, engaged a Ferengi ship and was abandoned due to fire. (See "The Battle")

McKINLEY ROCKET BASE: Where Gary Seven goes to prevent the launch of an orbiting bomb in the Twentieth Century. (See "Assignment: Earth")

MEMORY ALPHA: The Federation's primary library resource, it holds the sum of all accumulated information about all Federation planets, their histories and their cultures. It is located on a small planetoid unprotected by shields, in the spirit of freedom of knowledge. This leaves it wide open to attack by the deadly Lights of Zetar. Their attack kills everyone there and severely damages the information banks. (See "The Lights Of Zetar")

MERAK II: The planet that needs the substance Zienite to save its plant life, thus prompting the *Enterprise*'s trip to the world of Ardana. (See "The Cloud Minders")

MESOPOTAMIA: Ancient civilization on Earth where Flint was born in 3834 B.C. (See "Requiem For Methuselah")

M43 ALPHA: The star shared by Zeon and its neighboring planet Ekos, the Nazi world. (See "Patterns Of Force")

MIDOS V: The planet where Dr. Roger Korby planned to launch his dispersal of the androids throughout the galaxy. (See "What Are Little Girls Made Of?")

MINARA: A star orbited by several worlds that support life. One is the planet inhabited by the Empaths (not their original home) and another is home of the Vians, who test the Empath McCoy calls Gem. Minara soon goes nova, but not before Gem's actions convince the Vians to relocate her race to another, safer location elsewhere in the galaxy. (See "The Empath")

MINARA II: The planet where the Vians torture humanoids to test Gem, in a cavern deep under the planet's surface. Not the home of the Empaths but perhaps that of the Vians. (See "The Empath")

MINOS: A dead world where the *U.S.S. Drake* disappeared, but this world is still fully automated and trying to sell armaments by demonstrating their deadly effectiveness to anyone who visits this planet. Located in the Lorenze Cluster, this is the planet where the *Enterprise* almost falls prey to the same weapons systems that destroyed all civilization on Minos many years before. (See "The Arsenal Of Freedom")

MINOS KOVA: The Cardassians want the defense plans of this Federation world. They torture Jean Luc Picard but he refuses to reveal them. (See "Chain Of Command")

MINTAKA THREE: A planet with a primitive society of proto-Vulcan inhabitants. (See "Who Watches The Watchers?")

MIRA SYSTEM: A six-planet system where mining operations are run on the planet Dytalix-B. (See "Conspiracy")

MIRROR UNIVERSE: Captain Kirk, Dr. McCoy, Lieutenant Uhura and Scotty find themselves in a savage world remarkably like our own in the characters found there, but totally different in the brutality of its character. Only the bearded Spock-Two of that world, who realizes that Kirk is different from the one he serves under, seems to have some glimmer of civilized behavior. (See "Mirror, Mirror")

MIZAR II: This is the home world of a Mizarians. In the previous 300 years this world has been conquered 6 times. (See "Allegiance")

MOAB FOUR: The location of a closed society called a Genome colony. When a stellar core fragment threatens that world the *Enterprise* has to help them to survive, but contact with outsiders proves threatening to the stability of the society. (See "The Masterpiece Society")

M113: A planet whose race is all but extinct; only one of its members, a vampire-like creature that draws salt from other living creatures, survives. It killed Nancy Crater, but her husband Robert protected it in the interests of science — and also perhaps because it could take the shape of his wife. But when the *Enterprise* comes to check up on the Craters, its shapeshifting powers enable it to pick off members of the *Enterprise* crew to sate its hunger. A pitiable being when exposed, it is killed by a reluctant Leonard McCoy. (See "The Man Trap")

MORDAN IV: A hostage situation demands the presence of Admiral Mark Jameson, a retired Federation negotiator who secretly armed both sides in that bitter war many years before, a situation which returns to haunt him when he is lured back in his old age by his foe Karnas. (See "Too Short A Season")

MORGANA QUADRANT: The destination of the *Enterprise* upon departing Tango Sierra. (See "Where Silence Has Lease")

MOUNT SELEYA: The place on the planet Vulcan where the fal tor pan takes place with Spock. (See "Star Trek III: The Search For Spock")

MS ONE COLONY: A Federation colony which is attacked by the Borg. (See "Descent")

M24 ALPHA: The three-star system that contains the planet Triskelion. (See "The Gamesters Of Triskelion")

MUDD'S PLANET: The planet where the androids serve Harry Mudd — but he's really nothing more than a prisoner of their compulsive need to serve his every whim. (See "I, Mudd")

M-33 GALAXY: Where the Traveler unintentionally propels the *Enterprise*; it is located nearly three million light years from our galaxy, the Milky Way. (See "Where No One Has Gone Before")

M-ZED FIVE: Where the fugitive Klingons falsely claim to have been going. (See "Heart Of Glory")

NARENDRA THREE: The location of a Klingon outpost which was attacked by Romulans but defended, to the death, by the *Enterprise-C*.

NAZRELDINE: An *Enterprise* crewman is exposed to an influenza virus at this stopover which the *Enterprise* makes on its way to Starbase Montgomery. (See "The Icarus Factor")

NELVANA THREE: A world inside the Romulan neutral zone which was used to lure the *Enterprise* with a phony story about a base being built there from which to launch an attack on the Federation. (See "The Defector")

NERVALA FOUR: A planet ringed by an intense distortion field. Will Riker had been an officer on the *U.S.S. Potemkin* when he helped evacuate a Federation outpost from there. A transporter accident created a duplicate Will Riker who was not discovered until eight years later. (See "Second Chances")

NEURAL: A primitive planet where Kirk must contest with Klingons who are providing advanced weaponry to the natives. (See "A Private Little War")

NEUTRAL ZONE: A wide border area between Federation territory and Romulan space. Officially forbidden to both sides, but the Romulans seem to run pretty freely inside the Neutral Zone, as they're always right there to attack any Federation ship that happens to cross the border. The Zone was established after the war with the Romulans. (See "Balance Of Terror") Iconia turns out to be located here, which leads to the inevitable Romulan involvement in the events surrounding that planet's rediscovery. (See "Contagion")

NEW MARTIN VAZ: An underwater city in the Atlantic Ocean on Earth. Kevin Uxbridge and his wife Rishon met here and were married. (See "The Survivors")

NIMBUS III: The world where Sybok creates an incident in order to lure a Starfleet vessel there which he can hijack to take him to Sha Ka Ree. (See "Star Trek V: The Final Frontier")

NORKAN OUTPOST: Admiral Jarok was responsible for a massacre there. (See "The Defector")

NORPIN FIVE: A planet on which a retirement colony is located. Montgomery Scott was on the way there when his shuttle, the *Jenolan,* crashed. (See "Relics")

NOVACHRON: Because Guinan is so mysterious about her past, she is told by Wesley Crusher that many people believe she is from this world. (See "The Child")

OBIE SYSTEM: Dr. Susan Noress developed a plasma plague strain here. (See "The Child")

OHNIAKA THREE: The site of a non-strategic Federation outpost. The *Enterprise* is summoned there when it is attacked by the Borg. The *Enterprise* arrives to find that all 274 crewmen on the base have been killed. (See "Descent")

OMEGA CYGNI: The sun of the Malurian solar system. (See "The Changeling")

OMEGA IV: A planet occupied by two groups apparently descended from Earth colonists: the Yang (Yankees) and Kohms (Communists). They carried their ideological battles from Earth to their new world, where they have continued for centuries. Captain Tracey makes matters worse by coming in on the side of the Kohms. (See "Omega Glory")

OMEGA SAGITTA 12 SYSTEM: The Coalition of

Madina is located there. (See "The Outrageous Okona")

OMICRON IV: Gary Seven refers to this world, which experienced a nuclear arms race much like that on Earth in the 20th Century. (See "Assignment: Earth")

OMICRON CETI III: A planet where the Federation sets up five farming colonies. Unfortunately, Berthold rays make it all but uninhabitable. A certain variety of indigenous spore provides an antidote, but the cure is perhaps even worse than the illness, and the settlements must move off this particular planet. (See "This Side Of Paradise")

OMICRON DELTA: The galactic region that contains the system of the planet where thoughts become reality, as experienced by a group of *Enterprise* crew members taking shore leave. (See "Shore Leave")

OMICRON PASCAL: The *Enterprise*'s last stop before going to Starbase 74. (See "11001001")

OMICRON THETA FOUR: The planet where Dr. Noonian Soong created the androids Lore and Data. Its colony was destroyed by the Crystalline Entity. Soong escaped. (See "Datalore", "Brothers")

OMICRON THETA SYSTEM: The planetary system containing the planet where Data was created by Dr. Noonian Soong. (See "Datalore")

ONEAMISU SECTOR: This is where the Braslota system can be found. (See "Peak Performance")

OPRALINE: Where the *Enterprise* goes after departing Ornara. (See "Symbiosis")

ORELIOUS NINE: This world was destroyed in the war between the Promellians and the Menthars a thousand years ago. (See "Booby Trap")

ORGANIA: An Earth-like planet whose peaceful natives seem to be passive hicks who accept the worst abuse without so much as a shrug or a grimace. The occupying Klingons, as might well be expected, hold the Organians in contempt. James Kirk is baffled by their attitude; he goes to heroic lengths to rouse the Organians to resistance against the Klingons, but it is all in vain. The truth, when it is revealed, is staggering. The physical forms of the Organians are merely disguises assumed for dealing with Klingons and other humanoids; they are really energy beings of staggering power who have left physical concerns behind long, long ago. In fact, one can only imagine what it took to rouse them to the slight annoyance that prompted them to get fed up with the Klingons and the Federation. There's not much either side can do once the apparently omnipotent Organians make up their minds. (See "Errand Of Mercy")

ORNARA: Located in the Delos system, this planet's entire population is addicted to Felicium, provided to them by their neighboring planet, Brekka, in return for all their natural resources. The Ornarans think they still need the drug to fight a plague; the Brekkans know that the disease was cured generations before, but haven't bothered to mention this. (See "Symbiosis")

OTAR TWO: The location of a Federation starbase. (See "The Offspring")

OUTPOST DELTA 0-5: A Federation outpost which has been obliterated from the surface of the planet it was on. At the time there is no explanation for the incident, but events much later seem to indicate that this was an early indication of a Borg incursion into Federation space. (See "The Neutral Zone")

OUTPOSTS 1, 3, 4 AND 8: Asteroid outposts along the Neutral Zone border that are destroyed by a Romulan attack; four other outposts remain. (See "Balance Of Terror")

OUTPOST SERAN-T-1: Where Dr. Leah Brahms designed the *Enterprise's* dilithium crystal chamber on stardate 40052.

PACIFICA: A planet largely covered by water; the *Enterprise* is on its way there when the events surrounding the alien conspiracy in Starfleet divert them to Dytalix and Earth. (See "Conspiracy") The *Enterprise* is transporting two Antedians to this planet for a conference which will be the site for a Federation treaty negotiation. Deanna's mother, Lwaxana, is named an ambassador to this conference. (See "Manhunt")

PARADISE CITY: The place on Nimbus III where Sybok creates an incident in order to lure a starship into his clutches. (See "Star Trek V: The Final Frontier")

PARLIAMENT: A planet belonging to the Federation, where diplomatic matters are dealt with. (See "Lonely Among Us")

PAULSON NEBULA: An area of space consisting of 82% dilithium hydroxyls, chromium and magnesium. (See "The Best Of Both Worlds" part one)

PEGOS MINOR SYSTEM: Where the *Enterprise* investigates a distress call from the scientist Mannheim. (See "We'll Always Have Paris")

PELIUS FIVE: Where the *Enterprise* heads after the events at Starbase 74. (See "11001001")

PENAL PLANETS: Although social improvements and developments in mental health have made both crime and madness much rarer in the 23rd Century, they still exist — and in some extreme cases, it is necessary to sequester the criminally insane in such isolated places as Elba II (which has a mere fifteen prisoners) and Tantalus V. These planets are shut off from the rest of the galaxy with force fields. Medical and scientific personnel work hard to provide humane treatment and a search for a cure. (See "Dagger Of The Mind")

PENOLOGY, CENTRAL BUREAU OF: Administration of the penal world is undoubtedly centered in this bureau, located in what used to be Sweden. (See "Dagger Of The Mind")

PENTARUS FIVE: The planet to which Wesley accompanies Captain Picard right before the youth is scheduled to leave the *Enterprise* to begin attending Starfleet Academy. (See "Final Mission")

PENTHARA FOUR: A world which is endangered when a type C asteroid strikes the planet. The *Enterprise* goes to render aid. (See "A Matter Of Time")

PERSEPHONE V: Where Admiral Jameson boards the *Enterprise* for passage to Mordan IV. (See "Too Short A Season")

PHEBAN: The Klingon vessel the *Pagh* goes to this system to conduct maneuvers. (See "A Matter Of Honor")

PHOENIX CLUSTER: The *Enterprise* is on its way to an uncharted area when the crew start coming under the pernicious influence of a virtual-reality device (See "The Game")

PLANET 892-IV: An Earth-like world with a parallel historical development, this planet had a culture very close to Earth's Roman Empire. The primary difference here is that the Empire never died. This planet has reached a technological level similar to Earth's in the mid-20th Century, complete with television programming and automobiles. The commercial craft *Beagle* disappeared in this area; its entire crew wound up as fodder for the gladiatorial television shows favored by the general populace, except for its captain, who rose to high governmental rank. The *Enterprise* crew almost falls into the same situation. It also turns out that there is another key parallel: a religion similar to Christianity exists on Planet 892-IV as an underground movement. (See "Bread And Circuses")

PLANET Q: A planet visited by the Karidian players. Lenore Karidian murders Dr. Thomas Leighton, who recognizes her father, on Planet Q. (See "The Conscience Of The King")

PLATONIUS: A planet occupied by a cruel and capricious race of telekinetic humanoids whose power, it turns out, is derived from the substance kironide. All but immortal, these people visited Earth during the time of the ancient Greek philosophers. Their home world was destroyed by a nova. Thirty-eight refugees moved to the planet they now call Platonius, including Plasus, Philana and the dwarf Alexander. They almost get the better of Kirk and his crew, but he manages to turn the tables on them all. The good-natured Alexander, the only decent Platonian, leaves with the *Enterprise*. (See "Plato's Stepchildren")

PLEASURE HAVEN: When Picard goes on shore leave, he visits this resort on Risa. (See "Captain's Holiday") Apparently Riker visits this same resort. (See "The Game")

PLEIADES CLUSTER: The *Enterprise* was surveying this region of space before it was sent to investigate trouble at the terraforming base of Velara Three. (See "Home Soil")

POLLUX IV: A planet in the Pollux system with no indigenous life forms, where the ancient Greek deity Apollo plans to relocate the entire crew of the *Enterprise* in order that they might worship him— he needs worshippers to continue his existence. Unfortunately for him, the humans in question are not particularly amenable to this plan. (See "Who Mourns For Adonais?")

POLLUX V: A planet in the Pollux system that hosts no sentient forms of life. (See "Who Mourns For Adonais?")

PRAXIS: A Klingon moon responsible for a large portion of the Empire's energy needs. When it explodes, it serves as the impetus for Chancellor Gorkon to sue the Federation for peace. (See "Star Trek VI: The Undiscovered Country")

PSI 2000: A frozen planet which is the origin point of a virus that unleashes the innermost feelings and inhibitions of humanoid species. Spock is particularly affected in a profound and devastating fashion by the effects of the Psi 2000 virus. (See "The Naked Time")

PYRIS VII: The planet occupied by the apparently sorcerous entities that call themselves Sylvia and Korob, who subject the *Enterprise* crew to some interesting ordeals. (See "Catspaw")

QUADRA SIGMA II: The site of a rescue mission the *Enterprise* is dispatched to. Although Riker has been given the powers of the Q, he has vowed not to use them and as a result a small girl dies. (See "Hide & Q")

QUADRA SIGMA III: Q interferes with the *Enterprise* while it is on its way to provide relief after a mining disaster there. (See "Hide and Q")

QUADRANT 904: A desolate, starless area of space, where the *Enterprise* encounters Gothos, a planet without a sun. (See "Squire Of Gothos")

QUALOR TWO: The Vulcan ship the *T'Pau* is supposed to be in storage at the Qualor Two space yards. (See "Unification")

QUAZULU EIGHT: The planet where an infectious disease is brought aboard the *Enterprise* by Wesley and other youngsters. (See "Angel One")

RACHELIS SYSTEM: The site where a plague is ravaging the system. In order to find an antidote, the *Enterprise* transfers samples of the plague virus to the Tango Sierra station. (See "The Child")

RAHM-IZAD SYSTEM: The false lead Data gives the Cardassian Gul Ocett when they are searching for the final links in Prof. Galen's genetic program. (See "The Chase")

RAMATIS THREE: The homeworld of the famed Federation negotiator Riva. (See "Loud As A Whisper")

RANA IV: A planet with three moons. It had a Federation colony of eleven thousand which was destroyed by a Husnock battle cruiser. (See "The Survivors")

RAYNA VI: Sonya, a scientist experienced in doing phase work with antimatter, is from here. (See "Q Who")

REGULA ONE: The research space station utilized by Carol and David Marcus in the development of Genesis. (See "Star Trek II: The Wrath Of Khan")

REKAG-BIRONI: A planet divided by political conflicts. These conflicts have expanded to the point that they begin to threaten Federation trading routes. (See "Man Of The People")

RELVA VII: The planet where Wesley goes to take the entrance exam for Starfleet Academy. (See "Coming Of Age")

REMMLER ARRAY: A space station in orbit above the Arkaria Base. (See "Starship Mine")

REMUS: One of the two main planets of the Romulan system. (See "Balance Of Terror")

REX'S BAR: A tavern which Picard goes to during a Dixon Hill holodeck excursion. (See "Manhunt")

RIGEL SYSTEM: A star system with numerous colonized planets, all of which are threatened by the doomsday machine Berserker if the *Enterprise* cannot halt its inexorable destructive progress. (See "The Doomsday Machine")

RIGEL II: A planet whose recollection inspires the creation of two exquisite female companions for Leonard McCoy on the shore-leave planet. (See "Shore Leave")

RIGEL IV: The world where Hengist, a functionary

on Argelius II, was born; the hilt of the knife used in the murders he commits while possessed by the Jack-the-Ripper being is made of a mineral from Rigel IV, which leads to this discovery and frees Scotty from suspicion. (See "Wolf In The Fold")

RIGEL V: A world whose people are similar to Vulcans in their internal body chemistries; this enables McCoy to use a drug from Rigel V when he must perform a transfusion from Spock to his father Sarek. (See "Journey To Babel")

RIGEL VII: A planetary system where the residents are barbarous, violent and roughly medieval in cultural and technological development. Captain Christopher Pike has just lost three *Enterprise* crew members on a disastrous landing there when he responds to what seems to be a simple distress call from the planet Talos IV. (See "The Cage")

RIGEL XII: A dismal desert planet with no indigenous life forms but a great supply of dilithium crystals. Mudd's women wind up getting married to three miners who live and work on Rigel XII. (See "Mudd's Women")

RISA: A pleasure planet and resort world which is a popular stopover for shore leave. (See "Captain's Holiday" and "The Game")

ROMBOI DRONEGAR SECTOR 006: A Pakled vessel in this sector sends a distress signal which is picked up by the *Enterprise*. (See "The Samaritan Snare")

ROMII: A star in the system that is home to the Romulans; according to Spock, they have two suns and two planets. Names such as "Romulus" and "Remus" are Federation translations of the real Romulan names, if these are in fact known; details of the Romulan home world are sketchy at best. (See "Balance Of Terror")

ROMULUS: The Federation name that refers to both a star in the Romulan system and one of its main planets. The home world of the Romulan empire. Sights on the world include the fire-falls of Galga'thong and the Apnex Sea. (See "The Defector")

ROUSSEAU FIVE: This is a planet partially recreated on the holodeck by Wesley and Salia. It is a shattered world which is held together via neutrino clouds. (See "The Dauphin")

ROYALE: A hotel created on an alien world from a novel owned by Colonel S. Richey, a NASA astronaut who died 283 years before the *Enterprise* encounters the place, and finds that it is still functioning. Apparently it was built by long-departed aliens. (See "The Royale")

RUAH FOUR: A fertile, uninhabited world in the Ruah system. (See "The Chase")

RUAH SYSTEM: An unexplored and unpopulated star system. (See "The Chase")

RUBICAM III: A class M planet inhabited by the Edo, a hedonistic race ruled by a mysterious god device which invisibly orbits the planet. (See "Justice")

RUTIA FOUR: A planet beset by terrorist attacks organized by a group calling itself the Ansata. (See "The High Ground")

SANDARA: The Platonians came from a planet which orbited the star Sandara. When Sandara went nova, the Platonians fled and settled on a new world, which they dubbed Platonia. (See "Plato's Stepchildren")

SARONA EIGHT: The planet where the *Enterprise* is headed for shore leave; they are called away to go to Vandor Four instead. (See "We'll Always Have Paris")

SARPEIDON: A planet orbiting the sun Beta Niobe. Its inhabitants, the Sarpeids, use the atavachron to travel back in time when Beta Niobe threatens to go nova. (See "All Our Yesterdays")

SARTHONG FIVE: Famous ruins are located on this world but they are watched over by the Sarthongians who don't like trespassers. (See "Captain's Holiday")

SCALOS: This planet once boasted a fine civilization, but substances unleashed by severe volcanic activity have ravaged their world: now all their children are dead, the Scalosian men have all become incapable of fathering new children, and, to make matters worse, the Scalosians now move so fast that they can't even be seen by the human eye. The *Enterprise* landing party on Scalos hears the voices of the natives as some sort of faint insectoid buzzing.

The distress signal that brings the *Enterprise* to Scalos is a ruse; the women of Scalos have been luring humanoids there in an as-yet-unsuccessful effort to get some new blood, so to speak, and get their race going again. Kirk becomes a prime target of this campaign, but he prefers to distribute his vital bodily fluids in a more traditional fashion, and resists. Besides, acceleration, induced by drinking Scalosian water, is generally fatal to humans, although Kirk risks it in order to get this whole mess straightened out. (See "The Wink Of An Eye")

SECTOR 23: This is the region of Federation space which lies in the closest proximity to the Romulan Neutral Zone. Philipa Louvois is the representative for this sector's JAG office. (See "Measure Of A Man")

SECTOR 30: A sector on the Neutral Zone, where two Federation outposts were mysteriously destroyed. (See "The Neutral Zone")

SECTOR 31: Another sector near the Neutral Zone, where two Federation outposts were mysteriously destroyed. (See "The Neutral Zone")

SECTOR 39J: The region of the galaxy where the giant space amoebe is first encountered. (See "The Immunity Syndrome")

SECTOR 63: Where the starship of Walker Keel is found destroyed under mysterious circumstances. The sector where the *U.S.S. Horatio* is destroyed. (See "Conspiracy")

SECTOR 108: When the Enterprise is inside the place known as the "void," a Romulan ship mysteriously appears in this sector. (See "Where Silence Has Lease")

SECTOR 396: The location of the Selimi Asteroid Belt. (See "The Offspring")

SECTOR 9569: In "Transfigurations," this is the sector where the Zalkonian ship and the *Enterprise* have their encounter.

SELAY: A planet whose people are reptilian humanoids, at war with the wolf-like humanoid residents of nearby Antica; located in the Beta Renner system. (See "Lonely Among Us")

SELCUNDI DREMA SECTOR: The five star systems in this sector have fallen victim to destructive geological disturbances over the previous

150 years, although until the *Enterprise* visited there no one in the Federation knew that there was intelligent life (the Dremens) on the fourth planet in one of the systems. (See "Pen Pals")

SELIMI ASTEROID BELT: The *Enterprise* is charting this when Data creates his child, which he names Lal. (See "The Offspring")

SENTINEL MINOR FOUR: This was the destination of the *U.S.S. Lalo* before the Borg attacked it. (See "The Best Of Both Worlds")

SEPTIMIS MINOR: The *S.S. Artemis* was headed here but instead wound up on Tau Cygna V. (See "The Ensigns Of Command")

SHA KA REE: The legendary planet which Sybok believes is the origin of all life and the home of "God." (See "Star Trek V: The Final Frontier")

SHELIUS: The home plant of the Sheliak Corporate as described in "The Ensigns Of Command."

SHERMAN'S PLANET: An Earth-like world near Space Station K-7, currently disputed by the Klingons and the Federation, and undergoing an agricultural crisis. The Klingons try to sabotage Federation grain shipments in an attempt to convince the Organians that they would be better suited to running the planet. This scheme is foiled by hungry tribbles. (See "The Trouble With Tribbles")

SHIKAHR: Spock's home city on Vulcan. (See "Yesteryear")

SHORE-LEAVE WORLD: A beautiful planet which turns out to conceal hidden technology which turns the imaginings of visitors into reality. Although this is strictly for amusement, visitors unaware of this situation can, and do, think of dangerous things which complicate their visit. Fortunately, the fatal results of such thoughts turn out to be quite temporary. (See "Shore Leave")

SIERRA SIX OUTPOST: This outpost provides the identification of the Romulan scout ship in "The Defector."

SIGMA DRACONIS: A star; three of its nine worlds host intelligent life.

SIGMA DRACONIS III: An inhabited planet in the Sigma Draconis system, with technology on a level comparable to Earth in the 15th Century.

SIGMA DRACONIS IV: Another planet in the same system; it has reached a level comparable to Earth in the early 21st Century.

SIGMA DRACONIS VI: An inhabited planet in the Sigma Draconis system which has regressed culturally due to a renewed ice age. Vestiges of a formerly advanced technology remain but the inhabitants do not understand it very well. The women, or "Eymorgs," run things; the males, or "Morgs," are passive servants. The Eymorgs steal Spock's brain to keep their ancient computer going. (See "Spock's Brain")

SIGMA DRACONIS VII: For some reason, both Kirk and Sulu call Sigma Draconis VI by the wrong number— a remarkable consistency of error. (See "Spock's Brain")

SIGMA ERANI SYSTEM: According to "The Most Toys", this is the only source of Hytritium.

SIRRIE FOUR: The vase that Fako displays was carved here by Mark Off-Zel. (See "The Most Toys")

SOLAR SYSTEM L370: A planetary system consumed by the doomsday machine Berserker. (See "The Doomsday Machine")

SOLAR SYSTEM L374: Another system attacked by the doomsday machine berserker; its two innermost planets were spared. This is the system where the crew of the *Constellation* was killed. (See "The Doomsday Machine")

SOLARIAN FOUR: The Federation colony here was attacked, supposedly by the Bajoran terrorist Orta, but in point of fact the Cardassians attacked the colony in order to try to force the Federation to find and dispose of Orta. (See "Ensign Ro")

SOLEIS FIVE: Homeworld of the Solari, a race experiencing a civil war which requires the great Federation mediator Riva to end it. (See "Loud As A Whisper")

STARBASE ARMUS NINE: Where the *Enterprise* was headed for maintenance when it was diverted to Data's home world. (See "Datalore")

STARBASE G6: Federation Starbase where Deanna Troi disembarks to take a shuttlecraft to Betazed. (See "Hide and Q")

STARBASE 2: A Starbase located near Beta Aurigae and Camus II. (See "Turnabout Intruder")

STARBASE 4: A Starbase located near Triacus. Lokai steals a shuttle from Starbase 4, and would have returned there if Kirk had been able to transport Lokai and Bele back for a hearing. Instead, he returned there with the *Enterprise* after the two Cheronians finally brought their ancient battle back to the shattered ruins of their home world. (See "Let That Be Your Last Battlefield")

STARBASE 6: The Starbase closest to the events surrounding the arrival and destruction of the giant spacefaring amoeba. (See "The Immunity Syndrome") After picking her up on Graves' World, the *Enterprise* transports Kareen Brianon to this Starbase. (See "The Schizoid Man")

STARBASE 9: Located ten days from Pyris VII, this is the Starbase the *Enterprise* was headed towards when a black hole cast the ship back in time. (See "Tomorrow Is Yesterday")

STARBASE 10: A Starbase, under the command of Commodore George Stocker, located rather close to the border of the Neutral Zone between Federation space and Romulan territory. (See "Balance Of Terror")

STARBASE 11: The *Enterprise* takes refuge here after being damaged by an ion storm. Kirk is court-martialed here when he appears to have been negligent in the death of an *Enterprise* crewman, Finney. In truth, the charges are erroneous, for Finney is not really dead. At the time, the commander of Starbase 11 was Commodore Stone; later, he is replaced by Commodore Mendez. The base is the point of origin of mysterious and troubling events when Spock abducts the injured Christopher Pike from the base hospital and takes him to the forbidden planet of Talos IV. (See "Court Martial" and "The Menagerie")

STARBASE 12: A Starbase in the Gamma 400 solar system, near Pollux. (See "Space Seed") The mysterious evacuation of this Starbase tips Walker Keel off to the alien conspiracy. (See "Conspiracy")

STARBASE 14: The Starbase that sends the *Enterprise* the message informing Picard of the plague on the planet Styris Four. (See "Code of Honor")

STARBASE 24: According to "Sins Of The Father," after the Khitomer Massacre Kahlest was brought to this Starbase for treatment.

STARBASE 29: Under the command of Admiral Budron. (See "Frame Of Mind")

STARBASE 39 SIERRA: Where Picard is ordered to take the three humans revived from the cryogenic sleeper satellite. (See "The Neutral Zone")

STARBASE 45: Admiral Jameson deflects all attempts at examination by claiming that he's had a recent medical evaluation at this Starbase. (See "Too Short A Season")

STARBASE 67: Where the *Enterprise* goes for repairs after striking two quantum filaments. (See "Disaster")

STARBASE 73: The *Enterprise* picks up some Owan eggs here before continuing on to Endicor. (See "Time Squared") The *Enterprise* visits this starbase again on its way to the Ficus Sector. (See "Up The Long Ladder")

STARBASE 74: Where the *Enterprise* stops to undergo the required diagnostic work following their holodeck problems in "The Big Goodbye" (See "11001001")

STARBASE 82: Picard captures Etana and the Ktarian ship she is piloting in a tractor beam and takes her prisoner to be delivered to this Starbase. (See "The Game")

STARBASE 83: After Q returns the *Enterprise* to Federation space, Picard has the ship proceed to this Starbase. (See "Q Who")

STARBASE 84: Where the *Enterprise* heads after its encounter with the *Kartag*, a Klingon vessel. (See "Heart Of Glory")

STARBASE 103: Where the *Enterprise*'s saucer section, commanded by Logan, is sent after the *Enterprise* is attacked at Minos. (See "The Arsenal Of Freedom")

STARBASE 105: Destination the *Enterprise* was originally going to take the crippled *Enterprise-C* (See "Yesterday's Enterprise")

STARBASE 121: In order to rid the *Enterprise* of invidium, Geordi suggests that this Starbase is the place to do the necessary systems and biodecontamination. (See "Hollow Pursuits")

STARBASE 123: This Starbase detects two Romulan D'daridex class cruisers headed towards Beta Stromgren. (See "Tin Man")

STARBASE 133: The *Enterprise* heads for this Starbase after departing Rana IV. (See "The Survivors")

STARBASE 152: Following the encounter with the Romulans and the nova at Beta Stromgren, the *Enterprise* proceeds to this Starbase for repairs. (See "Tin Man")

STARBASE 153: Worf's former lover, K'Ehleyr, journeys from here to the *Enterprise* on a Class 8 Probe due to the lack of available ships at Starbase 153. (See "The Emissary")

STARBASE 157: This Starbase receives the *U.S.S. Lalo's* distress call. (See "The Best Of Both Worlds")

STARBASE 173: This is a new outpost on the border with the Romulan Neutral Zone commanded by Admiral Nakamura. (See "Measure Of A Man")

STARBASE 179: As part of the Officer Exchange Program the *Enterprise* stops here and picks up Ensign Mendon. (See "A Matter Of Honor")

STARBASE 185: When the *Enterprise* first encounters the Borg in System J25, they determine that at maximum warp the Borg threat is two years, seven months, three days and 18 hours away from Federation space in the form of this Starbase. (See "Q Who")

STARBASE 212: Lt. Aquiel is assigned here after the mystery of the communications relay station is resolved. (See "Aquiel")

STARBASE 336: Two days before K'Ehleyr reaches the *Enterprise*, Starbase 336 received a distress call from the T'Ong. (See "The Emissary")

STARBASE 324: Admiral Hanson comes here for a strategy meeting with Starfleet Command. (See "The Best Of Both Worlds")

STARBASE 343: The *Enterprise* proceeds here to have shore leave following the signing of the Gatherer Treaty. (See "The Vengeance Factor")

STARBASE 515: Where Jean-Luc undergoes an emergency heart operation when his artificial heart begins to malfunction. Dr. Katherine Pulaski, a cardiac expert, is brought in to assist in the operation. Up until then Jean-Luc had kept the knowledge that he had an artificial heart secret from his fellow officers. (See "Samaritan Snare")

STARBASE 718: Site of a conference about the mysterious outpost destructions near the Neutral Zone; Picard is in attendance. (See "The Neutral Zone")

STARBASE MONTGOMERY: When the *Enterprise* stops here for engineering consultations, Kyle Riker beams aboard to meet with his son in an official capacity. (See "The Icarus Factor")

STARBASE SCYLLA 515: A branch of Starfleet Academy is located here along with medical facilities. (See "Samaritan Snare")

STARBASE ZENDI NINE: The Starbase where the *Stargazer* is taken after the events surrounding its return to Picard by a Ferengi captain. (See "The Battle")

STAR CLUSTER NGC 321: Star system that includes the "warring" planets of Vendikar and Eminiar VII. (See "A Taste Of Armageddon")

STARFLEET ACADEMY: The officers' training school for Starfleet. James Kirk and Spock were two of its most notable graduates. Kirk returned there to teach at some point in his career (perhaps a standard requirement); Gary Mitchell was among his students. (Earlier on, Finney, who later framed Kirk for murder, was one of Kirk's teachers.) Pavel Chekov was also a student there. Historian John Gill, who introduced Naziism to the planet Ekos, was a civilian professor there earlier in his illustrious career. Starfleet Academy clearly offers an arduous course of study, designed not merely to educate but to detect and develop the leadership potential of its classmen. An institution with a long and distinctive history. Headquartered on Earth, but with various branches throughout Federation space, such as the Academy facility on Scylla 515 where Wesley goes for testing.

STARFLEET MEDICAL: The medical administration branch of Starfleet. Dr. Beverly Crusher served as its head for about a year (perhaps in an interim capacity) before returning to her duties on the *Enterprise*. (See "The Child", "Evolution")

STAR STATION INDIA: The Enterprise gets a call from the *U.S.S. Lantree* while it is en route to Star

Station India. (See "Unnatural Selection")

STAR SYSTEM 6-11: The star system that includes the planet Beta III, where the *U.S.S. Archon* crashed a century before the visit of the *Enterprise*. (See "The Return Of The Archons")

STATION SALEM ONE: In "The Enemy," the incident here is regarded as a possible preamble to war on a par with Galorndon Core and Pearl Harbor.

STRALEB: The planet on which Okona is wanted for stealing the Jewel of Thesia, a national treasure. (See "The Outrageous Okona")

STRATOS: The capital city of the planet Ardana. Stratos is kept afloat in the clouds above the surface of Ardana by highly advanced antigravity technology. Unfortunately, this "perfect" city is the center of a truly unjust social structure that oppresses the miners on the surface through the spurious argument of evolutionary inferiority. In fact, the miners are on precisely the same evolutionary level as the aristocrats of Stratos, but they've been affected by their daily exposure to the mind-numbing element Zienite. (See "The Cloud Minders")

STRNAD: Located near Rubicam, this planet was recently settled by a Federation colony. (See "Justice")

STYRIS IV: Where the Anchilles Fever strikes, sending the *Enterprise* in quest of a rare antidote (See "Code Of Honor")

SURATA FOUR: When the *Enterprise* sends down a survey team to explore here, Riker becomes infected with alien microbes. (See "Shades Of Gray")

SYSTEM J-25: In "The Best Of Both Worlds," this is referred to as where the *Enterprise* first encountered the Borg (see "Q-Who") seven thousand light years away from the previous position of the *Enterprise*. It is described as being identical with the Jouret Four incident.

TAGRA FOUR: A planet which suffers from ecological devastation until it is cured of all its problems by Amanda Rogers who uses her Q powers. (See "True Q")

TAGUS 3: The planet the *Enterprise* orbits so that it can be the site of an archeological expedition at which Picard gives the keynote speech. (See "Q-pid")

TALOS STAR GROUP: A dual-star system with a total of eleven planets. (See "The Menagerie")

TALOS IV: The fourth planet in the Talos Star Group. Long ago, its culture destroyed itself through atomic warfare. The survivors of this large-skulled race moved underground. In their subterranean homes they diverted themselves from their tragedy by creating false worlds with their incredible mental powers of illusion, and amused themselves by collecting alien species for their planetary zoo. Their race is slowly dying out, fading into more and more illusion and failing to reproduce. Their attempts to add a human specimen — Captain Christopher Pike — to their menagerie failed, and led to a Federation ban on all visits to the planet. This is the only Federation law whose violation still carries the death penalty, although punishment was waived due to special circumstances in the case of Spock, who undertook the only known expedition to Talos IV after Pike was there. (See "The Menagerie")

TANGO SIERRA: Patterned on the Regula-type station, this is a Federation medical facility in the Rachelis system. (See "The Child")

TANTALUS V: A planet whose sole colony is the penal institution run by Dr. Tristan Adams. After Adams' abuses were brought to a timely end, Dr. Simon van Gelder was appointed head of Tantalus V. (See "Dagger Of The Mind")

TANUGA FOUR: The Tanuga Research Station is located here. The legal system holds that a person is guilty until proven innocent. (See "A Matter Of Perspective")

TANUGA RESEARCH STATION: This is a Regula-type facility in orbit around Tanuga Four. The station is under command of Dr. Nel Apgar who believes that Riker is a threat to his plans and attempts to kill him in a phony transporter accident which backfires. (See "A Matter Of Perspective.")

TAROD 9: One of the Neutral Zone outposts destroyed by a mysterious force. (See "The Neutral Zone")

TARSUS III: Starbase 74 orbits this planet. The *Enterprise*, there for maintenance, is stolen by the Bynars. (See "11001001")

TARSUS IV: The planet where Governor Kodos "saved" the colonists from famine by executing more than half of them, based on an arbitrary judgment. It was believed that mass starvation was coming and that the relief ships would arrive far too late to prevent it. But shortly after the executions were completed, the relief ships arrived. In the confusion that resulted, Kodos fled the planet. (See "The Conscience Of The King")

TARTARES 5: A world in the Gamma Quadrant where ancient ruins have just been discovered. (See "Q Less")

TAU ALPHA-C: The supposed planet of origin of the assistant to Mr. Koszinski, the Federation propulsion expert sent to modify the engines of the *Enterprise-D*. No one is really certain, although Riker puts this theory forward. (See "Where No One Has Gone Before")

TAU CETI THREE: Walker Keel has a rendezvous with Picard in a bar on this planet, to test his loyalty or possible involvement in the alien conspiracy within Starfleet. (See "Conspiracy")

TAU CYGNA V: In "Ensigns Of Command," this world was settled by the colony ship *Artemis* when it accidentally arrived there instead of at its proper destination. The Sheliak Corporate demands that the colony be evacuated or else they'll destroy it.

TELARIA: Origin of the Batris. (See "Heart Of Glory")

TELLUN STAR SYSTEM: The system which contains two inhabited planets: the relatively civilized Troyius and the more barbarous Elas. These two planets have wasted their capacity for interplanetary flight in a useless war, which the marriage of Elaan to the Troyian monarch is intended to end. The Klingons claim jurisdiction in this region, but with little evidence to back the claim. (See "Elaan Of Troyius")

TERELLA: A planet ravaged by a plague weapon, its survivors wandered space in plague ships; the last known such ship is encountered by the *Enterprise* near the planet Haven. (see "Haven")

TERRA: The more common galactic name for Earth (being the Greek word for Earth). Birthplace of the human race in all its contradictory glory, which has finally stepped forth to take its place in galactic

civilization as part of the United Federation of Planets.

THALOS SYSTEM: Thalian chocolate mousse can be found here. (See "The Dauphin")

THANDAUS FIVE: People on this world are born without limbs. (See "Loud As A Whisper")

THASUS: The Earthlike planet where the native Thasians raised the human child Charles Evans, and where they take him back when they claim him from the *Enterprise*. The *Enterprise* is only too happy to see him go. (See "Charlie X")

THETA CYGNI XII: A planet whose inhabitants were all destroyed by the flying parasites later encountered by the *Enterprise* on Deneva. (See "Operation: Annihilate")

THETA VII: James Kirk ignores a mission to this planet in order to pursue the vampiric cloud that he first encountered as an ensign. (See "Obsession") The NASA vessel *Charybdis* was taken to this world in the Theta 116 system and the Earth environment known as the Hotel Royale was created by unknown alien beings. (See "The Royale")

THETA 116 SYSTEM: The planet Theta VIII is located there. (See "The Royale")

THIRD MOON OF VALO: A point on this moon is the location of the *Enterprise* rendezvous with Orta, the Bajoran terrorist wrongly blamed for an attack on a Federation colony. (See "Ensign Ro")

TIBURON: Birthplace of the Eden-seeking Dr. Sevrin. (See "The Way To Eden")

TILONUS FOUR: A world where the planetary government has collapsed and several factions are vying for power. When Will Riker is captured by one of the factions, they attempt to probe him for information. (See "Frame Of Mind")

TOKYO BASE: Kyle Riker developed tactics for Starfleet to deal with the Ferengi while he was assigned there. (See "The Icarus Factor")

TORONA IV: The planet where the Jarada expect Jean-Luc Picard to greet them flawlessly in their own language. (See "The Big Goodbye")

TRA'NUSAH: The father of the tactics officer on the

Klingon vessel the *Pagh* died in battle here. (See "A Matter Of Honor")

TRIACUS: Final resting place of the adult members of the ill-fated Starnes expedition; the "Friendly Angel" Gorgan drove them all to suicide and exerted his evil influence over their children. Gorgan was the last inhabitant of Triacus, who may in fact have waited countless years to find people who would enable him to spread out across the galaxies, wreaking destruction and conquest everywhere. Fortunately, Kirk is able to bring a halt to this before it can go too far. (See "And The Children Shall Lead")

TRIANGULUM SYSTEM: A renegade group of Andorians dismantled their ship and hid it here. (See "The Survivors")

TRISKELION: Located in the three-star system of M24 Alpha, this planet is occupied by the three Providers, alien brains which, like the Talosians of Talos IV, collect species from different planets. They operate more than a zoo, however. Their slaves, or thralls, are trained to take part in gladiatorial combat. The Providers amuse themselves by betting on the outcome. (See "The Gamesters Of Triskelion")

TROYIUS: One of the planets in the Tellun solar system. The king of Troyius agreed to a state marriage to Elaan of Elas, the neighboring planet that has warred with Troyius for years, in order to bring an end to that war. (See "Elaan Of Troyius")

TULA: An inhabitant of Beta III, Tula is the daughter of Reger. She is brutally assaulted during the Landru-sanctioned festival. (See "Return Of The Archons")

TURKANA FOUR: The birthplace of Tasha Yar and her younger sister Ishara. (See "Legacy")

TYCHO IV: The site of the *Farragut*'s deadly encounter with the vampiric cloud, and apparently that entity's native habitat. The *Enterprise* tracks it back to Tycho IV. (See "Obsession")

TYKEN'S RIFT: A tear in space where the crew of the trapped *Enterprise* slowly begin to go mad due to sleep deprivation. (See "Night Terrors")

TYPERIAS: A planet where certain soils have coagulant properties; these can be used to staunch the flow of blood. (See "A Private Little War")

TYPHON EXPANSE: An unexplored region of space which the *Enterprise-D* is the first to explore. (See "Cause And Effect")

TYRUS 7-A: A planet on which a huge project called the Tyan Fountain has been constructed. (See "Quality Of Life")

UTOPIA PLANITIA: The *Enterprise* was constructed at these shipyards located in Mars orbit. (See "Booby Trap")

VAGRA TWO: The planet located in the Zed Lapis system where the Armus was exiled, and where it killed Tasha Yar. (See "Skin Of Evil")

VALO ONE: The third moon of this planet is where the *Enterprise* meets with the Bajoran terrorist named Orta. (See "Ensign Ro")

VALO THREE: The site of a Bajoran refugee camp in the days before the Cardassians left Bajor. (See "Ensign Ro")

VANDOR FOUR: Dr. Manheim carried his time distortion experiments to the limit on this planetoid located in a binary star system. (See "We'll Always Have Paris")

VAYTAN: A star which is used to test the effectiveness of Dr. Reyga's metaphasic field technology. (See "Suspicions")

VEGA IX: Where Captain Christopher Pike was taking the *Enterprise* crew for medical treatment after the events on Rigel VII, only to be diverted to Talos IV by a fake distress call. (See "The Cage" and "The Menagerie")

VEGA OMICRON SECTOR: The *Ares* is patrolling this sector of space in search of intelligent life. (See "The Icarus Factor")

VELARA III: A planet where terraformers are at work transforming the world to make it suitable for colonization when it is discovered that a primitive native lifeform has been overlooked. (See "Homesoil")

VENDIKAR: A former colony of Eminiar VII, still called Eminiar III by the people of that planet. A computer-operated war has decimated both planets for half a millennium. (See "A Taste Of Armageddon")

VENTAX 2: The people of this world are led to believe that an impending apocalypse is about to occur. They experience earthquakes and other signs, as predicted in the Legend of Ardra, a thousand-year-old document. Ardra turns out to be a scam artist planning to rob the Ventaxans. (See "Devil's Due")

VOID: A new area of space which lacks dimension and where the strange alien being Nagilum lives. (See "Where Silence Has Lease")

VULCAN: The Vulcan homeworld. Vulcan is one of the founding members of the United Federation of Planets. A moonless Earthlike planet with a hot, arid atmosphere, largely desert-like in its geological terrain. The Vulcan ecosphere is very low in sodium chloride, so it's a safe bet that Spock is salt-free. (See "Amok Time")

VULCANA REGAR: A planet colonized by Vulcans; origin of T'Shalik. (See "Coming Of Age")

WOLF-359: In "The Best Of Both Worlds" this star local to the Terran system is the site of Starfleet's stand against the invading Borg vessel. (See also "Emissary")

XANTHRAS SYSTEM: In "Menage A Troi," the *Enterprise* leaves orbit here to meet with the *U.S.S. Zapata.*

ZALDAN: A world whose inhabitants have a marked disdain for good manners; they consider it rude to

cover the truth behind socially acceptable behavior. (See "Coming Of Age")

ZALKON: The Zalkonians, a race of fascists, live here. Zalkon is in the Zeta Gelis Cluster. (See "Transfigurations")

ZANZA MEN'S DANCE PALACE: An establishment located near the Blue Parrot Café on Sarona Eight. (See "We'll Always Have Paris")

ZEDAK FOUR: A primarily aquatic world colonized by the Federation; Harry, a young child kidnapped with Wesley and the others, is from there. (See "When The Bough Breaks")

ZED LAPIS: Location of the planet Vagra Two, where Armus kills Tasha Yar. (See "Skin Of Evil")

ZENDI SABU: Star system where the Ferengi Daimon Bock returned the *Stargazer* to Picard as part of his vengeance scheme. (See "The Battle")

ZEON: The planet Ekos' nearest neighbor in the solar system M43 Alpha. Its peaceful people become the focus of the Ekosian Nazi's genocidal schemes, but are saved by the intervention of the *Enterprise.* (See "Patterns Of Force")

ZETA ALPHA TWO: In "The Best Of Both Worlds", the *U.S.S. Lalo* is attacked after leaving here for Sentinel Minor Four.

ZETA GELIS CLUSTER: In "Transfigurations" the *Enterprise* is here charting a previously unknown star system.

ZIBALIA: The homeworld of Kivas Fajo. (See "The Most Toys")

ZYTCHIN THREE: In "Captain's Holiday," Picard takes shore leave here.

ALIENS

ACAMARIANS: The inhabitants of Acamar Three, these beings have a composite of iron-copper in their blood which is unusual. The Gatherers used to be a part of the Acamarian culture until they split off from them a hundred years before. (See "The Vengeance Factor")

ALLASOMORPHS: The scientific term for species with true shapeshifting abilities, such as the Daledi. (See "The Dauphin")

ALLIANCE: One of the warring factions on Tasha Yar's homeworld. (See "Legacy")

AMOEBA: An 11-thousand-mile-long, single-celled organism that destroys entire planetary systems, not to mention the *U.S.S. Intrepid*, by drawing off all their energy. (See "The Immunity Syndrome")

ANDORIANS: A member race of the Federation. Blue skin, white hair and their short, knobby antennae (two per Andorian) are their most prominent features. A warlike race, they generally manage to keep their latent hostilities under control, but their low-key demeanor masks a potential for real violence. Andorians are very prolific and are constantly looking to colonize other worlds because of their rapidly increasing populations. (See "Journey To Babel")

ANSATA: A terrorist separatist group fighting for their own homeland on the western continent on Rutia Four. The Ansata have been fighting for 70 years and have resorted to increasingly violent acts in order to force the government to surrender to their demands. They are led by Kyril Finn and their secret base is discovered to be 300 kilometers from the capital city on the southern tip of the continent. When they kidnap Beverly Crusher and Captain Picard, the *Enterprise* sides with the government in finding the Ansata in order to rescue their own personnel. (See "The High Ground")

ARCHONS: The name given by the Betans to the surviving members of the crew of the *Archon*, who spread the idea of insurrection. By extension, the Betans expect more Archons to come along and save them from tyranny, and see Kirk and his crew as the realization of this ancient hope. (See "Return Of The Archons")

ARGELIANS: Inhabitants of Argelius II. (See "Wolf In The Fold")

BANDI: The humanoid race that inhabits Deneb IV, or Farpoint. (See "Encounter At Farpoint")

BENZITE: A bluish-grey skinned humanoid race, apparently hairless, who need a special device to help them breathe the Earth-type atmosphere in Starfleet vessels. (See "Coming Of Age")

BENZITES: The indigenous peoples of the planet Benzar.

BETAZOID CATS: Deanna Troi recalls having such a pet when she was a child. (See "Pen Pals")

BETAZOIDS: A humanoid species native to the planet Beta Zed. The Betazoids possess empathic powers that verge on the telepathic. Full Betazoids are telepathic although Ferengis are immune to Betazoid mind reading. While these powers generally manifest only at the onset of adolescence, a few Betazoids are born with full power at birth, which makes life very difficult for them. Such cases find the influx of thoughts painful and overwhelming. Tam Elbrun is such an individual. (See "Tin Man"). Betazoid Deanna Troi, being half human, only has reduced empathic powers, very useful for her job as ship's counselor but apparently not enough to satisfy her full Betazoid mother Lwaxana. (See "Haven," "Manhunt," etc.) Betazoid pregnancies last a month longer that those of humans.

BODY, THE: The collective name for those people of Beta III (that is, most of them) under the control of the computer known as Landru. (See "Return Of The Archons")

BOLIANS: A humanoid race that belongs to the Federation. These are the inhabitants of Bolius Nine. Like many other races in the Federation, they are humanoid but differ from humans in that they have green skin and a ridge down the center of their skulls. Examples of Bolians are Captain Rixx ("Conspiracy") and Mitena Haro ("Allegiance")

BORG: The Borg are from hundreds of light years away and are cyborgs. They start out as normal humans but soon after birth have mechanisms attached to them which turn them into cyborgs and make them a part of the Borg collective. Although they apparently visited Federation space before (as indicated by some mysteriously destroyed outposts in "The Neutral Zone"), they were first encountered by the *Enterprise* in "Q Who". They subsequently attempted to invade the Federation ("The Best Of Both Worlds") but were defeated. An injured Borg was later discovered by an Away Team mission and brought back to the *Enterprise*, where it was exposed to emotions and then returned to the collective Borg consciousness in the hope that it would teach the others compassion. (See "I, Borg") A group of renegade Borg, under the leadership of Lore, returned years later but were defeated by other Borg and *Enterprise* personnel. (See "Descent") Probably the most deadly species yet encountered by the Federation. According to Guinan, they probably would not have come across the Federation and surrounding areas for many years if Q had not mischievously thrown the *Enterprise* into their path. Guinan's own home world was destroyed by the Borg sometime in the distant past. The threat of the Borg leads Starfleet to instigate wargames. (See "Peak Performance")

BREKKA: The people of this world have for centuries kept the people of Onara addicted to Felicium, a drug which the Onarians believe they need to control a plague. (See "Symbiosis")

BYNARS: Four dually linked aliens (11, 00, 10 and 01) who steal the *Enterprise* and try to distract Picard and Riker on the holodeck in the process. They come from a world where the humanoid race has become closely linked with the computers and they cannot survive without the computers. When their world is in danger they steal the *Enterprise* in order to reboot their own world's computer because they feared being turned down had they asked official permission. (See "11001001")

CALAMARAIN: A disembodied alien race which consists of ionized gas. Q once tormented them and when he is stripped of his powers and made a human mortal, the Calamarains attempt to exact revenge on Q. Data helps to protect the human Q from them. (See "Deja Q")

CALDONIANS: Aliens who are among the competitors for the rights to the Barzan wormhole. (See "The Price")

CAPELLANS: The inhabitants of Capella IV. Prone to sudden violence: they interpret almost any movement as a threat, and respond accordingly. (See "The Cloud Minders")

CARDASSIANS: Their homeworld is Cardassia and they are a race of conquerors who believe in harsh subjugation and a take-no-prisoners policy in combat. Apparently they were not always this way and were, in fact, a peaceful race until the military took over the ruling of their society, which makes them similar to the Romulans in many ways. The Cardassian military authority claims that only after they took over did they relieve the suffering the populace had been enduring, but ending the widespread starvation of the Cardassians was apparently accomplished at the cost of exploiting other worlds.

This is a humanoid race with rigid exoskeletons and some black slick hair on the tops of their heads. Senior officers carry the title Gul in their names (such as Gul Madred and Gul Ocett) and subordinates bear the title Glin. This warlike race subjugated Bajor for 25 years. They now have a peace treaty with the Federation, but it is more in the nature of an armed truce. When Captain Maxwell correctly recognized that the Cardassians were rearming for war, he took it upon himself to attack them without Starfleet authorization. When the *Enterprise* is forced to halt Maxwell's act of war, Picard warns the Cardassians that they are aware of what Maxwell discovered and will be watching them. Picard is later captured by Cardassians and tortured, but refuses to break. Simultaneously with this, Captain Edward Jellico in temporary command of the *Enterprise* heads off a planned Cardassian invasion of Minos Corva. The Cardassians are a continuing presence to those serving on Deep Space Nine. Introduced in "The Wounded". (See also "Ensign Ro", "Chain of Command", "The Chase" and DEEP SPACE NINE)

CETI EEL: Native to Ceti Alpha V, this tiny creature crawls inside a person's head through the ear, wraps itself around the cerebral cortex and remains there, growing. The host goes mad with the pain, finally becoming paralyzed. A side effect is that they become very susceptible to suggestion. Captain Clark Terrell becomes a victim and finally kills himself. Pavel Chekov is victimized but his eel chooses to finally exit his head. (See "Star Trek II: The Wrath Of Khan")

CHALNOTH: The beings who come from the world of Chalna, of which Esoqq is one. They are anarchists and spend their lives fighting among themselves. (See "Allegiance")

CHANDRANS: The Inhabitants of Chandra Five, they are reportedly a gentle people with untroubled, placid minds who have a three-day ritual for saying "Hello." (See "Tin Man")

CHILDREN OF TAMA: An alien race that communicates by means of metaphors. (See "Darmok")

CHRYSALLIANS: A race of neutral people who have enjoyed ten generations of peace. At the negotiations for the Barzan wormhole the Chrysallians are represented by Ral. (See "The Price")

CLOUD CREATURE: An amorphous, sentient entity in space; when part of this being was caught on the *Enterprise,* it unwittingly killed some crew members in its efforts to get back to its main body. (See "Lonely Among Us")

COALESCENT: An organism which needs to absorb other life forms to survive, and it duplicates whatever it absorbs, even down to the cellular level. (See "Aquiel")

CONTINUUM: The name of the body of individuals who comprise all of the entities who call themselves the "Q."

COUNCIL OF ELDERS: The leaders of the Organians, who appear to be docile hicks but who are really super-evolved energy beings. (See "Errand Of Mercy")

COUNCIL OF NOBLES: Chief Council of Elas — the body that marries Elaan off to the ruler of Troyius. (See "Elaan Of Troyius")

"CREATURES": The name given to those who reach puberty on the world where childhood lasts three hundred years; arriving so late, it produces monsters on the verge of death. (See "Miri")

CRYSTALLINE ENTITY: A gigantic alien being which lives on energy and can destroy all life on a world by absorbing the energy patterns into itself. Although only one such entity has ever been found by the Federation, the fact that more may exist has not been ruled out. Lore formed an alliance with such a creature and destroyed the colonists of Omicron Theta; his attempt to repeat the procedure with the *Enterprise* fails. (See "Datalore") The *Enterprise* later encounters the creature and is on the verge of communicating with it when a vengeful scientist destroys it. (See "Silicon Avatar")

CYTHERIANS: Aliens who explore other cultures by having representatives of the cultures come to them. (See "The Nth Degree")

DACHLYDS: A culture on a planet near Gemaris Five, among whom Picard mediated a trade dispute. (See "Captain's Holiday")

DAL'ROK: A creature which threatens a Bajoran tribe each harvest time. Only the storyteller, the Sirah, can drive the thing away. (See "The Storyteller")

DOHLMAN: Leaders of Elas, powerful but subject to decisions of the Council of Nobles on that world, as in the decision to marry off the Dohlman Elaan to the Troyian ruler. (See "Elaan Of Troyius")

DOPTERIAN: A type of alien who, like the Ferengi, are immune to Betazoid mind reading abilities. A Dopterian is caught stealing Lwaxana Troi's latinum hair brooch when she visits Deep Space Nine. (See "The Forsaken")

DOUWD: An immortal, all-powerful being about whom little is known. They are comparable to the Q although only one Douwd has ever been encountered by the Federation. (See "The Survivors")

DRILL THRALLS: Triskelion slaves who train new gladiators, such as the *Enterprise* landing party. (See "Gamesters Of Triskelion")

THE EDO: The simple people of a Class M planet, Rubicum III, who are friendly, affectionate and ruled by a strange orbiting "god" who dispenses harsh justice. (See "Justice")

EDO LORD: The "god" of the Edo, it seems to be a satellite that exists partially in our dimension, and partially in another. (See "Justice")

ELECTED ONE: The leader of the inhabitants of Angel One. When the Enterprise visits that world, the position is held by Beata. (See "Angel One")

EMPATHS: A race of unknown origin, which occupies the planet Minara II. They are tested by another race, the Vians, to see if they deserve to be rescued before their planet is destroyed in a solar nova. The test involves the abduction of James Kirk and McCoy, who are tortured. A single female Empath, who McCoy calls "Gem," must decide to use her healing powers to save them despite the risk to herself. Fortunately, she succeeds, and saves her people. (See "The Empath")

EMPATHIC METAMORPH: A being who can sense what a mate wants and needs. Female metamorphs are rare and highly prized. (See "The Perfect Mate")

ENNIS: The warrior people who are prisoners on a moon surrounded by a satellite defense network capable of returning the dead to life. But once the slain have walked again, they can never leave that planetoid and survive. Their leader is Golin Shel-la. (See "Battle Lines")

EYMORGS: The women of Sigma Draconis, who rule over their men as docile servants fit only for breeding. When their central computer begins to fail, they steal Spock's brain to keep it going. (See "Spock's Brain")

FABRINI: Builders of *Yonada,* the asteroid-sized vessel that allowed them to escape the destruction of their planet when the star Fabrina went nova. Only the most useful Fabrini were able to escape. A computer failure would have destroyed *Yonada* if not for the timely arrival of the *Enterprise.* (See "For The World Is Hollow And I Have Touched The Sky")

FEEDERS OF VAAL: Those who, on Gamma Trianguli VI, provide the computer with the various materials that it converts into its power source. (See "The Apple")

FERENGI: A race of dwarf aliens who pride themselves on being ruthless businessmen and live for nothing else. The ultimate capitalists. They subjugate their females (who are forced to go naked) and only the males are allowed to engage in business activities. (See "The Last Outpost", "The Nagus") They are often at odds with the Federation but apparently not an enemy or a member. A Ferengi vessel intrudes on Starfleet wargames when its captain misconstrues them as a battle between the *Enterprise* and the *Hathaway,* and assumes that the strife is over something of immense value. (See "Peak Performance")

FERENGI PHYSIOLOGY: Ferengi brains are composed of four different aspects which in combination make it impossible for Betazoids to read Ferengi minds. (See "Menage A Troi")

FIRST FEDERATION: Balok's civilization. (See "The Corbomite Maneuver")

GATHERERS: A tribe of nomads who departed from Acamar Three a century before due to blood feuds which were decimating their clans. They are raiders who disrupt trade routes with their outlaw activity. An attempt to end hostilities and work out a peace accord involving an amnesty was attempted unsuccessfully eighteen years before. In order to return in peace to Acamar Three, the Gatherer leader, Chorgon, wants not only autonomy for his people but also three seats in the ruling council. (See "The Vengeance Factor")

GEMARIANS: A trade dispute between the Gemarians and their planetary neighbor, the Dachlyds, was settled by Captain Picard. (See "Captain's Holiday")

GILVOS LIZARD: A harmless lizard which Alexander makes friends with. It is kept in a cage in the biolab. (See "New Ground")

GLOB FLY: A small and apparently harmless insect on the Klingon planet, known for its irritating sound. Seems to bother those surly Klingons no end. (See "The Outrageous Okona")

GORGAN: An evil entity sealed for ages on the planet Triacus until the Starnes expedition frees him. After driving the adults to killing themselves, he takes over the affections of the children, who call him the "Good Angel." He is anything but, and tries to use the *Enterprise* to launch his conquest of the galaxies. Kirk is able to defeat him only with extreme difficulty. (See "And The Children Shall Lead")

GORN: A tall, reptilian creature with humanoid posture. After a Gorn attack wipes out the Federation outpost on Cestus III, the Metrons pit a representative Gorn against James Kirk in a one-to-one struggle that will determine the outcome of a possible war — at considerably less expense in lives. (See "Arena")

GRIZELLAS: When the Sheliak Corporate pressures the Federation to live up to the Treaty of Armens, Picard finds a loophole which allows him to name the Grizellas to be the arbiters. But since the Grizellas are currently in their six month hibernation phase, the Sheliaks reluctantly agree to give Picard the additional time he requests to meet their demands. (See "The Ensigns Of Command")

GUARDIANS OF BORETH: Another name for the High Clerics, the Klingon religious leaders who live on Boreth and study the history of Kahless as they await his return. (See "Rightful Heir")

GUARDIAN OF FOREVER: The time portal on an unnamed planet, a living being created by some unknown source. Kirk and Spock travel to the 1930s through it in their pursuit of the temporarily unhinged McCoy. (See "City On The Edge Of Forever")

HAHLILIAN: An exotic humanoid alien race. (See "Aquiel")

HALKANS: A peaceful race whose character remains unchanged between the "real" universe and the mirror universe. In our world, their refusal to provide dilithium crystals to the Federation is no big deal; in the mirror world it leads to some serious complications. (See "Mirror, Mirror")

HARADA: An alien race which will only open negotiations with the Federation when Picard welcomes them in their own language, without making any errors of speech. The Harada consider such errors to be highly insulting and the last time the Federation made an attempt to open negotiations, the ambassador made an error and the Harada broke off all contact with the Federation for years. (See "The Big Goodbye")

HIGH CLERICS: The Klingon religious leaders who live on Boreth and study the history of Kahless as they await his return. (See "Rightful Heir")

HORNBUCK: An animal which is hunted by the Mintakans. (See "Who Watches The Watchers?")

HORTA: A silicon-based being on Janus VI that seems to be an indiscriminate killer of humans until Spock discovers, courtesy of the Vulcan mind meld, that it is merely protecting its eggs, which the miners mistook for mineral formations. Fifty-six humans die before this gets straightened out, however, but the Horta decides to help in mining operations in return for being left in peace. The Horta looks, basically, like a large crawling rock, and is not a very pretty sight to human eyes. (See "Devil In The Dark")

HUSNOCK: An alien race that wantonly destroyed all life on Rana IV. In reprisal, the mysterious alien who had adopted human form and called himself Kevin Uxbridge, destroyed every Husnock in the universe. (See "The Survivors")

I-CHAYA: Spock's pet sehlet when he was a boy. (See "Yesteryear")

ICONIANS: The extinct inhabitants of Iconia, whose race and culture perished 200 millennia ago. Captain Varley discovers the location of their planet. The Iconians held the secret of instantaneous transportation, a technology that survives until Picard, perhaps wisely, destroys it. (See "Contagion")

IOTIANS: Inhabitants of Iotia, the planet forever altered by the accidental leaving behind of the book *Chicago Mobs of the Twenties* (see **Intrepid, U.S.S.**), it developed a culture based on philosophies best represented by the likes of Al Capone. Kirk manages to get matters back on track by unifying the rival gangs, but is less than pleased to learn that McCoy accidentally left a communicator on Iotia — who knows what the Iotians will do with this jump in technological information? (See "A Piece Of The Action")

JARADA: An alien race Riker refers to in passing; all that we know is that they have little in common with the Pakleds. (See "Samaritan Snare")

J'NAII: An androgynous race. They possess both male and female sexual characteristics and favor neither one over the other emotionally. But occasionally there is a throwback to an earlier time when the J'Naii were divided into males and females and the majority of modern J'Naii regard these throwbacks with repugnance and employ mind control techniques to alter them and make them like everyone else. (See "The Outcast")

KALANDANS: A long-dead race. The outpost discovered by the *Enterprise* was the origin site of the disease that spread and wiped out the entire Kalandan civilization, but the outpost's defense mechanisms still operate, with deadly results. (See "That Which Survives")

KANUTU: One of the many tribes of the planet Neural, known for healing abilities. Nona, wife of Tyree, is a member of this tribe. (See "A Private Little War")

KLINGONS: A warlike race, inherently opposed to the ideals and interests of the Federation. Their government is an Empire, united and maintained by force; at the time of James Kirk's initial mission with the *Enterprise*, they are relentlessly expansionist, determined to take over or subvert the power structure of as many worlds as they can. Sometimes direct force is their main tactic; it's certainly their favorite. But they find themselves outclassed when they think they've conquered the pacifistic Organians. The resulting forced treaty between the Empire and the Federation doesn't stop them from trying to subvert Federation influence by selling arms to underdeveloped planets (no Prime Directive for the Klingons!)

or by providing the Romulans with Klingon ships and cloaking devices. Notable Klingons encountered by James Kirk include Kang, Koloth, Kor, and a recreation of the historical Kahless. As these name suggests, their language is as harsh and guttural as can be, obviously a reflection of their barbaric ways— although leaders such as Kor and Koloth are very sophisticated adversaries in their own inimitable fashion. Other unnamed Klingons met by the *Enterprise* include the captain of the ship that interferes, ill-advisedly as it turns out, with the *Enterprise* as it takes Elaan to Troyius, and a variety of underlings and associates. The expansionist attitude has a lot to do with the lack of natural resources on the worlds they inhabit. One Klingon in particular (Kruge) was responsible for the death of Kirk's son, David Marcus. Late in James T. Kirk's career, the Klingons made peace with the Federation.

KLINGON AGE OF ASCENSION: A Klingon rite of passage, reenacted on certain anniversaries. A typical Klingon test of pain and endurance, it involves having your friends beat you with pain sticks. Worf's human friends, led by Geordi, help him observe his tenth anniversary on the holodeck. (See "The Icarus Factor")

KLINGON DEATH RITUAL: When a Klingon is about to die, his living companions perform this, crying out loud warnings to the dead so they'll know a Klingon is headed their way. (See "Heart Of Glory")

KLINGON TEA CEREMONY: Another dangerous Klingon ritual involving an apparently distasteful beverage, which is toxic to humans. Pulaski takes the antidote in advance so she can share the ceremony with Worf. (See "Up The Long Ladder")

KOBLIAD: A dying alien race which requires deuridium to stabilize their cell structure in order to extend their life span. (See "The Passenger")

KOHMS: Asian humans encountered on Omega IV, apparently offspring of an old Chinese colony still indoctrinated with Communist ideology. It is never adequately explained why they should have wound up on the same planet with a colony of real gung-ho right wing American types, but it seems likely that one group or the other followed the other there in an effort to continue their ideological conflict. They have extremely long life spans. (See "Omega Glory")

KOINONIANS: There were two such races which

were destroyed in the Koinonian War. One of the races was non-corporeal and some members of that Koinonian race have survived and are non-violent. (See "The Bonding")

KURL: This ancient alien civilization believed that an individual was actually a community of individuals as inside a person are many voices, each with its own desires. (See "The Chase")

LAPLING: An extinct creature which burrowed in the sand. The last living one of the species is in the Kivas Fajo collection. (See "The Most Toys")

LEGARANS: The inhabitants of Legara Four, they exists in a strange substance which must be maintained at 150 degrees Celsius. Sarek negotiates the final treaty of his career with this race. (See "Sarek")

LIGHTS OF ZETAR: Strange, nonphysical life forms that take the form of lights that can possess humanoids — which is usually fatal to their hosts unless the exposure is very brief. Even then it is generally unhealthy. Their presence seriously disrupts the entire nervous system. Insane, they have no qualms about killing other life forms; they are themselves destroyed when their latest host, Mira Romaine, is put in a pressure chamber. (See "The Lights Of Zetar")

LORNACK CLAN: One of the clans of Gatherers, Volneth and Chorgon are its remaining survivors. Their rivals were the Tralestas which they massacred eight years before. (See "The Vengeance Factor")

LUMERIAN: Ves Alkar is a Lumerian who claims that their religious beliefs prohibit an autopsy being performed on one of their dead. (See "Man Of The People")

LYSIANS: A race not as technologically advanced as Starfleet. The Satarrans are at war with them and try to trick the *Enterprise* into attacking the Lysians. (See "Conundrum")

MAKERS: An extinct race, which left behind the

subservient androids of the outpost world later known as Planet Mudd, named after the new (if somewhat unwilling) master of the androids, who exist only to serve. (See "I, Mudd")

MALKORIANS: The people of Malkor, a planet on the verge of the space age but which is thus far unaware of the existence of the Federation and all that it implies. (See "First Contact")

MARCOFFIAN SNOW LIZARD: When Q's powers are taken away, his choice is to become either a human being or a Marcoffian snow lizard. (See "Deja Q")

MARIPOSANS: The descendants of the five survivors of the *U.S.S. Mariposa*. Upon reaching a Class M planet they started reproducing by cloning. After generations of this, their gene pool is quite weak. (See "Up The Long Ladder")

MEDUSANS: A remarkable telepathic race. It is uncertain whether or not they have bodies in the sense of most species. What is certain is that humanoids cannot look upon a Medusan with the naked eye without going completely mad. Telepathic communication is possible for races like the Vulcans, although they must wear special visors to protect themselves. A special case is Dr. Miranda Jones, a rare human telepath who develops a close relationship with one Medusan, Ambassador Kollos. Her secret, concealed from humanity for years, is that she is blind. Medusans can navigate in interstellar space, a region that also drives humanoids out of their minds. (See "Is There In Truth No Beauty?")

MELKOT: The name, both collective and individual, used to describe an alien race; however, humanoids tend to refer to them as **Melkotians.** They do not care for other races to intrude on their planet, and devise cruel and unusual punishments for anyone who does; the *Enterprise* crew winds up reliving the famous gunfight at the OK Corral in Tombstone, Arizona. Obviously, they are able to create convincing and potentially fatal illusions. After the *Enterprise* crew manages to think their way through the Tombstone scenario, the Melkotians begrudgingly agree to some interaction with the Federation. (See "Spectre Of The Gun")

MENTHARS: A race which died out hundreds of years ago as the result of a war they engaged in with the Promellians. The Menthars used Aceton assimilators in order to trap Promellian ships in the debris of the shattered planet Orelious Nine. (See "Booby Trap")

METRON: The alien race, vastly advanced over ours, that pits a single human – Kirk – against a single Gorn adversary. Also the individual Metron seen by Kirk and the *Enterprise* crew. (See "Arena")

MICROBIOTIC BACTERIA: A microscopic, metal-eating creature that (in sufficient numbers) threatens the *Pagh* and the *Enterprise* with serious hull integrity problems. Destroyed by a neutrino beam. (See "A Matter Of Honor")

MIKULAKS: Tissue samples from this race are being transported to Nahmi Four to battle an outbreak of Correllium Fever. (See "The Price")

MINTAKANS: Proto-Vulcan humanoids whose culture is at the level of the Bronze Age. They are a peaceful culture. Physiologically their lyzome levels are such that the mind-erasing technique employed by the *Enterprise* medical personnel will not work on them. (See "Who Watches The Watchers?")

MIRADORNS: Aliens who exist as twins. They are each one half of a single being and one cannot live long once his twin dies. (See "Vortex")

MISTRESSES: The elite class of the planet Angel One, led by the Elected One. (See "Angel One")

MIZARIANS: The inhabitants of the planet Mizar Two. This race is peaceful and nonviolent and as a result has been conquered six times in three hundred years. (See "Allegiance")

MORGS: The males of Sigma Draconis VI, kept docile and primitive by the dominant females, or Eymorgs. (See "Spock's Brain")

MUGATO: A shaggy, albino, horned gorilla-like creature native to the planet Neural. Its bite is poisonous, as James Kirk finds after tangling with one of the vicious brutes. He is saved by the healer-woman Nona, who uses mako root as an antidote. (See "A Private Little War")

NAUSICAANS: Nasty aliens with whom Picard got into a fight years ago when he was a cocky young

ensign and nearly lost his life, although he did get an artificial heart as a result of the brutal encounter. (See "Samaritan Snare" and "Tapestry")

NAVOT: A Bajoran faction which is in a territorial dispute with the Paqu, another Bajoran faction. Benjamin Sisko is asked to mediate the dispute. (See "The Storyteller")

NOL-ENNIS: The counterparts of the Ennis. They are prisoners on a moon surrounded by a satellite defense network capable of returning the dead to life. But once the slain have walked again, they can never leave that planetoid and survive . (See "Battle Lines")

OLD ONES, THE: The apparently extinct beings who left behind the androids of Exo III. Korob on Pyris VII also refers to his masters as the Old Ones, but they were probably a different group of Old Ones; the androids of Exo III claim to have destroyed their creators. (See "What Are Little Girls Made Of?")

ONLY: Miri and her fellow "children" call themselves this because they were the "only" ones to remain when the adults of their world died, centuries ago. (See "Miri")

ORGANIANS: The inhabitants of Organia. The physical forms of the Organians are merely disguises assumed for dealing with Klingons and other humanoids; they are really energy beings of staggering power who have left physical concerns behind long, long ago. (See "Errand Of Mercy")

ORION WING SLUGS: A creature referred to by Deanna Troi when she says that she'd rather eat them than have to deal with a toad-faced troll like the Ferengi Tog. (See "Menage A Troi")

PAKLEDS: A dim-witted alien race who need the assistance of others in order to operate the technology they have acquired. Their apparent helplessness leads the *Enterprise* to help them, only to have them kidnap LaForge. The Pakleds are smart enough to steal technology from other races for their own use, but not understanding the science behind it, they are easily impressed by a simple ruse devised by Riker. (See "Samaritan Snare")

PAQU: A Bajoran faction which is in a territorial dispute with the Navot, another Bajoran faction. (See "The Storyteller")

PARASITES: Flying entities, apparently forming a crude collective mind, that can control people through extreme pain. The collective mind grows and learns as more hosts are accumulated. Contact can be, and often is, fatal. The parasites have traveled quite a bit, ravaging world after world, and are encountered by the *Enterprise* on the planet Deneva. There the *Enterprise* crew manages to find the weakness of these deadly beings: ultraviolet light. After this, the parasites are finally eradicated for once and for all. They probably originated somewhere beyond the reaches of our own galaxy. (See "Operation: Annihilate")

PLANET COUNCIL: This is the central governmental assembly of the planet Ardana, in the cloud-borne Stratos City. (See "The Cloud Minders")

PLATONIANS: A cruel and capricious race of telekinetic humanoids whose power, it turns out, is derived from the substance kironide. All but immortal, these people visited Earth during the time of the ancient Greek philosophers. Their home world was destroyed by a nova. Thirty-eight refugees moved to the planet they now call Platonius, including Plasus, Philana and the dwarf Alexander. They almost get the better of Kirk and his crew, but he manages to turn the tables on them all. The good-natured Alexander, the only decent Platonian, leaves with the *Enterprise*. (See "Plato's Stepchildren")

PRAETOR: The very highest rank in the Romulan Empire. (See "Balance Of Terror")

PRAETORIAN GUARD: The imperial guard in ancient Rome, and the translation of the equivalent group in the Roman-style culture of Planet 892-IV. The *Enterprise* landing party is briefly mistaken for members of this elite military group. (See "Bread And Circuses")

PRESERVERS: A highly developed alien race that seems to have been in the habit of relocating primitive cultures to other planets. They brought the American Indian tribes to the world where Kirk had amnesia, and left an obelisk there to protect them. So far, the Federation has yet to find any more evidence of the Preservers. It is not known if they still exist, are extinct, or even if they came from our galaxy — one of the great mysteries of deep space. (See "The Paradise Syndrome") Although unidentified, these are apparently the same aliens revealed in the climax of the TNG episode "The Chase."

PROMELLIANS: A vanished alien race apparently destroyed a thousand years before in a war with the Menthars. The *Enterprise* is lured into an ancient booby trap when they detect a Promellian warship which is fully intact. (See "Booby Trap")

PROVIDERS: Another name for the Gamesters of Triskelion, three disembodied brains with apparently nothing better to do than pit their human slaves against each other in various forms of combat and bet on the outcome. Kirk convinces them that freeing their slaves and helping them develop their own forms of government might in fact be a more interesting challenge. (See "The Gamesters Of Triskelion")

Q CONTINUUM: The race of omnipotent beings whose true appearance is unknown to anyone in the Federation. The one who calls himself Q periodically takes on human form to bedevil the *Enterprise,* and in particular Jean-Luc Picard. (See "Encounter at Farpoint", "Hide & Q", "Q Who?", "Deja Q", "Q-Pid", "Tapestry", "Q Less")

RAKHAR: An alien society which is a virtual police state in which its people have few rights. (See "Vortex")

RAZORBEAST: The imaginary friend Guinan had as a child that purred her to sleep at night. (See "Imaginary Friend")

ROMULANS: A race related to the Vulcans, the Romulans seem to have developed a radically different culture. It is obvious that they split from the Vulcans before the Vulcans mastered their emotions and embraced logic, which would seem to indicate that the Vulcans achieved space travel long before their philosophical breakthrough. The Romulans also have no telepathic powers. Perhaps they have diverged evolutionarily since the split. Culturally, the Romulans are imperialistic, having a highly militarized empire that seems bent on expansion. A century before the missions of Kirk's *Enterprise*, the Federation and the Romulans fought a war which ended when the Neutral Zone was established, apparently after the Federation got the upper hand in the conflict. The space ships used at the time did not allow the combatants to see each other. Only more recently, after the Romulans obtained ships of obvious Klingon design (see **Romulan/Klingon Alliance**, below), did either side see the face of the other. Romulans are not prone to capturing enemies, or enduring capture themselves; they are prepared at all times to go down with their ships. Despite the fact that their culture is pointlessly aggressive and is backwards in many ways, the Romulans apparently hold their women in high regard, as female commanders serve effectively on Romulan vessels. Kirk and Spock will both attest to that fact. Romulans kept to their own space for quite some time after the war, but in Kirk's time they renewed their aggressive ways (with Klingon vessels) and attacked Federation outposts, leading to several encounters between the *Enterprise* and Romulan ships. (See "Balance Of Terror" and "The Enterprise Incident")

ROMULAN EMPIRE: A foe of the Federation, which stopped all contact, hostile or otherwise, for 53 year, perhaps as a matter of some internal problem, although they did destroy their alliance with the Klingons with their attack on Khitomer. Their reasons for reappearing are also unknown, but they are clearly still hostile. (See "The Neutral Zone," etc.)

ROMULAN/KLINGON ALLIANCE: Unconfirmed at the time of "The Enterprise Incident", but widely suspected, since Romulan ships suddenly seemed to be of Klingon design.

SALTAH'NA: An ancient race which once existed in the Gamma Quadrant and which was destroyed in a power struggle. (See "Dramatis Personae")

SANDBATS: Deadly denizens of the planet Maynark IV. They blend in flawlessly with rocky surfaces until they are ready to attack. By then, it's usually too late. (See "The Empath")

SATARRAN: An alien race at war with the Lysians who attempt to trick the *Enterprise* into attacking them, as the Federation has far more advanced technologically than either the Lysians or the Satarrans. (See "Conundrum")

SCALOSIANS: The inhabitants of Scalos, a planet which once boasted a fine civilization, but substances unleashed by severe volcanic activity have ravaged their world: now all their children are dead, the Scalosian men have all become incapable of fathering new children, and, to make matters worse, the Scalosians now move so fast that they can't even be seen by the human eye. The *Enterprise* landing party on Scalos hears the voices of the natives as some sort of faint insectoid buzzing. The distress signal that brings the *Enterprise* to Scalos is a ruse; the women of Scalos have been luring humanoids there in an as-yet-unsuccessful effort to get some new blood, so to speak, and get their race going again. Kirk becomes a prime target of this campaign, but he prefers to distribute his vital bodily fluids in a more traditional fashion, and resists. Besides, acceleration, induced by drinking Scalosian water, is generally fatal to humans, although Kirk risks it in order to get this whole mess straightened out. (See "The Wink Of An Eye")

SEHLET: A Vulcan house pet. It is like a large bear which has protruding fangs, but it quite gentle unless aroused in protection of its master. (See "Yesteryear")

SENTINELS: On Ardana, Troglytes are sometimes taken from the surface and trained as sentinels for security duty in the cloudborne city of Stratos. (See "The Cloud Minders")

SHAKAAR: The Bajoran resistance under the brutal occupation of the Cardassians. Kira Nerys was a member of the Shakaar resistance. (See "Duet")

SHELIAK CORPORATE: A race of aliens found in the Shelius star system. The Federation has attempted to negotiate with them, without success, for 111 years. They are crystalline entities who know some of the languages of the Federation although no one outside of the Sheliak Corporate knows their tongue. The only contact the Federation has had with the Sheliak is through the Treaty of Armens. (See "The Ensigns Of Command")

SOLARI: The natives of the planet Soleis Five. They may hold the record for duration of warfare: fifteen centuries. They call in the famous negotiator Rivato to help them work out their long-standing conflicts. (See "Loud As A Whisper")

SPORES, OMICRON CETI III: Alien spores of unknown origin which drifted through space before arriving at a hospitable host planet, Omicron Ceti III. The spores found the Berthold Rays that assail that planet to be quite amenable to their existence. The spores used native flowering plants as their hosts until humans arrived to colonize Omicron Ceti III. Humans served as even better hosts, and the initial influence of the spores seemed beneficial, if unusual. The first symptom was highly desirable: immunity to the Berthold Rays, which are generally deadly to humanoids. Peace of mind, improved health and an almost-telepathic rapport with other humanoids affected by the spores were also, in themselves, not negative effects — except that the effects were so intense that the colonists were left with little or no motivation to work. While some might see this as a perfectly desirable state, it was really quite a problem, as the crew of the *Enterprise* — especially Spock — can attest. Fortunately, the spores can be driven out by powerful human emotions, and the colonists of Omicron Ceti III were released from the spores, and then moved on to create a new colony on some other world. (See "This Side Of Paradise")

TAKARAN: An alien species which is capable of simulating a death-like state. This is enabled by the fact that Takaran physiology doesn't have important separate organs but rather every system is equally distributed throughout their body and they can control their physiology at a cellular level. (See "Suspicions")

TALARIANS: Aliens who were once at war with the Federation. They were known to take the children of their slain enemies and raise them to be Talarians. (See "Suddenly Human")

TALOSIANS: The inhabitants of Talos IV, the fourth planet in the Talos Star Group. Long ago, its culture destroyed itself through atomic warfare. The survivors of this large-skulled race moved underground. In their subterranean homes they diverted themselves from their tragedy by creating false worlds with their incredible mental powers of illusion, and amused themselves by collecting alien species for their planetary zoo. Their race is slowly dying out, fading into

more and more illusion and failing to reproduce. Their attempts to add a human specimen — Captain Christopher Pike — to their menagerie failed, and led to a Federation ban on all visits to the planet. This is the only Federation law whose violation still carries the death penalty, although punishment was waived due to special circumstances in the case of Spock, who undertook the only known expedition to Talos IV after Pike was there. (See "The Menagerie")

TAMARIANS: See Children of Tama. (See also "Darmok")

TELLERIANS: A race of aliens who were once at war with the Federation. They are a humanoid race with a very Spartan lifestyle. (See "Suddenly Human")

TELLARITES: Piggish in appearance, the Tellarites are one of the alien races that belong to the Federation. A fairly disagreeable people whose participation in any diplomatic conference seems fairly absurd. (See "Journey To Babel")

TERELLIANS: The race all but destroyed by their own biological warfare weapons; the survivors wander space in sealed plague ship and are generally treated as pariahs. (See "Haven")

TETRARCH: Sul Varis, the magistrate of the Paqu. She is a 15-year-old girl. (See "The Storyteller")

THASIANS: Non-physical beings who raised the child Charles Evans when he was left alone on their planet, Thasus. They taught him their amazing mental powers, but did not mean for him to leave their world before he learned the maturity to use those powers wisely. (See "Charlie X")

THOLIANS: A very reclusive, protective alien race with minimal contact with the Federation. They seem to be somewhat insectoid in nature, but the quality of their video transmissions leaves much to be desired, and this remains mere conjecture. An offhand comment by Spock suggests that the Vulcans may have had more significant contact with the Tholians than any other Federation race. (See "The Tholian Web") First encountered by Kirk about a century earlier. Very elusive; they attacked a Starbase and Kyle Riker was the only person to survive. (See "The Icarus Factor") Will Riker has also encountered them, but only in a battle training simulation. (See "Peak Performance")

THRALLS: Slaves of every galactic variety, assembled by the Providers of Triskelion to take part in the deadly games which the Providers gamble on. (See "The Gamesters Of Triskelion")

TILONIAN: An inhabitant of Tilonus Four. (See "Frame Of Mind")

TIN MAN: A reference to the Oz character, used to refer to Data. (See "The Schizoid Man", "The Measure of a Man") Also the code name given a mysterious sentient spaceship encountered in deep space: a living creature used by a mysterious race as transportation through space. The only living one ever found is known as Gomtuu. It is a spaceborne creature which lives on certain types of galactic matter. Its crew was apparently killed in an explosion and the radiation which resulted. The creature, code named "Tin Man," is in orbit around the planet Beta Stromgren which will soon self-destruct. Tam Elbrun, a Betazoid who was a full telepath from birth (a rarity), is brought in to attempt contact with the creature in order to warn it of the impending danger. Tam Elbrun joins with Gomtuu, thereby giving the lonely creature a reason to live. (See "Tin Man")

T'KON EMPIRE: An ancient alien empire which was destroyed by a supernova centuries ago. A defunct political entity that ruled a large part of the known galaxy, 600 thousand years ago. At least one outpost of their empire survived to the 24th Century (Federation reckoning). (See "The Last Outpost")

TRALESTA CLAN: A clan of Gatherers who are the rivals of the Lornacks of Acamar III. The Lornacks attempted to massacre the Tralesta but five people survived. Finally only Yuta remains of the Tralesta Clan and Chorgon from the Lornacks, so Yuta tries to kill Chorgon. Riker finds that the only way to stop Yuta is to kill her. (See "The Vengeance Factor")

TRIBBLES: Small, relatively shapeless and completely covered with fur, these are very gregarious beasts indeed, the perfect pets for anyone in the entire galaxy, except if you're a Klingon. Tribbles hate Klingons, and Klingons hate tribbles. Humans, by and large, love the little furballs, although their highly accelerated reproductive rate can cause serious problems, especially in enclosed spaces such as space stations. This, combined with their innate hunger and limitless capacity for eating, provide two major flaws in the otherwise perfect tribble scenario. (See "The Trouble With Tribbles")

TRILL: A symbiot which can live on and on in a series of host bodies. (See "The Host")

TROGLYTES: The sub-surface inhabitants of the planet Ardana, miners for the most part, although some are trained to serve the upper class in Stratos. Their constant exposure to Zienite has impaired their mental abilities and given rise to a class division based on a spurious evolutionary difference between the Troglytes and their masters. In fact, both groups are equal, and the effects of Zienite are reversible. This discovery shakes the foundations of Ardana's society. (See "The Cloud Minders")

ULANS: Residents of Margaritus Six, mentioned by Lwaxana Troi, who have unusual dining habits. (See "Manhunt")

ULLIANS: Telepathic humanoids. (See "Violations")

VAAL: The subterranean computer system that controls the lives of the natives of Gamma Trianguli VI and provides for their every need. Its interface with the surface looks like a huge Mayan serpent. Kirk destroys it and sets the natives on the path to civilization. (See "The Apple")

VAMPIRIC CLOUD: A gaseous being that absorbs the red blood cells from humanoids with an iron-based blood. Needless to say, Spock is not on its menu. Capable of interplanetary and interstellar travel, it seems to originate on the planet Tycho IV. It is not known whether the one destroyed by Kirk was unique or if there are others still out in space. (See "Obsession")

VIANS: The race, based on Minara II, that abducts Kirk, Spock and McCoy to act as torture subjects in an experiment that is cruel in its execution but strangely humane, in a misguided fashion, in its intent: to test the Empath "Gem" and find if her race "deserves" to be spared the nova of their sun. The Vians do save the Empath's race, but it is unclear whether they saved themselves as well; it seems unlikely that they could have passed their own empathy test. (See "The Empath")

VORGONS: Criminals from this race, Boratus and Ajur, come back in time from the 27th Century in order to try to find the dangerous device known as the Tox-Uthat. They are the ones whom the inventor, Kal Dano, hid the device from. (See "Captain's Holiday")

VULCANS: Also known as VULCANIANS (an outdated and inaccurate terminology). The native race of the planet Vulcan: tall humanoids with pointed ears, arched eyebrows and skin that is faintly green due to the copper-based blood. A less obvious physical trait is their second eyelid, apparently evolved to protect their eyes from the extremely bright sun of their dry, desert-like world. (When Spock is ill he increases his room's temperature to a cozy 125 degrees Fahrenheit.) In the distant past the Vulcans were much like their relatives, the Romulans, an aggressive people who colonized other planets but whose violent ways threatened to destroy them. The entire Vulcan character changed radically after a period of upheaval; out of the chaos, serene Vulcan philosophers like Surak led the Vulcans into a new age dominated by logic rather than by base, uncontrolled passions. (Vulcan colonies either died out, created their own cultures that have yet to be rediscovered, or, like the Romulans, became a completely separate race with a different way of life.) Since their new philosophy took hold, the Vulcans have taken a great lead in science, excelling in such fields as subatomic physics. In character, they are very stoical, logical and can be very exasperating to humans used to expecting an emotional component to all conversations and arguments. (This is best exemplified by Dr. Leonard McCoy.) Humor is rumored to be totally absent from the Vulcan character, although Spock shows the occasional flash of dry wit which may not be entirely derived from his mother's side of the family. Vulcans are also vegetarians, with no interest in intoxication, although they apparently will accept alcohol on social occasions; perhaps they metabolize it differently and do not get drunk, or can control its effects with their minds. A fascinating race, the Vulcans provide an intriguing counterpoint to the wild extremes of illogical human behavior.

WADI: A new race recently encountered by the Federation in the Gamma Quadrant beyond the Bajoran wormhole. They are a people who love to play games. (See "Move Along Home")

YANGS: The humanoids of Omega IV who possess strange relics that turn out to be the American Pledge of Allegiance and other items of Earth origin. They are the enemies of the Kohm, another group of humanoids who apparently derive their own culture from Earth's communist ideologies. (See "Omega Glory")

YRIDIAN: The type of alien who approaches Worf when he is visiting Deep Space Nine. (See "Birthright") An Yridian destroyer attacks the shuttle of Prof. Galen, who dies from the injuries he sustains. (See "The Chase")

ZAKDORNS: Somewhat arrogant aliens whose long-standing reputation as strategists has been taken for granted for thousands of years; Sohlrami meets his match in Data. (See "Peak Performance")

ZALKONIANS: The people of the planet Zalkon who are attempting to prevent those of their people who are evolving into noncorporeal beings. They unleash a weapon on the *Enterprise* which causes everyone aboard to begin choking, although "John Doe" has the ability to halt the effect. (See "Transfigurations")

ZIBALIANS: The inhabitants of the world of Zibalia, one of whom is the mad collector Kivas Fajo. (See "The Most Toys")

CHARACTER INDEX

AARON, ADMIRAL: One of the senior Starfleet officers infested by the alien parasites. (See "Conspiracy")

ABRAMSON: A famous 22nd Century figure who was really the immortal human being from Earth who called himself Flint. (See "Requiem For Methuselah")

ABROM: Older brother of the Zeon Isak.

ACCOLAN: The Aldean given Harry Bernard as his "son" after the *Enterprise* children are kidnapped. (See "When The Bough Breaks")

ACHILLES: McCoy's opponent on the gladiatorial game show *Name The Winner*. (See "Bread And Circuses")

ADAM: One of Dr. Sevrin's band of space-wandering youths in search of the mythical planet of Eden. (See "The Way To Eden")

ADAMS, DR. TRISTAN: In "Dagger Of The Mind," he is the head of the Tantalus penal settlement who, despite his once-justified reputation as an advocate of human prison practices, has become power mad. His brain-control seat proves to be his own undoing.

AGENT 201: A benevolent alien agent who preceded Gary Seven. (See "Assignment: Earth")

AGENT 347: Agent 201's cohort. Both are killed off screen in a car crash on their way to a vital mission in "Assignment: Earth," which brings Gary Seven into the picture.

AH-KEL: A Miradorn alien, one half of a whole being as Miradorns are twin entities. When his twin, Rok-Kel, is killed, Ah-Kel vows vengeance. (See "Vortex")

AJUR: A 27th Century Vorgon security agent who

wants to steal the Tox-Uthat which Picard and Vash have located on Risa. (See "Captain's Holiday")

AKAAR: The leader of the tribes of Capella IV. He is murdered by a rival, Maab, who sides with the Klingons (Akaar prefers the Federation). (See "Friday's Child")

AKAAR, TEER LEONARD JAMES: The son of Akaar, born after his father's death; he is named after McCoy and Kirk by the grateful widow, Eleen. (See "Friday's Child")

AKHARIN: The original identity of the immortal Flint: born in Mesopotamia in 3834 B.C., he developed from a simple soldier to a great genius in his long, long life. (See "Requiem For Methuselah")

AKUTA: The link between the computer Vaal and the people of Gamma Trianguli IV, and thus their leader. His metal antennae keep him directly interfaced with Vaal. (See "The Apple")

ALANS: A specialist in geomechanics and vulcanology, married to Hildebrant. He is a member of Wesley's Selcundi Drema team. (See "Pen Pals")

ALBERT, JOSH: A teammate of Wesley Crusher's in the Nova Squadron at Starfleet Academy. Josh is killed when the squadron practices a dangerous and forbidden maneuver in their one-man ships which they had intended to perform at the Starfleet graduation ceremonies. (See "The First Duty")

ALEXANDER: The dwarfish recipient of all the abuse the telekinetic Platonians can muster, Alexander is a key player in the struggles of Kirk and crew to escape the sadistic rulers of that world. Alexander declines their powers when McCoy unearths the secret behind them, and instead leaves his world behind to go where the *Enterprise* will take him. (See "Plato's Stepchildren")

ALEXANDER: The Klingon son of Worf. The boy's mother is K'Ehleyr, who was killed by Duras when he realized that she knew about his plotting against the Klingon High Council. (See "Reunion")

ALEXANDRA: Another child abducted from the *Enterprise*. (See "When The Bough Breaks")

ALICE: The shared name of the five hundred indistinguishable androids whose only purpose is to make Harry Mudd happy. (See "I, Mudd")

ALKAR, RAMID VES: A Lumerian ambassador who goes to the planet of Rekag-Bironi to try to find a way to end the bitter conflict there. (See "Man Of The People")

ALLENBY, ENSIGN TESS: An ensign aboard the *Enterprise*. (See "Final Mission" and "The Loss")

ALRIK: A Ferengi who gets aboard the *Enterprise* under false pretenses so he can attempt to steal a rare, female metamorph. (See "The Perfect Mate")

ALVA: A murder victim for whose killing her boyfriend was indicted. Part of the Dixon Hill computer hologram program. (See "Manhunt")

ALVIN: A victim of the accelerated aging disease on Gamma Hydra IV, whose body scares Chekov when he finds it — saving Chekov in the process. (See "The Deadly Years")

AMANDA: Spock's mother, the human woman who married the Vulcan ambassador, Sarek. She met her husband-to-be when he represented his world on Earth, and gave up her teaching career to marry him. She gave her son his human side, and even though he tends to favor the Vulcan side it is a key component in his makeup. (See "Journey To Babel") Sarek's first human wife, played thus far only by Jane Wyatt. In "Sarek" it is clear that she died some years before.

AMARIE: The four-armed widow of a dead smuggler who somehow came into possession of the stolen Vulcan shuttle the *T'Pau*. (See "Unification")

ANAN 7: On Eminiar VII, he is the head of the planetary Union — who almost lures the *Enterprise* crew to its doom. (See "A Taste Of Armageddon")

ANARA: O'Brien's Bajoran assistant. (See "The Forsaken")

ANAYA, APRIL: A crew member of the *Enterprise-D*. (See "The Nth Degree")

ANDREA: Dr. Korby's android creation, which falls in love with him; destroyed when Korby does himself in. (See "What Are Little Girls Made Of?")

ANTEDIAN DELEGATE: An assassin from Antede Three whose robe is lined with ultretium. (See "Manhunt")

ANYA: An allasomorph as is Salia whom she is the guardian of. Anya is from Daled's third moon. She opposes Salia's involvement with Wesley Crusher. (See "The Dauphin")

APELLA: Leader of the village where the Klingons come to sell armaments. (See "A Private Little War")

APGAR, DR. NEL: The creator of a Krieger wave converter, this Tanugan scientist has been secretly planning to sell the Federation-funded project to the highest bidder. He attempts to kill Will Riker to cover up his own intrigue. (See "A Matter Of Perspective")

APGAR, MANUA: The wife of Dr. Nel Apgar who stands by her late husband and claims that Riker killed him after Dr. Apgar caught the Starfleet officer trying to rape his wife. (See "A Matter Of Perspective")

APOLLO: Supposedly the ancient Greek god of the same name, encountered by Kirk and crew when he decides he needs to be worshipped again — not an idea to Kirk's liking, to say the least. Apollo, as is the habit of Greek gods, falls for a mortal: Lt. Carolyn Palamas. (See "Who Mourns For Adonais?")

APPEL, ED: A leader of the miners on Janus VI, on hand when the Horta appears. (See "Devil In The Dark")

APRIL, CAPTAIN ROBERT: The first man to hold command of the starship *Enterprise*. (See "The Counterclock Incident")

AQUINO, ENSIGN: A missing crewman who apparently died working on a power conduit aboard Deep Space Nine. It turns out that he was murdered by phaser fire and his death was made to look like an accident. (See "In The Hands Of The Prophets")

ARAN: Aldean who is meant to get Alexandra as his daughter. (See "When The Bough Breaks")

ARDAN: A terrorist on Mordan. Admiral Jameson is duped into believing that Ardan is still alive and behind the abductions of Federation diplomats. (See

"Too Short A Season")

ARDRA: A legendary being who brought peace to Ventax a thousand years before. In the 24th Century a woman appears claiming to be Ardra and demanding riches in tribute to her powers, until Picard exposes her as a fraud. (See "Devil's Due")

ARGYLE, BLAKE: An engineering officer on the *Enterprise*. (See "Where No One Has Gone Before". "Datalore")

ARIANA: A young woman on the Terellian ship who has been seeing Wyatt in her dreams just as Wyatt has been seeing Ariana in his dreams. A medical student, Wyatt decides to beam over to the Terellian ship and spend the rest of his life trying to find a cure for the plague. (See "Haven")

ARIEL: A resident of Angel One, she goes against her society when she falls in love with Captain Ramsey, a love that almost costs her her life. (See "Angel One")

ARMUS: An evil being marooned on an unexplored world called Vagra II. When an Away Team arrives there, Armus kills Tasha Yar. Created by a race that cast off all its evil aspects into one being, Armus looks like an animated tar slick. A truly vicious creature. (See "Skin Of Evil")

ARON: An *Enterprise* officer. (See "The Dauphin")

ARRIDOR, DR.: A Ferengi scientist who pilots a shuttle through a wormhole and is then marooned on the other side when the unstable wormhole abruptly closes. (See "The Price")

ASTER, JEREMY: Jeremy's mother is killed on an Away Team mission by an ancient land mine. His father died five years before of a Verustin infection, so Jeremy becomes an orphan on the *Enterprise*. A disembodied alien, called a Koinonian, feels concern and takes the form of Jeremy's mother to attempt to replace her. Ultimately Picard convinces the Koinonian that this is not how humans deal with grief. Jeremy finally agrees to join with Worf in the R'uustai, known as The Bonding. (See "The Bonding")

ASTER, LT. MARLA: The mother of Jeremy Aster. She is an archeologist aboard the *Enterprise* who is killed while on an Away Team mission to the surface of the planet Koinonia, a planet devastated by war eons before.

ATOZ: More properly, Mr. Atoz: keeper of the Atavachron, last Sarpeid to go back in time, he erroneously sends Kirk, McCoy and Spock back to different eras. (See "All Our Yesterdays")

AYLEBORNE: A leader of the Organians, an old man who is really, like his fellow Organians, an entity that has shed all physical trappings and assumed a pure energy state. He puts a quick end to Federation/Klingon squabbles. (See "Errand Of Mercy")

AZETBER: Daughter of Klingon Chancellor Gorkon, who takes his place after he is assassinated on the eve of a truce between the Empire and the Federation (See "Star Trek VI: The Undiscovered Country")

BADAR: The chief Antican delegate traveling to Parliament on the *Enterprise*. (See "Lonely Among Us")

BA'EL: A young woman who is half Klingon, half Romulan (she has pointed ears), a fact which would make her an outcast in normal Klingon society. For this reason she remains on the benevolent Romulan prison planet with her parents while some of the younger Klingons choose to experience the richness of their heritage back on the Klingon homeworld. Her father is the Romulan named Tokath. Her mother is the Klingon named Gi'ral. (See "Birthright")

BAILEY: The *Enterprise* navigator who stays with Balok as an emissary between cultures. (See "The Corbomite Maneuver")

BALLARD, LIEUTENANT: A teacher aboard the *Enterprise-D*. (See "The Offspring")

BALOK: A harmless, short humanoid who hides behind a huge ship and a monstrous appearance until he determines that Kirk and the *Enterprise* are on a peaceful mission — he is on a similar mission for his culture, known as the First Federation. (See "The Corbomite Maneuver")

BALTRIM: An unauthorized resident of Jeraddo who refused to evacuate when the government of Bajor ordered it. His family had suffered under the torture of the Cardassians before they escaped to Jeraddo 18 years before. (See "Progress")

BARASH: An alien child who had been hidden in a cavern beneath the surface of a mysterious planet. He has devices similar to the holodeck instruments for creating a variety of scenarios. He also claims to be a boy named Ethan as well as Riker's son, Jean-Luc, before admitting the truth about himself. (See "Future Imperfect")

BARCLAY, LT. ENDICOTT REGINALD: An *Enterprise* crewman who has trouble dealing with his fellow officers and attempts to work this out on the holodeck. He previously served under Captain Gleason on the *Zhukov*. In spite of his personality quirks, he is an expert diagnostic engineer. His drink of choice in Ten Forward is warm milk. Has appeared in several episodes. (Introduced in "Hollow Pursuits")

BAREIL, VEDEK: A Bajoran cleric who had hopes of being the next Kai. (See "In The Hands Of The Prophets")

BARIS, NILZ: A Federation agricultural bureaucrat whose jurisdiction includes Space station K-7, site of the narrowly-averted tribble disaster. (See "The Trouble With Tribbles")

BARRETT, LIEUTENANT: An *Enterprise* officer. (See "Yesterday's Enterprise")

BARRON, DR.: When there is an explosion in the Mintakan Anthropological Station, Dr. Barron, the Chief Scientist, is one of the only two survivors. The other survivor, Palmer, is reported missing. (See "Who Watches The Watchers?")

BARROWS, YEOMAN TONIA: One of the *Enterprise* crew members who takes a fateful shore leave on a planet where thoughts become reality. (See "Shore Leave")

BARSTOW, COMMODORE: A high-ranking Starfleet officer who is on hand when Lazarus A invades our dimension. (See "The Alternative Factor")

BARTHOLOMEW, COUNTESS REGINA: A persona created by Data on the holodeck to be the lover of Prof. James Moriarty. (See "Ship In A Bottle")

BASHIR, DR. JULIAN: The chief of medical operations aboard Deep Space Nine.

BATAI: After Picard is hit by a beam from a strange space probe and awakens a thousand years in the past on the planet Kataan, he finds that his best friend there is named Batai. His friend dies a few years later and Kamin/Picard names his newborn son after his departed friend. (See "The Inner Light")

BATANIDES, MARTA: A close friend of Jean-Luc's from his Academy days. (See "Tapestry")

BATES, HANNAH: A scientist at the Genome colony on Moab Four. After the crisis passes she is one of those who elects to leave on the *Enterprise* in order to be exposed to those advances the Federation has made in the past decades. This poses a threat to the stability of the colony as every colony member fits into a specific and important niche. (See "The Masterpiece Society")

BATES, BROTHER JOHN: Only a simulated character who appears in a holodeck simulation of the play "Henry V." (See "The Defector")

BATESON, CAPTAIN: The Captain of the *U.S.S. Bozeman,* a 23rd century Federation starship, Soyuz class, which vanished without a trace. The mystery was solved when it emerged from a break in the time-space continuum in the 24th century. (See "Cause And Effect")

BEACH: An unseen character who tries, unsuccessfully, to call Dixon Hill. (See "The Big Goodbye")

BEATA: The leader of Angel One, she relaxes her strict way of running things after Riker charms her. (See "Angel One")

BEAUREGARD: Yeoman Rand's name for Sulu's semi-sentient plant pet, which he calls Gertrude. (See "The Man Trap")

BEHAN, JOHNNY: The sheriff Kirk encounters in the Melkotians' deadly recreation of the gunfight at the OK Corral. (See "The Spectre Of The Gun")

BELE: The hunter of Lokai, a dedicated fanatic who's been on this job for fifty thousand years. He's the one whose face is black on the *right* side. (See "Let That Be Your Last Battlefield")

BELL, LT. DAN: Chief of Police of 1941 San Francisco in the Dixon Hill holodeck stories. (See "The Big Goodbye")

BENBECK, MARTIN: A member of the Genome

colony on Moab Four. He is totally opposed to contact with any outside agencies and regards them as a threat to the stability of the colony. He seems to be an extremist but he turns out to be right. (See "The Masterpiece Society")

BENDER, SLADE: A character in a Dixon Hill program on the holodeck. (See "Manhunt")

BENNETT, ENSIGN: A crewman aboard the *Enterprise-D*. (See "Captain's Holiday.")

BENSON, BJORN: The engineer in charge of the terraforming project on Velara Three. (See "Home Soil")

BENZAN: The son of Kushell of Streleb. (See "The Outrageous Okona")

BEREL: A Malkorian who becomes aware that Riker is an "alien" trying to pass as a Malkorian. (See "First Contact")

BERNARD, DR. HARRY : A doctor serving on the *Enterprise*; his son is kidnapped by the Aldeans. (See "When The Bough Breaks")

BERNARD, HARRY (JR.): Son of the doctor (see above); abducted by the Aldeans. (See "When The Bough Breaks")

B'ETOR: The sister of Lursa, the two Klingon sisters claim that a youth, Toral, is the illegitimate son of Duras. Through him they hope to gain control of the Klingon High Council. Unknown to the council the sisters are secretly working with the Romulan, Sela, so that the Romulans can gain influence over the Klingons. (See "Redemption")

BHAVANI, PREMIER: The planetary leader of Barzan II who negotiates for rights to the Barzan wormhole. (See "The Price.")

BLACK KNIGHT: An unfortunate product of McCoy's imagination, which kills him, albeit temporarily, on the shore-leave planet. (See "Shore Leave")

BOCK, DAIMON: A Ferengi commander bent on destroying Picard as revenge for his son's death at the Battle of Maxia, nine years earlier. He returns the *Stargazer* to Jean-Luc Picard as a means of setting Picard up for destruction. (See "The Battle")

BOCHRA: A Romulan lost on Galorndan Core with Geordi; they form an alliance in order to survive. (See "The Enemy")

BOMA, LIEUTENANT: A member of the group in the *Galileo* shuttlecraft when it crash-lands on Taurus II. He doesn't get along with Spock at all. (See "The Galileo Seven")

BONAVENTURE, RUTH: One of Mudd's women. (See "Mudd's Women")

BONES: Leonard McCoy's nickname, used by James Kirk with considerable frequency.

BOOTHBY: The groundskeeper at Starfleet Academy. He was there when Jean-Luc Picard was a cadet and is still there when Wesley Crusher attends the Academy many years later. Boothby once did cadet Jean-Luc a favor when he was at the Academy. (See "The First Duty")

BORATIS: A 27th Century Vorgon security agent who wants to steal the Tox-Uthat which Picard and Vash have located on Risa. (See "Captain's Holiday")

BOYCE, DR. JOSEPH: The doctor on the *Enterprise* when it was under Captain Pike's command. (See "The Menagerie")

BRACK: The most recent identity of the immortal Flint. (See "Requiem For Methuselah")

BRACKETT, ADMIRAL: The Starfleet officer who gives Captain Picard the mission to discover whether Spock has defected to the Romulans. (See "Unification")

BRACTOR, DAIMON: The commander of the Ferengi vessel *Krik'ta* which comes upon the *Enterprise* during Federation wargames and attacks it. (See "Peak Performance")

BRADLEY, ARTHUR GLINTON: A very rich man in the holodeck version of 1941 San Francisco; his wife seeks help from Dixon Hill. (See "The Big Goodbye")

BRADLEY, JESSICA: Wife of Arthur Glinton Bradley; when this young, beautiful woman is killed, the blame is placed on Picard — a.k.a. Dixon Hill. (See "The Big Goodbye")

BRAHMS, JOHANNES: Famous German composer who was really the identity adopted by the immortal Flint between 1833 and 1897. (See "Requiem For Methuselah")

BRAND, ADMIRAL: The head of the board of inquiry looking into the death of Josh Albert, a member of the Nova Squadron at Starfleet Academy. (See "The First Duty")

BRENT: The lieutenant who takes over Uhura's position when she covers for Kevin Riley. (See "The Naked Time")

BRIAM: The Kriosian ambassador whom the *Enterprise* is assigned to escort to a peace conference at Valt Minor. (See "The Perfect Mate")

BRIANON, KAREEN: The former assistant to Dr. Ira Graves. When he transfers his mind from his old, dying body into the young powerful form of Data, he confesses his love for her, which she cannot accept. (See "The Schizoid Man")

BROOKS, JANET: A crew person aboard the *Enterprise-D*. (See "The Loss")

BROWER, ENSIGN: A crew member of the *Enterprise-D*. (See "The Nth Degree")

BROWN, DR.: Doctor Korby's dead assistant; the Brown that Captain Kirk meets is really an android replacement, courtesy of Korby. (See "What Are Little Girls Made Of?")

BRULL: The leader of the encampment of Gatherers on Gamma Hromi II. (See "The Vengeance Factor")

B'TARDAT: A representative of Kaelon-2 who demands that Dr. Timicin return to the planet to undergo the Age of Resolution (ritual suicide at age 60). (See "Half A Life")

BUCK BOKAI: A legendary baseball player whom Jake Sisko likes to play with in the holosuite. (See "If Wishes Were Horses")

BUDRON, ADMIRAL: The commander of Starbase 29. The Tilonians claim that Budron stated there was no such person in Starfleet as William T. Riker. (See "Frame Of Mind")

BURKE, ENSIGN: A tactical officer on the *Enterprise* who stands in for Worf when he temporarily goes to assist Riker on the *Hathaway* during wargames. (See "Peak Performance")

CARAPLEDES, UNA: An officer who is killed to prevent her from uncovering the conspiracy. (See "Conspiracy")

CARETAKER: An ancient humanoid male (at least in appearance), he runs the planet encountered in "Shore Leave."

CARLISLE, LIEUTENANT: A member of the *Enterprise's* security team.

CARTER, DR.: Ship's doctor on board the *Exeter*.

CASTILLO, LT. RICHARD: The Helmsman of the *Enterprise-C*. He becomes involved with Tasha Yar and when Commander Garrett is killed in battle, he becomes the senior officer who leads the *Enterprise-C* back through the temporal rift to Narendra Three. (See "Yesterday's Enterprise")

CATULLAN, AMBASSADOR: Father of Tongo Rad, who has fallen in with Dr. Sevrin's band of spacefaring youths. (See "The Way To Eden")

CHANDRA, CAPTAIN: One of the presiding officers at James Kirk's court martial for the apparent murder of Finney. (See "Court Martial")

CHANG, GENERAL: A Klingon officer who likes to quote Shakespeare. He also conspires to prevent the Federation and the Klingon Empire from signing a peace accord. (See "Star Trek VI: The Undiscovered Country")

CHANG, TACTICAL OFFICER: One of the testing officers at the Relva VII facility who oversees the examinations when Wesley Crusher is trying out for the Academy entrance. (See "Coming Of Age")

CHAPEL, CHRISTINE: McCoy's head nurse, who has an unrequited interest in Spock. She first joined the *Enterprise* to take part in the search for Dr. Roger Korby, who was her fiancé. Although she works as a nurse, she has advanced degrees in biology.

CHEKOV, ENSIGN PAVEL ANDREIVICH : The young, Russian officer who comes on board as the *Enterprise's* permanent navigator.

CHEKOV, PIOTR: Chekov's non-existent brother, a

memory-implant created by an alien that feeds off hatred and pits Klingons and Federation personnel against each other. In the false memory, Piotr was killed in a Klingon assault. (See "Day Of The Dove")

CHEKOV-TWO: The mirror-universe Chekov, who attempts to kill Kirk-One. (See "Mirror, Mirror")

CHILDRESS, BEN: One of the Rigellian miners who ultimately marries one of Mudd's women. (See "Mudd's Women")

CHORGON: A member of the Lornack clan and a leader of the tribes known as the Gatherers. (See "The Vengeance Factor")

CHORUS: The three empathic/telepathic humanoids who served, prior to their untimely deaths, as the translators of the mute diplomat Riva's thoughts and emotions. (See "Loud As A Whisper")

CHRISTOPHER, DR.: The human husband of T'Pan, the director of the Vulcan Science Academy and a scientist who agrees to visit the *Enterprise* to witness a test of Dr. Reyga's metaphasic field technology. (See "Suspicions")

CHRISTOPHER, CAPTAIN JOHN: The Air Force captain taken on board the *Enterprise* during its brief sojourn in the 20th Century. (See "Tomorrow Is Yesterday")

CIANA, VICE-ADMIRAL LORI: James T. Kirk's love interest during the years he lives in semi-retirement after completing his five-year mission on the *Enterprise* and before going off into space again when V'ger threatens Earth. Lori is killed in a transporter accident right before Kirk leaves Earth on the refitted *Enterprise*. (See "Star Trek: The Motion Picture")

CIRL THE KNIFE: One of Krako's henchmen on Iotia. (See "A Piece Of The Action")

CLAIBORNE, BILLY: One of the Clanton boys at the OK Corral, portrayed by Pavel Chekov in the Melkotian reenactment of the famous gunfight. (See "Spectre Of The Gun")

CLANCY, ENSIGN: An assistant engineer aboard the *Enterprise* who is later promoted to Ops. (See "Elementary Dear Data" and "The Emissary")

CLANTON, BILLY: Another OK Corral participant, a role assigned to Scotty by the Melkotians. (See "Spectre Of The Gun")

CLANTON, IKE: Head of the Clantons, and thus the role assigned to James Kirk by the Melkotians. (See "Spectre Of The Gun")

CLARKE, DR. HOWARD: His opinion is sought when "Ardra" supposedly returns to Ventax-2 after an absence of a thousand years. (See "Devil's Due")

CLAUDIUS MARCUS: The leader — Proconsul — of planet 892-IV, where the Roman Empire of that world never died. (See "Bread And Circuses")

CLAYMARE: One of the Organian elders who baffle both James Kirk and the Klingons with their apparent passivity. (See "Errand Of Mercy")

CLEMONS, L.Q. ("SONNY"): One of the 20th Century humans frozen cryogenically and revived by the *Enterprise* centuries later; his death was drug related. (See "The Neutral Zone")

CLOUD, WILLIAM: A leader of the Yang, and James Kirk's cellmate as a prisoner of the Kohm. (See "Omega Glory")

COCHRANE, ZEFREM: Inventor of warp drive, dead a century and a half before James Kirk, or so it is believed until he turns up on Gamma Canaris N, kept living by the gaseous Companion that loves him. (See "Metamorphosis")

COGLEY, SAMUEL T.: James Kirk's lawyer in his court martial, who gets him acquitted of murder charges by proving that the "victim" had staged his own death — and then defends Kirk's enemy. (See "Court Martial")

COLEMAN, DR. ARTHUR: Easily the worst physician in the 23rd Century, he lets Janice Lester's victims die. Passive and weak but madly in love with Lester, he does her every bidding. But he cannot quite pull off a multiple murder at her request. (See "Turnabout Intruder")

COLT, YEOMAN: A young officer on board Captain Pike's *Enterprise*, she is beamed down by the Talosians as one of Pike's potential mates. (See "The Cage")

COMPANION: The sentient, cloudlike being that saved warp drive inventor Zefrem Cochrane and extended his life by a century and a half. Realizing that this love is flawed, the entity joins with the dying Nancy Hedford and, becoming human, decides to live out a human lifespan with the now-mortal Cochrane. (See "Metamorphosis")

COMPIO FROM CONSTELAINE: A dignitary who comes aboard the *Enterprise* and prepares to wed Lwaxana Troi, who is all for it even though she has never met him in person before they finally get together on the *Enterprise*. Ultimately Lwaxana decides against marrying Compio and scandalizes him by showing up at their wedding naked, which is the Betazoid tradition. (See "Cost Of Living")

COMPTON: The first victim of the waters of Scalos, this *Enterprise* crewman becomes radically accelerated and becomes a pawn of the Scalosians when he helps them take over the *Enterprise*. He is killed accidentally, being rendered more fragile by his acceleration. (See "The Wink Of An Eye")

CONOR, AARON: The leader of the Genome colony on Moab Four. (See "The Masterpiece Society")

CONSTABLE: A lawman of the Sarpeidian "Restoration" period. He arrests James Kirk as a sorcerer and throws him into prison. (See "All Our Yesterdays"). Also a nick-name for the shape-shifting security chief Odo on Deep Space Nine.

CORY, DONALD: The benign administrator of the asylum colony at Elba II, who is overthrown by his shapeshifting patient Garth of Izar. The forgiving sort, he does not hold his imprisonment and torture against Garth after James Kirk defeats him. (See "Whom Gods Destroy")

COSTA: A diagnostic engineer. (See "Hollow Pursuits")

CRATER, NANCY: Leonard McCoy's ex-girlfriend, who later married archeologist Robert Crater. When the *Enterprise* visits their archeological site on the planet M113, McCoy looks forward to seeing his old flame — not realizing that she has died and been replaced by the last survivor of the indigenous race of M113, a being that thrives on salt and draws it from the bodies of other living creatures. (See "The Man Trap")

CRATER, PROFESSOR ROBERT : Husband of Nancy Crater, who protects the being that took her place after she died — with disastrous results for the *Enterprise* crew. (See "The Man Trap")

CREATOR: The space probe *Nomad's* name for James Kirk after it confuses him with its real creator, Jackson Roykirk. (See "The Changeling")

CRODEN: An alien who attempts to perpetrate a theft on Deep Space Nine, resulting in the death of a Miradorn. He is from Rakhar, a world which considers him an enemy of the people. (See "Vortex")

CROMWELL: Head of the McKinley Rocket Base on Earth in the 20th Century, where Gary Seven must stop a dangerous launch. (See "Assignment: Earth")

CROSIS: A wounded Borg captured at the Federation outpost on Ohniaka Three. He is in alliance with Lore and helps to alter Data's program so that the android will rescue Crosis and flee the *Enterprise* and go straight to Lore. (See "Descent")

CRUSHER, DR. BEVERLY: Senior officer aboard the *Enterprise-D*. For one year she transferred to Starfleet Medical and was replaced by Dr. Pulaski.

CRUSHER, JACK: The deceased husband of Beverly Crusher and father of Wesley. He was a close friend of Jean-Luc Picard. (See "Family")

CRUSHER, WESLEY: Son of Jack and Beverly Crusher. For a time he was an acting Ensign on the *Enterprise-D* before being accepted into Starfleet Academy.

CUZO, JIMMY: A character in a Dixon Hill program on the holodeck. (See "Manhunt")

DAILY, CAPTAIN JON: Commanding officer of the *Astral Queen*, who allows James Kirk to pick up his passengers, the Karidian Players. (See "Conscience Of The King")

D'AMATO: An ensign put on report by Worf during an unsettling visit to the *Enterprise* by Sarek. (See "Sarek")

D'AMATO, LIEUTENANT: The first victim of the Losira projection at the Kalandran outpost; the ship's head geologist. (See "That Which Survives")

DANAR, GUL: The commanding officer of a

Cardassian vessel who wants the escaped terrorist Tana Los turned over to him. (See "Past Prologue")

DANAR, TOGA: A supersoldier and veteran of the Tarsian War. He was physiologically amplified, along with some fellow Angosians, to fight for his world in that war. Once the war ended, he and his kind were considered unfit for polite society and were forced to live on Lunar Five. His war record is impressive with 84 confirmed kills and two promotions to the rank of Subhadar. But he doesn't love fighting and only wants to live as an equal on his home world. (See "The Hunted")

DANO, KAL: The inventor of the mysterious Tox Uthat. A 27th Century scientist, he went back in time and hid it in the 22nd Century on Risa where it is found by Vash and Picard in the 24th Century. (See "Captain's Holiday")

DAR, CAITHLIN: A Romulan consul who is taken hostage by Sybok and his gang, and then converted to his cause. (See "Star Trek V: The Final Frontier")

DARA: The daughter of Timicin who insists that her father not disgrace his family. She wants him to return home and follow through on the ritual called The Resolution which requires that Timicin commit suicide because he has reached the age which makes it mandatory. (See "Half A Life")

DARAS: Liberation fighter on Ekos who manages to pass as one of the fascistic overclass. (See "Patterns Of Force")

DAREN, NELLA: The chief of the stellar sciences department on the *Enterprise-D*. Captain Picard and she become romantically involved. Because of the disruptions this ultimately creates in their professional lives, Nella decides to transfer to another vessel. (See "Lessons")

DARHE'EL, GUL: A brutal Cardassian official during the Bajoran occupation, also known as the "butcher of Gallitepp." When he is seemingly captured on Deep Space Nine, Bajor prepares for a war crimes trial. But when Dul Dukat states that Gul Darhe'el has been dead for five years, Odo is allowed access to the Cardassian data banks to verify the claim. (See "Duet")

DARNELL: The first *Enterprise* crew member to fall prey to the salt vampire of planet M113, while it posed as Nancy Crater. It tried to pass off his death as a result of poisoning by the Borgia plant. (See "The Man Trap")

DARSON, CAPTAIN: The Captain of the *U.S.S. Adelphi*, a Starfleet board of inquiry found him guilty of causing the Ghorusda Disaster. Tam Elbrun was there and says that it was because Captain Darson ignored his advice that the disaster occurred. (See "Tin Man")

DARVIN, ARNE: A Klingon spy, disguised as a human, who is well situated as the assistant to the bureaucrat Nilz Baris until he is unmasked, as it were, by the tribbles, which have an innate antipathy towards Klingons. This foils his plan to poison the triticale. (See "The Trouble With Tribbles")

DATA, LT. COMMANDER: An android created by Dr. Noonian Soong. He is the Second Officer on the *Enterprise-D*. He is the only android in Starfleet. He has a brother android, named Lore, who has human emotions which twisted him with hatred against all humanity. Data is the most advanced android known to exist. Discovered on Omicron Theta IV by the *U.S.S. Tripoli*, he passed all tests of sentience and was accepted by Starfleet Academy. Has performed exemplary service on numerous ships. A remarkable individual who is far more human than he gives himself credit for.

DATHON: One of the Children of Tama, he is a commander who meets with Picard in order that the two peoples might finally learn a means of communicating. Dathon dies in the attempt, but his death is not in vain. (See "Darmok")

DAUPHIN: Salia, a young woman on her way to rule her home planet of Daled IV. Wesley Crusher becomes attracted to her, unaware that her true form is anything but that of an adolescent human female. (See "The Dauphin")

DAVID: The child from the Darwin Science Station whom Pulaski takes aboard a shuttlecraft in order to examine. (See "Unnatural Selection")

DAVIES, ENSIGN: A geochemistry specialist and Wesley's assistant on the Selcundi Drema team. (See "Pen Pals")

DA VINCI, LEONARDO: Famous painter and inventor from Earth (1452-1519) who was really another front identity for the immortal human, Flint. (See "Requiem For Methuselah")

DAX, CURZON: The name of the Trill which has merged with Jadzia to become Jadzia Dax.

DAX, LT. JADZIA: The Science Officer on Deep Space Nine. She is a Trill whose name is Curzon.

DAYSTROM, DR. RICHARD: A brilliant scientist, inventor of the computer used on the *Enterprise* and other Federation ships. A bit past his prime, he unveils the M-5 computer, a new development with disastrous results: the entire crew of the *Excalibur* is killed by the M-5. Computer and inventor alike cannot cope with the results of this horrible action. (See "The Ultimate Computer")

DEALT, HESTER: A medical trustee and Lieutenant Commander at the Federation Medical Collection Station at 'aucdet Nine. (See "The Child")

DEAN, LIEUTENANT: Practices fencing with Picard. (See "We'll Always Have Paris")

DEBIN: The leader of the planet Atlek who believes that Yanar, his daughter, was made pregnant by Okona. (See "The Outrageous Okona")

DECIUS: An officer on the Romulan vessel that attacks the *Enterprise*. (See "Balance Of Terror")

DECKER, COMMODORE MATTHEW: Captain and sole survivor of the *Constellation,* he is obsessed with destroying the doomsday machine. Ultimately, he dies in his efforts. (See "The Doomsday Machine")

DECKER, CAPTAIN WILLARD: The son of Matt Decker. Will is assigned the command of the refitted *Enterprise* until Admiral Kirk overrides those orders and assumes command himself, with Will given a temporary reduction to First Officer. He and Ilia choose to merge with V'ger when that entity decides it wants to find out what the next level of existence is like beyond being just a machine. (See "Star Trek: The Motion Picture")

DEELA: Female ruler of the high-speed Scalosians, she lures the *Enterprise* to her world to provide men for mating purposes: the radiation that speeds up the Scalosians also makes their men sterile. (See "The Wink Of An Eye")

DEEM: One of Maab's followers on the planet Capella IV. (See "Friday's Child")

DEHNER, DR. ELIZABETH: The woman who helps defeat Gary Mitchell when she develops telekinetic, reality-altering powers like his own. Unfortunately, she dies in the process, but enables James Kirk to save the day. (See "Where No Man Has Gone Before")

DESALLE, LT. VINCENT: A crewman on the *Enterprise*, first a backup navigator, later Scotty's main assistant in engineering.

DESEVE, STEFAN: A Federation ensign who years before defected to the Romulans. Finally seeing the error of his ways he returns from exile in order to give Picard a message from Spock about an important mission. (See "Face Of The Enemy")

DESOTO, CAPTAIN: He commands the *U.S.S. Hood*; Will Riker was his First Officer before his transfer to the *Enterprise*. (See "Encounter At Farpoint")

DEVOR: A technician who is actually one of a group of pirates who steal aboard the *Enterprise* to obtain trilithium resin, a toxic waste material produced by warp engines and which can be used to manufacture a powerful explosive. It is a very unstable substance and must be transported with great care. (See "Starship Mine")

DEVOS, ALEXANA: The Director of the Rutia Police who is fighting against the terrorist group called the Ansata. (See "The High Ground")

DICKERSON, LIEUTENANT: The member of the *Enterprise* security team who meets Abraham Lincoln in the transporter room. (See "The Savage Curtain")

DIOYD: A young-looking but ancient Platonian. (See "Plato's Stepchildren")

DIRGO: A shuttlecraft captain whose craft crashlands on a desert planet and who is killed by an automatic defensive system around a natural spring inside a cave. (See "Final Mission")

DOE, JOHN: A Zalkonian who is the first one of his race to be allowed to live long enough to begin to evolve into the noncorporeal state. He was originally stricken with amnesia when found by the *Enterprise*. His transformation is completed successfully and he returns to his homeworld to support others like himself who are on the verge of evolving. (See

"Transfigurations")

DOKACHIN, KLIN: The alien being who is in charge of the junkyard in space at Qualor Two. (See "Unification")

DOMINGUEZ, COMMANDER JOSE: Commander of the Corinth V Starbase; a good friend of James Kirk. (See "The Man Trap")

DON JUAN: One of the legendary figures encountered by the *Enterprise* crew on the shore-leave planet. (See "Shore Leave")

DREA: One of the Kelvans who take over the *Enterprise*. (See "By Any Other Name")

DRELLA: The cloudlike being of Alpha Carinae V that loves Zefrem Cochrane and keeps him alive. (See "Metamorphosis")

DROXINE: One of the Cloud-Dwellers of Stratos City, whose father is the High Adviser of the Planetary Council, Plasus. She is as prejudiced as the rest of her people, but is interested in the alien Spock nonetheless. (See "The Cloud Minders")

DRUSILLA: The female slave of Claudius Marcus. (See "Bread And Circuses")

D'SORA, JENNA: A young *Enterprise* engineer whom Data attempts to have a romance with as an experiment in trying to understand what romance is all about. (See "In Theory")

DUANA: The Aldean woman assigned to be Wesley Crusher's adoptive mother after he is abducted. (See "When The Bough Breaks")

DUFFY: An engineer aboard the *Enterprise-D*. (See "Hollow Pursuits")

DUKAT, GUL: A Cardassian and the former Prefect of Bajor when it was occupied by Cardassia. (See "Emissary")

DUMONT, ENSIGN SUZANNE: An ensign whom Wesley has a date with. But because of the strange influence of Sarek's mental disorder, Geordi blurts out that Wesley will fail with her. (See "Sarek")

DURAS: The son of Ja'rod, the actual traitor at the Khitomer Massacre. (See "Sins Of The Fathers")

DURKIN, CHANCELLOR: The ruler of Malkor, a world on the verge of space flight which is unaware of the Federation or other inhabited worlds until Picard comes to him for help. Durkin ultimately decides that his people are not yet prepared for the culture shock of discovering that their world is not alone in the universe. (See "First Contact")

DUUR: One of Maab's Capellan followers, killed by a Klingon named Kras. (See "Friday's Child")

DYAPLANE: The governor of the planet Pacifica, who reports to the alien-controlled Savar. (See "Conspiracy")

EARP, MORGAN: One of the enemies faced by Kirk and his friends at the reenactment of the OK Corral gunfight. (See "Spectre Of The Gun")

EARP, VIRGIL: Another one of the Earp brothers. (See "Spectre Of The Gun")

EARP, WYATT: The most famous Earp brother; he is the Marshal in the Melkotian version of history, although in reality he was not — his brother Virgil was. (See "Spectre Of The Gun")

ED: The bartender in the Melkotian version of Tombstone, Arizona. (See "Spectre Of The Gun")

EKOR: One of the Scalosians who takes over the *Enterprise*. (See "The Wink Of An Eye")

EINSTEIN: A crew member of the *Enterprise-D*. (See "The Nth Degree")

ELAAN: From the planet Elas, she's trouble for James Kirk, if ever there was any. Her tears contain a substance that make him fall in love with her, complicating an already complicated scenario: she's supposed to be married off to the ruler of Troyius, a plan she only accepts with great difficulty. A woman graced with truly bad manners when dealing with anyone she regards as her inferior — in other words, just about everybody she meets. (See "Elaan Of Troyius")

ELBRUN, TAM: A Betazoid telepath who dislikes dealing with other beings because it is difficult for him to block out all of the thoughts he receives. One of the foremost telepaths in the Federation. (See "Tin Man")

ELEEN: An inhabitant of the planet Capella 4, she is the wife of the leader Akaar, who is murdered. James Kirk and crew help her survive when it is discovered that she is pregnant; she names her son, the new leader, after Kirk and McCoy. (See "Friday's Child")

ELIG, DEKON: A Bajoran who was reported killed trying to escape from a Cardassian prison camp. (See "Babel")

ELINE: The name of the wife Picard discovers that he has, after he is hit by a beam from a strange space probe and awakens a thousand years in the past on the planet Kataan. (See "The Inner Light")

ELLIOT: A member of the party sent to examine the *Constellation* after its encounter with the doomsday machine. He was an engineering technician. (See "The Doomsday Machine")

MR. ELLIS: He served as the First Officer on board the *Antares*.

ENDAR, CAPTAIN: The Tellerian who adopted Jeremiah Rossa after the boy's parents were killed by the Tellerians. (See "Suddenly Human")

ENEG: Chairman of the underground anti-fascistic movement on Ekos. (See "Patterns Of Force")

EPSTEIN, PROFESSOR TERENCE : One of Beverly Crusher's teachers, stationed later at Starbase 74. (See "11001001")

ERACLITUS: One of the psychokinetic Platonians. (See "Plato's Stepchildren")

ESOQQ: A Chalnoth warrior whose name means "fighter." He can only go three or four days without food before he'll resort to cannibalism to survive. (See "Allegiance")

ESTEBAN, CAPTAIN J.T.: Commander of the *U.S.S. Grissom*. (See "Star Trek III: The Search For Spock")

ESTRAGON, PROF. SAMUEL: An archeologist who once spent many years unsuccessfully searching for the Tox-Uthat. Vash claims to have been his assistant but that remains unproven. (See "Captain's Holiday")

ETANA: A woman who gives Riker an item she calls "The Game" which is a mind control device used to enslave the crew of the *Enterprise*. The Ktarians are behind this conspiracy. (See "The Game")

EVANS: A security guard on board the *Enterprise* at the time the ship is transporting the Dohlman Elaan. (See "Elaan Of Troyius")

EVANS, CHARLES ("CHARLIE"): A human child raised by the non-physical Thasians on Thasus; they taught him their reality-bending abilities. He rejoined humanity prematurely, seemingly a young adult but really still a child in temperament. His powers, linked with his immaturity, make his readjustment rather difficult for his hosts on the *Enterprise*. Fortunately, the Thasians reclaim him in the nick of time. (See "Charlie X")

FAJO, KIVAS: A ruthless collector of rare objects who kidnaps Data and is willing to kill to keep his prize from escaping. Data nearly kills Fajo. (See "The Most Toys")

FALOR, KEEVE: The actual leader of the Bajoran refugees in the encampment on Valo Three. (See "Ensign Ro")

FALOW: Also known as Master Surchid of the Wadi, a new race recently encountered by the Federation in the Gamma Quadrant beyond the Bajoran wormhole. They are a race who love to play games. (See "Move Along Home")

FARALLON, DR.: The scientist in charge of the Tyan Particle Fountain on Tyrus 7-A. (See "Quality Of Life")

FAREK, DR.: A Ferengi doctor aboard the Krayton who dislikes Lwaxana Troi. (See "Menaga A Troi")

FARRELL: A denizen of the mirror universe, where he is an underling of that world's Kirk. (See "Mirror, Mirror")

FENTO: A Mintakan wise man. (See "Who Watches The Watchers?")

FERRIS: A high-ranking commissioner in the Federation who wants James Kirk to give up looking for the missing *Galileo* shuttlecraft. (See "The Galileo Seven")

FINN, KYRIL: The leader of the Ansata terrorists who is willing to go to any extreme to see justice done to his people, whether it means his own death or the death of others. (See "The High Ground")

FINNEGAN: An older student during James Kirk's Academy days, Finnegan made life hard for Kirk at every turn. One can only imagine Kirk's exasperation at meeting him again on the shore-leave world — until he gets him back — for once and for all. (See "Shore Leave")

FINNEY, JAMIE: Daughter of Kirk's old friend Finney, she turns against Kirk when he is charged with her father's murder, but later realizes his innocence. (See "Court Martial")

FINNEY, LT. COMMANDER BENJAMIN : Although he seems to be James Kirk's friend, Finney has long held a grudge against the Captain of the *Enterprise*, who rose in the ranks while Finney lagged behind. He frames Kirk for his own death, prompting Kirk's court martial for murder, but he is discovered alive. (See "Court Martial")

FISHER: A geologist who unwittingly beams up with the magnetic materials that cause the next person to beam up — Kirk — to split into two halves. For his troubles, Fisher is assaulted by the evil Kirk. (See "The Enemy Within")

FITZGERALD (ADMIRAL): He orders Spock not to beam down to Gideon and look for Kirk. Spock violates these orders willfully. (See "Mark Of Gideon")

FITZPATRICK (ADMIRAL): He orders the *Enterprise* to Space Station K-7, where the tribble situation unfolds. (See "The Trouble With Tribbles")

FLAHERTY, COMMANDER: The First Officer of the *U.S.S. Ares* who is an expert linguist fluent in 40 languages. (See "The Icarus Factor")

FLAVIUS MAXIMUS: An ex-gladiator on the "Roman" planet, 892-IV. He is pitted against Spock on the gladiatorial television show. (See "Bread And Circuses")

FLINT: A six-thousand-year-old human from Earth, born during the Babylonian Empire, who turns out to

have been many of Earth's most celebrated geniuses: DaVinci, Brahms and more. Under the pseudonym "Mr. Brack," he purchases the planet of Holberg 917G and lives in incredible luxury, surrounded by android companions of his own creation, for he can no longer stand the fact that those he gets close to will die long before him. His paradise is intruded upon by the *Enterprise* when it arrives looking for the cure for a plague. He allows a visit, but matters get complicated when James Kirk falls for his "ward" Reena, not realizing that she is an android. Reena dies, leaving Kirk in the lurch. McCoy discovers that Flint is dying. It seems that his immortality did not follow him when he left the atmosphere of his home planet, Earth. (See "Requiem For Methuselah")

FOLEY, LT.: When he finds Tog's pericules in a pond on Betazed, Picard realizes that the three people missing must have been kidnapped. (See "Menage A Troi")

FOX, ROBERT: The Federation ambassador to Eminiar VII. He brings a pause to their war with Vendikar. (See "A Taste Of Armageddon")

FREDERICKS: An officer aboard the *Enterprise-C*. (See "Yesterday's Enterprise")

FREEMAN: An ensign who unwittingly accepts one of the offspring of Uhura's pet tribble. (See "The Trouble With Tribbles")

FRIENDLY ANGEL: A name referring to the evil Gorgan. (See "And The Children Shall Lead")

GAETANO: A crewman killed on Taurus II after the crash of the shuttlecraft *Galileo*. (See "The Galileo Seven")

GALEN, PROF. RICHARD: Jean-Luc Picard's old archeology professor. Galen considered Jean-Luc his finest student and regretted that Picard chose Starfleet over a career in archeology. When Picard turns down what Galen regards as "the chance of a lifetime," Galen leaves in a huff, and a short time later dies when he is attacked by an Yridian destroyer. But Galen's death inspires Captain Picard to complete his mentor's work. (See "The Chase")

GALLIULIN, IRINI: A close female acquaintance

of Pavel Chekov at Starfleet Academy, she turns up again as one of Dr. Sevrin's youthful band of Eden-seekers. (See "The Way To Eden")

GALLOWAY, LIEUTENANT: Rather long-lived for a security officer, he shows up for duty on Miri's world, gets taken hostage on Eminiar VII, and is finally killed by Captain Tracey when he beams down to Omega IV with an *Enterprise* landing party. (See "Miri")

GALT: Chief thrall of Triskelion, he is in charge of the gladiators. (See "The Gamesters Of Triskelion")

GALWAY, LT. ARLENE: A victim of the accelerated aging disease contracted on Gamma Hydra IV, she was, before her death, the head biologist on board the *Enterprise*. (See "The Deadly Years")

GAREK: The last Cardassian on Deep Space Nine. He owns a clothing shop and is rumored to be a spy for Cardassia. (See "Past Prologue")

GARIN, DR.: The scientist in charge of the research team on Bre'el Four investigating the problem of their descending moon. (See "Deja Q")

GARRETT, CAPTAIN RACHEL: The Captain of the *Enterprise-C* who is killed in a battle with Klingons. (See "Yesterday's Enterprise")

GARRISON, CHIEF PETTY OFFICER: An officer who served on the *Enterprise* under the command of Captain Christopher Pike. (See "The Cage")

GARROVICK, CAPTAIN: James Kirk's commander on his first space duty, Captain Garrovick was killed (along with much of his crew) when the vampire cloud attacked the *U.S.S. Farragut*. (See "Obsession")

GARROVICK, ENSIGN: Son of Captain Garrovick, coincidentally assigned to the *Enterprise* just before it encounters the vampiric cloud; young Garrovick helps Kirk destroy the being once and for all. (See "Obsession")

GARTH OF IZAR: A famous Starfleet captain and renowned strategist, he has gone quite mad. Unfortunately, he has also learned the shapeshifting techniques of an alien race, and uses these powers to take over the asylum on Elba II, where he is imprisoned. James Kirk has a hard time of it outwitting this brilliant madman; luckily, a cure is also on hand, and

the defeated Garth is returned to sanity at last. (See "Whom Gods Destroy")

GAV: The Tellarite delegate to the Babel conference. After he loses a debate with Ambassador Sarek, the pig-like alien is murdered, and suspicion is cast on Sarek. The real murderer was an Orion in disguise, posing as an Andorian. (See "Journey To Babel")

GEM: The empathic Minaran chosen to represent her race in the cruel test performed by the Vians. Her real name is unknown, but McCoy dubs her "Gem." Observing the behavior of Kirk, Spock and McCoy under duress, she is moved to help them despite the extreme risk to herself. She saves McCoy with her almost miraculous healing powers, and by this also saves her entire race; impressed, the Vians will move her people away from their nova-doomed planet. (See "The Empath")

GIBSON, ENSIGN: The *Enterprise* operations officer. (See "The Dauphin")

GILL, JOHN: A renowned Earth historian, Gill errs drastically when, as a secret Federation observer on Ekos, he introduces governmental ideas from Nazi Germany. This form of Naziism is not altered enough to prevent history from almost repeating itself in its usual bloody fashion. Replaced by an underling, Gill barely manages to help undo the damage he has created before he passes away. (See "Patterns Of Force")

GILNOR: Another Mordan terrorist who is dead, but whom Jameson is duped into thinking is still alive. (See "Too Short A Season")

GIOTTO, LT. COMMANDER: On the mining planet of Janus VI, he leads the security detail that tries to hunt down the Horta. (See "Devil In The Dark")

GLADSTONE, MISS: The nursery attendant aboard the *Enterprise*. (See "The Child")

GLEASON, CAPT.: Reginald Barclay's previous commanding officer aboard the *U.S.S. Zhukov*. (See "Hollow Pursuits")

GOMEZ, ENSIGN SONYA: A recent Starfleet Academy graduate who has done phase work with antimatter. She is from Rayna VI and transferred to the *Enterprise* from Starbase 173. (See "Q Who" and "Samaritan Snare")

GORKON, CHANCELLOR: When he is assassinated on the eve of an armistice between the Federation and the Klingon Empire, Kirk and McCoy are charged with the crime and the peace negotiations are almost destroyed. (See "Star Trek VI: The Undiscovered Country")

GORO: A leader of the Indian-like tribe on Miramanee's world, who marries her to Kirk. (See "The Paradise Syndrome")

GOSHEVEN: The leader of the Tau Cygna V colony. When the Federation has to relocate that colony due to the world being claimed by the Sheliak, Gosheven opposes the relocation until Data demonstrates just how hopeless their opposition will be once the Sheliak arrive. (See "The Ensigns Of Command")

GOSS, DAIMON: An unscrupulous Ferengi leader who will stop at nothing to secure the rights to the Bhavani wormhole. He even poisons Mendoza, the UFP representative. (See "The Price")

GOWRON: The new head of the Klingon High Council and the successor to K'Mpec. (See "Reunion")

GRAK-TAY: A musician whose style Data can duplicate. (See "Sarek")

GRANGER: A reference to the Granger clones of *Mariposa*. Others include Victor Granger, the Minister of Health and Wilson Granger, the Prime Minister. (See "Up The Long Ladder")

GRANGER, CAPTAIN WALTER: Of the *U.S.S. Mariposa*. His descendants all are actually clones of him. (See "Up The Long Ladder")

GRANGER, WILSON: The head of a planet of scientists whose genetic material has become weakened because they have cloned themselves for so long. In order to strengthen their society they team up with a primitive farming community so that they can begin reproducing the old-fashioned way again. (See "Up The Long Ladder")

GRANT: An *Enterprise* security officer killed by the Klingon Kras on the planet Capella IV. (See "Friday's Child")

GRAVES, IRA: A cyberneticist and former student of Noonian Soong. When he dies he manages to transfer his consciousness into Data's positronic brain until convinced that this was morally wrong. (See "The Schizoid Man")

GRAX, REITTAN: The Betazoid conference director who tells Picard that Riker, Troi and her mother have been kidnapped. He has known Deanna Troi since she was a child. (See "Menage A Troi")

GRAYSON, AMANDA: Spock's human mother, first wife to Sarek. She has often been caught in the middle of the struggle between her husband and son (See "Journey To Babel"), and has encouraged Spock to explore his human half (See "Star Trek IV: The Voyage Home")

GREBNEDLOG: The Captain of the *Mondor,* a Pakled vessel. The Pakleds have bought or stolen all of the technology they have and therefore do not understand it very well. (See "Samaritan Snare")

GREEN, COLONEL: One of Earth's most notorious military villains, a genocidal maniac from the 21st Century who combats James Kirk on Excalbia. (See "The Savage Curtain")

GROMEK, ADMIRAL: The admiral of Starfleet who gives the *Enterprise* its orders to go to meet K'Ehleyr at Boratis. (See "The Emissary")

GUINAN: The hostess of Ten Forward. She comes from a long-lived race and is apparently at least 700 years old. Little is known about her. Guinan's abilities are also a secret except that when time is altered (see "Yesterday's Enterprise") she is the only one who is aware of the change.

HACOM: A cowardly resident of Beta XIIA. (See "Return Of The Archons")

HADEN, ADMIRAL: The commanding officer of the Lya Three Starfleet station. When Picard grants asylum to Admiral Jarok, Haden conveys the Romulan Empire's official protest over the incident, but he supports Picard's actions. (See "The Defector") Haden also contacts Picard when the *U.S.S. Phoenix* starts attacking Cardassian vessels. (See "The Wounded")

HAFTEL, ADMIRAL ANTHONY: Haftel comes aboard the *Enterprise* at Galor Four and is determined to take possession of Lal to study at Galor Four, but Picard protests the attempt. (See "The Offspring")

HAGON: Second-in-command to the Ligonian leader Lutan, Hagon becomes top dog when Lutan's wife Yareena dumps Lutan for him. (See "Code Of Honor")

HAHN, ADMIRAL: When Wesley is late returning to Starfleet Academy, Admiral Hahn contacts Picard to inquire about the delay. (See "Menage A Troi")

HAKI: A Mintakan child from whom Picard receives a gift of a woven cloth. (See "Who Watches The Watchers?")

HALI: When Palmer is wounded and separated from the science observation post, he is found by this Mintakan hunter. (See "Who Watches The Watchers?")

HALLOWAY, CAPTAIN THOMAS: He is in command of the *Enterprise* when Q shows Picard how different his future could have been. (See "Tapestry")

HANAR: One of the Kelvans who invade the *Enterprise*; McCoy injects him with Formazine, which makes him get into conflict with his fellow Kelvan, Rojan. (See "By Any Other Name")

HANSEN, LIEUTENANT: An occasional replacement at the helmsman's position. (See "Court Martial" and "Menagerie")

HANSON, COMMANDER: In charge of Federation Outpost 4 along the Neutral Zone, he dies in the Romulan attack on that outpost. (See "Balance Of Terror")

HANSON, ADMIRAL J.P.: The Starfleet tactical officer who accompanies Shelby to the *Enterprise* to investigate the threat posed by the Borg. He returns to Starfleet Headquarters to plan the defense of Earth and is in charge of the battlefleet which is decimated by the Borg ship. (See "The Best Of Both Worlds")

HARITATH: When Data informs the people of the Tau Cygna V colony that they must evacuate due to the demands of the Sheliak, he finds the few who support the Federation's position include Haritath and Ard'rian. (See "The Ensigns Of Command")

HARO, MITANA: An alien spy who infiltrates the real captives, who include Picard, Esoqq and Tholl. (See "Allegiance")

HAROLD, LIEUTENANT: Stationed on Cestus III, he survives the Gorn attack that destroys the settlement. (See "Arena")

HARPER, ENSIGN: The crewman from engineering who dies when he attempts to shut off the M-5 computer. (See "The Ultimate Computer")

HARRIS, CAPTAIN: Commanding officer of the *Excalibur*, whose crew (and he) dies when they engage in wargames with the M-5 computer. (See "The Ultimate Computer")

HARRISON, DR.: A victim of the Psi 2000 virus whose symptoms consist primarily of hysterical laughter. (See "The Naked Time")

HARRISON, TECHNICIAN 1/C: A member of the *Enterprise* bridge crew when Khan takes control and cuts off the air. (See "Space Seed")

HARRISON, WILLIAM B.: An officer from the *Beagle* who is killed in gladiatorial combat on Planet 892-IV. (See "Bread And Circuses")

HASKELL: The alien scientist Nagilum kills this bridge crewman on the *Enterprise* in order to study the nature of life and death among the humans. (See "Where Silence Has Lease")

HASKINS, DR. THEODORE: Leader of the Talos IV expedition. He died when their vessel was destroyed, but appears to Pike as an illusion generated by the Talosians. (See "The Cage")

HAWKINS, AMBASSADOR: Head of the Federation diplomatic mission held hostage by Governor Karnas of Mordan IV. (See "Too Short A Season")

HAYNE: A member of one of the warring factions on Turkana Four (Tasha Yar's homeworld). (See "Legacy")

HEDFORD, NANCY: A Federation commissioner who is afflicted with Sakuro's disease. She is near death when she is entered by the gaseous Companion; she is rejuvenated, and marries Zefrem Cochrane. They decide to stay together for the rest of their lives. (See "Metamorphosis")

HEIFETZ, JASCHA: A Russian concert violinist born in Vilna in 1901. In one performance Data does he blends Trenka Bron-ken's style with that of Heifetz. (See "Ensigns Of Command")

HENDORF: A security guard who beams down to Gamma Triunguli VI and dies when he is struck by deadly thorns. (See "The Apple")

HENGIST: The native of Argelius II who is taken over by the Jack-the-Ripper being. His mousy, officious manner makes this bureaucrat an unlikely suspect in the brutal murders that are almost pinned on Scotty. (See "Wolf In The Fold")

HENNESSY: Dr. Pulaski's patient whom she is treating for Andonesian encephalitis. (See "The Dauphin")

HENOCH: One of the three survivors of the planet Arret, who borrows Spock's body and decides to keep it. Fortunately, his nemesis Sargon helps outwit him, restoring Spock to himself. (See "Return To Tomorrow")

HENRY, ADMIRAL: The Starfleet officer who terminates the hearings into security breaches aboard the *Enterprise* when it becomes clear that Admiral Satie sees conspiracies everywhere. (See "The Drumhead")

HENSHAW, CHRISTY: A civilian aboard the *Enterprise* whom Geordi finally gets the nerve to ask out on a date. (See "Transformations")

HERBERT, ENSIGN: An *Enterprise* transporter officer. A transporter operator. (See "We'll Always Have Paris" and "The Icarus Factor")

HERMAN: The name of a model of android on Planet Mudd. (See "I, Mudd")

HILDEBRANT: Married to Alans and a specialist in geomechanics and vulcanology. She is a member of Wesley's Selcundi Drema team. (See "Pen Pals")

HILL, DIXON: A fictional detective on Earth c. 1941, of whom Jean-Luc Picard is a big fan. Besides reading about him, Picard also likes to relive the adventures on the holodeck. (See "The Big Goodbye")

HODIN: A leader of the planet Gideon. His daughter is the key player in his plan to reintroduce death to his world. Once she is infected with the lingering Vegan choriomeningitis bacteria in James Kirk's system, her doom is sealed, as is that of her entire race, which must now adapt to disease and an increased mortality rate. (See "Mark Of Gideon")

HOLLANDER, ELI: An outlaw character in the Deadwood, South Dakota holodeck program. (See "A Fistful Of Datas")

HOLLANDER, FRANK: An outlaw character in the Deadwood, South Dakota holodeck program. (See "A Fistful Of Datas")

HOLLIDAY, DOC: Another historical member of the Earp saga as reenacted by the Melkotians. (See "Spectre Of The Gun")

HOLMES, SHERLOCK: Popular character in Earth literature, created by Arthur Conan Doyle in the late 19th Century. His hold on the imagination is still strong in the 24th Century; Data is fascinated by the character. (See "Lonely Among Us". "Elementary, Dear Data")

HOLZA, JAS: A Bajoran spokesman at the refugee camp on Valo Three. Ensign Ro claims that he is just a figurehead trotted out to speak to any representatives of the Federation who happen by, and he has no genuine authority in the encampment. (See "Ensign Ro")

HOMN, MR.: The seven-foot-tall silent manservant and general factotum of Lwaxana Troi. (See "Haven", "Manhunt")

HON-TIHL: The lone Klingon survivor of the destruction of the Bird of Prey *Toh'Kaht,* but he only lives long enough to exclaim the one word "Victory!" before he dies. (See "Dramatis Personae")

HOVATH: The assistant of the Sirah. (See "The Storyteller")

HOY, ENSIGN: A transporter operator who relinquishes the controls to Picard so that he can beam up Nuria. (See "Who Watches The Watchers?")

HUMBOLT, CHIEF: Spock knocks out this Starbase 11 staffer in the course of his abduction of Captain Christopher Pike. (See "The Menagerie")

HUTCHINSON, COMMANDER: The Commander of the Arkaria Base. He is a master of small talk and can spend hours talking without saying anything of significance. He is killed by renegades planning to steal valuable material from the *Enterprise*. (See "Starship Mine")

IAN: An alien entity which impregnates itself in Deanna Troi and is born 36 hours later. It wishes to experience what human life is like. He allows his human body to die when he realizes he is emitting Eichner radiation, which is dangerous to humans, whereupon the noncorporeal entity leaves the *Enterprise*. (See "The Child")

IBODAN: A Bajoran black marketeer, and a murderer. Ibodan once allowed a child to die because the child's parents could not afford to purchase a life-saving medicine from him. Odo is accused of Ibodan's murder when actually it was a clone who was killed. (See "A Man Alone")

ILIA, LIEUTENANT: A Deltan navigator, like all of her race she has taken a vow of celibacy for the safety of the humans she works with. Deltans can control their own sex drive, and that of others, on a chemical level. Ilia was once involved with Will Decker and they choose to go together with V'ger to the next level of existence, whatever that may be. (See "Star Trek: The Motion Picture")

INAD: An older woman, a telepath and member of the Ullian delegation. (See "Violations")

INNIS, VALEDA: Leader of the planet Haven, she wants Picard to destroy the Terellian plague ship that is approaching her planet. (See "Haven")

ISABELLA: Little Clara Sutter's imaginary friend who becomes very real when an alien entity takes on Isabella's form. (See "Imaginary Friend")

ISAK: The younger brother of the Zeon Abrom. (See "Patterns Of Force")

ISHIKAWA, KEIKO: Now Keiko O'Brien, the wife of Miles O'Brien, former *Enterprise* Transporter Chief and now Chief of Operations on Deep Space Nine. They were wed in "Data's Day."

ISIS: A mysterious being associated with Gary Seven. It's a little unclear as to who is really in charge; Isis usually takes the form of a black cat but also is seen as a beautiful woman. Her real form is a matter of conjecture. (See "Assignment: Earth")

JACKSON: A crew member killed by Sylvia on Pyris VII. (See "Catspaw")

JACK THE RIPPER: Perpetrator of brutal, unsolved murders in London, Earth in 1888, he (or it) was really an energy being capable of possessing humanoid life forms and using them to kill. Some of its crimes can be traced: China in 1932, Russia in 1974 and, after moving into space, Mars in 2105. Over the centuries it has wreaked havoc on many other worlds; its planet of origin, if any, is unknown. Encountering it on Rigel IV, Kirk outwits it and casts it into space, but is really not certain that it is dead. (See "Wolf In The Fold")

JA'DAR, DR.: One of the developers of the Soliton Wave theory. (See "New Ground")

JAEGER, LT. CARL: A member of the Gothos landing team. (See "Squire Of Gothos")

JAHIL, CAPTAIN: An alien whose ship stops off at Deep Space Nine for repairs. (See "Babel")

JAHN: Chief of the gang of centuries-old children on the planet where adolescence arrives rather late. (See "Miri")

JAMAL, YEOMAN ZAHRA: One of the *Enterprise* crew members who beam down to parasite-plagued Deneva. (See "Operation: Annihilate")

JAMESON, ADMIRAL MARK: He violated the Prime Directive with the secret settlement he made on Mordan IV (supplying Federation technology to both sides and creating a balance of terror along with a balance of power) and 45 years later Karnas, the ruler of Mordan IV, decides to exact his revenge. (See "Too Short A Season")

JAMESON, ANNE: The wife of Admiral Mark Jameson. She opposes the use of the alien youth drug which does ultimately bring about her husband's death. (See "Too Short A Season")

JANOWSKI, MARY: One of the preadolescent survivors of the Starnes group, a young girl who falls into the sphere of Gorgan the "Friendly Angel." (See "And The Children Shall Lead")

JARED, ACOST: One of the Ventaxans who is taken in by the phony Ardra. (See "Devil's Due")

JARIS: The top ranking functionary on the planet of Argelius II. His wife is a victim of the Jack-the-Ripper being, which tries to possess Jaris when it is driven out of Hengist's body. (See "Wolf In The Fold")

JA'ROD: The actual traitor behind the Khitomer Massacre and the father of Duras. (See "Sins Of The Fathers")

JAROK, ADMIRAL ALIDAR: A high Romulan officer who poses as a sublieutenant named Setal when he defects to the Federation. He warns Picard that the Romulans have constructed a base near the edge of the Neutral Zone at Nelvana Three. (See "The Defector")

JARTH: A member of the Lumerian team that accompanies Ves Alkar to Rekag-Seronia for the peace negotiations. (See "Man Of The People")

JASAD, GUL: The Cardassian commander in charge of the battle fleet which threatens Deep Space Nine following the discovery of the wormhole. (See "Emissary")

J'DAN: A Klingon exchange officer, he is caught accessing security codes aboard the *Enterprise*. He is believed to be a spy who gave the Romulans the information. (See "The Drumhead")

JELLICO, CAPTAIN: He is assigned the command of the *Enterprise* in Jean-Luc Picard's absence. He is a harsh commander. (See "Chain Of Command")

J'LESTRA, SABIN: A full Betazoid aide who is brought aboard the *Enterprise* by Admiral Satie as she investigates damaging security leaks. (See "The Drumhead")

JENNA: An *Enterprise* officer with whom Data has an affair, of sorts, in order to determine what romance is like. Not having emotions, Data doesn't succeed in learning very much. (See "In Theory")

JEV: Part of the Ullian delegation of telepaths and Tarmin's son. Jev is a dangerous throwback who likes to indulge in mental rape. (See "Violations")

JOACHIM: Khan's trusted assistant. Although not revealed in the film, Joachim was Khan's son. (See "Star Trek II: The Wrath Of Khan")

JO'BRIL: A Takaran scientist who agrees to visit the *Enterprise* to witness a test of Dr. Reyga's metaphasic field technology. He kills the Ferengi and tries to make the metaphasic field test appear to be a failure. Dr. Crusher is forced to kill Jo'Bril when he attacks her in an effort to cover up his crimes. (See "Suspicions")

JOHNSON, ELAINE: A young woman who dies of the accelerated aging disease caused by the deadly radiation of Gamma Hydra. (See "The Deadly Years")

JOHNSON, LIEUTENANT: A young officer involved in the fight with the Klingons provoked by the hate-feeding entity. He is wounded, but the entity repairs him so that he can rejoin the fight. (See "Day Of The Dove")

JOHNSON, ROBERT: Husband of Elaine Johnson; he also succumbs to the accelerated aging disease of Gamma Hydra. He was the leader of the ill-fated Gamma Hydra expedition. (See "The Deadly Years")

JONES, CYRANO: The blustery, mercenary space trader who brings the tribbles to Space Station K-7, thus nearly triggering an agricultural crisis in the sector. (See "The Trouble With Tribbles")

JONES, DR. MIRANDA: The blind, telepathic human woman who serves as translator and companion to the Medusan, Kollos. Jones learned to control her telepathic abilities with Vulcan techniques, but is resentful of the fact that Spock's natural telepathy exceeds hers. Like Vulcans, she is disdainful of emotions. (See "Is There In Truth No Beauty")

J'ONN: One of Sybok's most devoted disciples. (See "Star Trek V: The Final Frontier")

JONO: A boy whose parents were killed in the Tellerian war and who was taken and raised by the Tellerians until all he knows is that way of life. His real name is Jeremiah Rossa. (See "Suddenly Human")

JOSEPHS, LIEUTENANT: The crewman who comes across the murdered Tellarian ambassador's body. (See "Journey To Babel")

JOVAL: An employee of the Risa Pleasure Haven who tells Jean-Luc the true meaning of displaying the Horga'hn. (See "Captain's Holiday")

KAHLESS: A legendary Klingon warrior who combats Kirk, Lincoln and the rest of the "good guys" as one of Yarnek's evil champions. The Klingons see him as a legendary hero and have an almost religious worship of what Kahless represents to them. (See "The Savage Curtain" and "Rightful Heir")

KAHLEST: When Worf was a child, she was his nurse at the Khitomer Outpost and along with Worf, was one of the only two survivors of the Khitomer Massacre. When Worf is threatened with disgrace, she comes out of hiding to speak on his behalf. (See "Sins Of The Fathers")

KAI: The Bajoran spiritual leader.

KAJADA, TY: A Kobliad security officer who had been tracking Rao Vantika, a serial killer, for 20 years. (See "The Passenger")

KALO: An Iotian native; part of the Oxmyx gang. (See "A Piece Of The Action")

KALOMI, LEILA: A young botanist who has been in love with Spock for several years. On Omicron Ceti II, she uses the disinhibiting spores to awaken Spock's emotions, and he reciprocates until James Kirk returns him to normal. (See "This Side Of Paradise")

KAMG: The Captain of the Klingon ship that the hate-feeding entity draws into its staged battles with the *Enterprise* crew. It takes all of Kirk's persuasive powers to convince Kang that they must cease all hostilities in order to defeat their real common enemy, the entity. (See "Day Of The Dove")

KAMIN: The name Jean-Luc is called by his wife, Eline, after he is hit by a beam from a strange space probe and awakens a thousand years in the past on the planet Kataan. (See "The Inner Light")

KAMALA: An empath who is to be a gift to the planetary leader, something which she has been raised to be all her life. She is an empathic metamorph who is in her final stages of sexual develop-ment when she will finally imprint herself on one man. As it turns out, she imprints on Picard but is willing to do her duty and become the mate of the planetary leader as she was intended to be. (See "The Perfect Mate")

KAPEC, RENA: The android woman that the immortal Flint designs as his companion. Passing her as human, he tries to use James Kirk to provoke real emotions in her, but the result is disastrous for all, and she "dies." Spock uses the Vulcan mind-meld to wipe these traumatic events from Kirk's memory. (See "Requiem For Methuselah")

KAPLAN: One of the crew members killed on Gamma Trianguli VI.

KARA: 1.) The woman who leads the Eymorgs of Sigma Draconis VI. ("Spock's Brain")
2.) A dancer on Argellius II. Scotty takes a liking to her and winds up accused of her brutal murder, actually committed by the possessed Hengist. ("Wolf In The Fold")

KARATOK: The author of a book which is given to Data titled "The Dream Of The Fire." (See "Measure Of A Man")

KARGAN, CAPTAIN: The commander of the *Pagh*, a Klingon Bird-of-Prey which Riker is temporarily transferred to under an officer exchange program. (See "A Matter Of Honor")

KARIDIAN, ANTON: The leader of the Karidian Players, a wandering troupe of actors. He is actually Kodos, known as Kodos the Executioner. Notorious for executing half the population of Tarsus IV (the "inferior"" half) during a famine, he is believed dead. Suspicion falls on Karidian when murders begin to occur around him, which leads Kirk to investigate the situation. (See "Conscience Of The King")

KARIDIAN, LENORE: Anton Karidian's daughter. Her father, although guilty of terrible draconian measures in his past, is innocent of the murders. Lenore, in fact, is the killer — she's been eradicating any witness who can identify her father as Kodos. Her father places himself between her and James Kirk when she tries to kill Kirk, and is killed by her phaser blast. She then loses her mind. (See "Conscience Of The King")

KARIDIAN PLAYERS: Under the aegis of the Galactic Cultural Exchange Project, Karidian's troupe has brought the classics of theater to remote regions of the galaxy for the better part of the decade — until his past begins to catch up with him. (See "Conscience Of The King")

KARNAS: The planetary leader of Mordan IV who creates a terrorist incident in order to force a confrontation and a final reckoning with retired Starfleet Admiral Jameson for whom he has a long-held hatred. (See "Too Short A Season")

KARTAN: One of the Denevans under the influence of the parasites; he attacks Kirk and crew. (See "Operation: Annihilate")

KATIE: One of the *Enterprise* children abducted by the Aldeans. (See "When The Bough Breaks")

KAYRON: One of the Ferengi encountered by the *Enterprise* Away Team on Delphi Ardu. (See "The Last Outpost")

KAZAGO: Second in command to Daimon Bock, he realizes that Bock is out for revenge; since this is a most unprofitable course of action that runs contrary to all Ferengi interests, he is perfectly justified, under Ferengi law, in arresting his superior and taking command of the ship. (See "The Battle")

KEEL, ANNE: A sister of Walker Keel. (See "Conspiracy")

KEEL, MELISSA: Walker Keel's other sister. (See "Conspiracy")

KEEL, CAPTAIN WALKER: Since serving with Picard on the *Stargazer*, Keel has been promoted and commands his own ship. After he warns Picard of the alien conspiracy within Starfleet, his ship is destroyed, killing him and his entire crew. (See "Conspiracy")

KEELER, EDITH: The central figure in the 1930s sojourn of McCoy, Kirk and Spock. She was, in fact, a truly kind person with a strong humanitarian impulse — but if she is not killed by a truck, she will live to head a peace movement which, although noble in intention, will keep America out of World War II for too long and allow the Third Reich to achieve lasting victory. Kirk falls in love with her but sacrifices her to history when he keeps McCoy from preventing her death. (See "City On The Edge Of Forever")

KEENA: An unauthorized resident of Jeraddo who refused to evacuate when the government of Bajor ordered it. She and Baltrim suffered under the torture of the Cardassians before they escaped to Jeraddo 18 years earlier. (See "Progress")

KEEPER: The chief Talosian and zoo-keeper on Talos IV. (See "The Cage")

K'EHLEYR: Worf's former lover and the mother of his son, Alexander. At the time Worf is first reunited with her (See "The Emissary") she says nothing about their child. She has an interesting background in that her mother was human and her father Klingon.

KELINDA: One of the Kelvans who take over the *Enterprise*. Kirk tries to put some moves on her in his efforts to regain control of his ship. (See "By Any Other Name")

KELL: The Klingon ambassador who accompanies Picard to Krios, a Klingon colony where a fight for independence is under way. The ambassador and Picard are headed there to investigate the planetary governor's claim that the Federation is supplying the rebels with armaments. Little do they know that the Romulans are supplying the weapons and they have brainwashed Geordi into becoming an instrument of assassination aimed at Kell so as to divert attention away from the Romulans and create a rift between the Federation and the Klingons. (See "The Mind's Eye")

KELLY: A crewman from the *Enterprise* who is killed by the Horta on Janus VI. (See "Devil In The Dark")

KELOWITZ, LT. COMMANDER: A security officer from the *Enterprise*. He helps look for Spock on Taurus II after the crash of the *Galileo*, is involved in the first firefight with the Gorn on Cestus III, and is affected by the spores on Omicron Ceti. He survives all these adventures. Perhaps this is because he didn't wear a red shirt?

KELSEY: A female pirate who leads a group of raiders who board the *Enterprise* during a baryon sweep so that they can steal a quality of trilithium resin. She ultimately dies in the attempt. (See "Starship Mine")

KELSO, LT. LEE: An *Enterprise* crewman killed by Gary Mitchell on remote Delta Vega. (See "Where No Man Has Gone Before")

KENNELLY, ADMIRAL: He conspires with the Cardassians to find a way to trap the Bajoran terrorist leader Orta. But in so doing, Kennelly breaks the Prime Directive and ends his Starfleet career. (See "Ensign Ro")

KENNER, COMMANDER: A rival officer in the mirror universe who has a fancy for James Kirk's woman, Marlena-Two. (See "Mirror, Mirror")

KENTOR: He was one of Data's supporters in the colony of Tau Cygna V when the Federation orders them to evacuate. (See "Ensigns Of Command")

KIM, DR. JOSHUA: His name is heard announced over the intercom as he is told to report to Cetacean Ops. (See "Yesterday's Enterprise")

KIM, Dr. LUISA: One of the head scientists involved in the terraforming of Velara III; her superior keeps the native life form a secret from her. (See "Home Soil")

KINGSLEY, DR. SARA: At the Darwin Genetic Research Station she is the Chief Researcher. She is an early victim of the old-age illness caused by the immune system of the special children they have there. (See "Unnatural Selection")

KIR: One of the high-speed Scalosians. (See "The Wink Of An Eye")

KIRK, AURELIAN: A colonist on Deneva, and James Kirk's sister-in-law. She dies as a result of the parasite invasion. She sends the message that brings James Kirk to Deneva. (See "Operation: Annihilate")

KIRK, GEORGE SAMUEL: James T. Kirk's older brother, known as Sam. He was a biologist, and died in the attack of the flying parasites. (See "Operation: Annihilate")

KIRK, CAPTAIN JAMES TIBERIUS: The third and most famous captain of the *Enterprise*, Kirk is the descendant of early American pioneers. A real leader, with an impressive string of accomplishments to his name both in war and in peace, he is the ideal man to lead the exploration of unknown regions of space. As adept in a rough-and-tumble fistfight as he is in a complex diplomatic situation or a baffling murder mystery, Kirk is a dedicated and driven officer with one eye always on the future. His career — just the parts that have been documented — holds enough adventure for several ordinary lifetimes.

His serial number is SC937-0176CEC. He has been decorated many times. A real ladies' man, he has broken hearts across the galaxy. His real affection is for his ship, the *Enterprise*. His admittedly large ego is generally held in check by his immense dedication to his job and by the awesome responsibility of running a starship with more than four hundred people on board. His closest friends seem to be Leonard McCoy and Spock, although there is often friction between them all.

KIRK, PETER: James Kirk's nephew, the sole survivor of the flying parasite attack on Deneva. His parents Aurelian and George were not so lucky. (See "Operation: Annihilate")

KIRK-TWO: The Kirk of the mirror universe, who takes James Kirk's place in our world. Luckily, Spock realizes that this mass killer is not the right Kirk and secures him in the brig. (See "Mirror, Mirror")

KIROK: Kirk's name as pronounced by Miramanee and her tribe; he can barely remember his name anyway. (See "The Paradise Syndrome")

KIROS: One of the pirates who board the *Enterprise* during a baryon sweep so that they can steal a quantity of trilithium resin. (See "Starship Mine")

KLAA, CAPTAIN: The Klingon starship commander who makes it his personal business to go after James T. Kirk. (See "Star Trek V: The Final Frontier")

KLAG, LIEUTENANT: When Riker is transferred to the Klingon Bird-of-Prey the *Pagh*, Klag is the Second Officer. Klag's father was captured by Romulans (and thereby disgraced since he didn't die in battle). (See "A Matter Of Honor")

KLOOG: One of the thralls encountered on Triskelion. (See "Gamesters Of Triskelion")

K'MPEC: Former leader of the Klingon High Council. He knew all along that Ja'rod was the real traitor at Khitomer. (See "Sins Of The Fathers") Jean-Luc Picard helps him choose his successor. (See "Reunion")

K'NERA: The Klingon commander whose ship proceeds to the *Enterprise* to pick up the renegade Klingons. (See "Heart Of Glory")

KOL: He and Arridor are marooned on the wrong side of the wormhole when it closes. (See "The Price")

KOLLOS: The Medusan ambassador, representative of a race so intense that no humanoid can glimpse one and remain sane. For this reason he is accompanied by Dr. Miranda Jones, who is blind and thus immune; her telepathy makes her the ideal translator for him. Kollos lives in a box and can be observed through special glasses, which Spock uses to approach him for a crucial mind-meld when the *Enterprise* is in dire need of the Medusan's almost-psychic navigational skills. Afterwards, Kollos and Miranda Jones form a permanent telepathic link, providing perhaps a solution to Jones' loneliness. (See "Is There In Truth No Beauty")

KOLOTH, CAPTAIN: The Klingon captain who is on hand during the tribble crisis at Space Station K-7. He and Kirk have met before, most likely before the Organian Treaty, and affect the attitude of friendly adversaries. (See "The Trouble With Tribbles")

KOLRAMI, SIRNA: A Zakdornian master strategist who works for Starfleet and comes aboard the *Enterprise* to advise on the battle simulation. (See "Peak Performance")

KOMACK, ADMIRAL: James Kirk defies a direct order from this top-ranking Starfleet officer in Sector 9, in order to take Spock to Vulcan when he is afflicted with *pon farr*. (The ordered destination was Altair VI.) Diplomatic requests from Vulcan deter his wrath, and Kirk is given permission — retroactively — to go to Vulcan after all. (See "Amok Time")

KONMEL: A wounded Klingon who is brought aboard the *Enterprise* where he dies. Worf helps perform his death ritual. (See "Heart Of Glory")

KORBY, DR. ROGER: The exobiologist who discovered the remnants of the ancient "Old Ones," who left their androids on Exo III. Learning this ancient technology, he builds new androids, which he plans to introduce to the galaxy, and builds himself a new android body after experiencing severe damage to his original body. When he realizes that this is destroying his humanity, he eradicates his androids and himself. Prior to this, his archeological/scientific discoveries were largely beneficial, especially when ancient alien medical records enabled him to establish new medical standards for humanity. He's yet another in the chain of so many good minds gone bad in the darker reaches of space. (See "What Are Little Girls Made Of?")

KORIS: One of two escaped Klingons who are found aboard a battered vessel which they stole because they oppose the new peace accords of the modern Klingon Empire. He dies aboard the *Enterprise* while attempting to escape before a Klingon vessel can come to return them to the home world. (See "Heart Of Glory")

KOROB: An alien whom the *Enterprise* encounters in human form on Pyris VII. With his less-moral partner Sylvia, he subjects the *Enterprise*'s key officers to a reign of terror marked by all the trappings of ancient Earth wizardry. Apparently an emissary of the same Old Ones who left behind the androids found by Dr. Roger Korby on Exo III, his goal is colonization, but his partner's capricious cruelty complicates matters unduly, and she kills him when he objects to her vicious abuse of the humans and Spock. (See "Catspaw")

KOROTH: The head cleric on the planet Boreth, a world in the Klingon Empire where the followers of Kahless study the history of this legendary Klingon warrior and await his return. As it turns out, Kahless does return to life on Boreth, and Koroth is very much involved in the reason why. (See "Rightful Heir")

KORRD, GENERAL: The old Klingon who is first imprisoned by Sybok and then joins him. When he sees the error of his ways he rescues Kirk from Captain Klaa. (See "Star Trek V: The Final Frontier")

KOSZINSKI: A Federation propulsion expert. An arrogant warp scientist who really doesn't know what he's doing; his sometimes miraculous results are really caused by the amazing mind powers of his assistant, the legendary Traveler. (See "Where No One Has Gone Before")

KRAG, INSPECTOR: When Dr. Apgar is killed, Riker is taken into custody for his murder by Inspector Krag of the Tanugan Security Force. (See "A Matter Of Perspective")

KRAKO, JOJO: One of the rival gang leaders of Iotia. (See "A Piece Of The Action")

KRAS: A truly shifty Klingon emissary. Kirk encounters him on Capella IV, where Kras' mission is to thwart the Federation's interests on this topaline-rich planet. He is killed, quite deservedly, by the Capellan Keel, a follower of Maab. (See "Friday's Child")

KRASNOWSKY, CAPTAIN: One of the presiding officers at James Kirk's court martial for murder. (See "Court Martial")

KRAX: The son of the Grand Nagus. (See "The Nagus")

KRELL: A Klingon who provides guns to the primitive people of Tyree's world. (See "A Private Little War")

KRISTIN: A crew person on the *Enterprise-D*. (See "Conundrum")

KRITE: One of the J'Naii. She reveals to Riker that the other J'Naii know about his affair with Soren and that Soren has been taken into custody to be put on trial. (See "The Outcast")

KRODAK: A high-ranking inhabitant of Gideon, who tries to counter Spock's suspicions about the disappearance of Captain Kirk. (See "Mark Of Gideon")

KROLA: Malkorian Security Minister who opposes all contact with aliens. (See "First Contact")

KRUGE: The Klingon commander who is determined to have the secret of Genesis. He has David Marcus killed to force Kirk to turn over the secret of Genesis from the *Enterprise* computer banks. Kirk and Kruge fight a duel to the death on the surface of Genesis, a fight from which Kirk emerges the victor. (See "Star Trek III: The Search For Spock")

KRYTON: One of the retinue that accompanies Elaan on her voyage to Troyius, he is in love with her, and conspires with the Klingons to stop her marriage. He also sabotages the antimatter pods of the *Enterprise*, and gets a guard to kill him rather than be taken prisoner. (See "Elaan Of Troyius")

K'TEMOC: Captain of the Klingon vessel the *T'Ong* who has been in cryogenic suspension for 75 years along with his ship and crew. He still believes that the Federation and the Klingon Empire are adversaries. (See "The Emissary")

KUDA, VING: The author of "Ethics, Sophistry and the Alternate Universe" (See "Captain's Holiday")

KULLNARK: An actor known for his portrayal of Henry V. (See "The Defector")

KUNIVAS: One of two escaped Klingons who are found aboard a battered vessel which they stole because they oppose the new peace accords of the modern Klingon Empire. He dies aboard the *Enterprise* while attempting to escape before a Klingon vessel can come to return them to the home world. (See "Heart Of Glory")

KURAK: A female Klingon scientist who agrees to visit the Enterprise to witness a test of Dr. Reyga's metaphasic field technology. (See "Suspicions")

KURLAND, JOSEPH: A student edged out of Academy competition by Wesley Crusher. He steals a shuttle from the *Enterprise* because he wants to relocate to a freighter, but when the shuttle malfunctions, Picard miraculously talks the shuttle in to safety by giving Kurland specific directions on how to save himself. (See "Coming Of Age")

KURN, COMMANDER: Worf's younger brother whom he didn't even know was still alive until he was an adult. Kurn had been raised by Lorgh, a friend of the family. (See "Sins Of The Father")

KUSHELL: From the planet Streleb, he is the leader of the Legation of Unity and thinks that Okona stole the Jewel of Thesia. (See "The Outrageous Okona")

K'VADA: The commander of the Klingon ship which sneaks Data and Picard to the planet Romulus. (See "Unification")

KYLE, LIEUTENANT: Occasional helmsman, transporter operator and general backup, he manages to avoid planet missions and thus survives a good, long time.

KYLE-TWO: The mirror world's Lieutenant Kyle is not so lucky as his Federation counterpart; a minor transporter problem earns him a dose of the agonizer, administered by Spock-Two. (See "Mirror, Mirror")

LAFORGE, LT. COMMANDER GEORDI: The Chief of Engineering aboard the *Enterprise-D*. LaForge has been blind all his life, but is able to see with the aid of a visor linked directly to his brain. This approximates human sight, and can also be adjusted to take in spectra not normally visible to humans: ultraviolet and infrared light, magnetic fields, thermal patterns and the like. An agreeable young man, Geordi has something of the innocent about him, and seems inclined to get along with everybody. Originally a bridge officer on the *Enterprise*, he was promoted to Chief Engineer after about a year of service. (See "The Child")

LAL: A Vian, one of those who tests Gem on Minara II, torturing Kirk, McCoy and other humans in the process. (See "The Empath")

LAL: An android built by Data which he succeeds in giving human emotions. Data refers to Lal as his "child." Lal is given self-determination by Data and she chooses her own sex and appearance. Her name is Hindi for "beloved." When a representative of Starfleet threatens to separate her from her "father," Lal's complicated feelings cause her to have a nervous breakdown and she begins to die. Data absorbs her memory patterns into his own positronic brain. (See "The Offspring")

LANDON, YEOMAN MARTHA: A young female officer with a liking for Ensign Chekov. On Gamma Trianguli VI, she kisses him, leading to trouble for the two natives, Sayana and Makora, who imitate this action. (See "The Apple")

LANDRU: The computer that has run things on Beta III for the past six thousand years. It projects itself with the human form of a dignified elderly man. James Kirk talks it into destroying itself by pointing out that it is really hurting the people of Beta III. (See "Return Of The Archons")

LANEL: When Riker is captured and exposed as an "alien" while on an observation mission on a world which has not yet achieved space flight, Lanel offers to help Riker escape in exchange for having sex with her, as she's never had sex with an alien. (See "First Contact")

LANG, LIEUTENANT: An early casualty of the Gorns on the planet Cestus III. (See "Arena")

LANGFORD: An unseen person in the mirror universe, who apparently had the misfortune of crossing the deadly Uhura-Two. (See "Mirror, Mirror")

LANGOR: A female Brekkian, en route to Ornara with a shipment of Felicium when the ship she's on is destroyed and she is beamed over to the *Enterprise*. (See "Symbiosis")

LAREN, ENSIGN RO: A Bajoran who was released from prison by Admiral Kennelly in an effort to trap the Bajoran terrorist, Orta. But when Ensign Ro tells Picard the truth about why she is there, they both expose Kennelly for conspiring with the Cardassians in violation of the Prime Directive. Picard then invites Ro to remain aboard the *Enterprise*, although Will Riker doesn't support the idea. (See "Ensign Ro")

LARS: One of the thralls of Triskelion, paired up with Uhura against her will. (See "Gamesters Of Triskelion")

LARSON: A crew member of the *Enterprise-D*. (See "The Nth Degree")

LATIMER: The first casualty after the crash of the *Galileo* on Taurus II, killed in by a primitive spear. (See "The Galileo Seven")

LAWGIVER: A representative of the computer Landru. (See "Return Of The Archons")

LAZARUS: Biblical figure raised from the dead; allegedly he was really the immortal Flint. (See "Requiem For Methuselah")

LAZARUS A: A deranged humanoid from another dimension, looking like an insane Biblical prophet. He destroyed his world and its alternative universe parallel when he encountered his counterpart in that world, Lazarus B, and became obsessed with destroying him. Their struggle has lasted for hundreds of years. (See "The Alternative Factor")

LAZARUS B: The good Lazarus, who helps Kirk in his plan to exile the evil Lazarus A to a dimensional limbo, but sacrifices himself there as well in order to ensure that Lazarus A will never be a threat again. (See "The Alternative Factor")

LEDA: The Aldean woman assigned the abducted Harry Bernard as her son. (See "When The Bough Breaks")

LEECH, FELIX: A henchman in the Dixon Hill holodeck recreation who gets angry and shoots Mr. Whelan, an *Enterprise* crewman. (See "The Big Goodbye")

LEFLER, ROBIN: A young woman whom Wesley befriends and who, along with him, discover the danger inherent in "The Game."

LEGER: Data observes that Jean-Luc's artwork seems to be an imitation of this artist. (See "A Matter Of Perspective")

LEIGHTON, DR. THOMAS: One of Lenore Karidian's murder victims; crippled in the reign of terror of Kodos the Executioner, he survived — unlike his family — and recognized Anton Karidian as Kodos the Executioner while watching a performance of Shakespeare's *Macbeth* on Planet Q. This, unfortunately, cost him his life. (See "Conscience Of The King")

LEIGHTON, MARTHA: Dr. Thomas Leighton's wife. (See "Conscience Of The King")

LEITJEN, COMMANDER SUSANNA: She had been part of an Away Team from the *U.S.S. Victory* along with Geordi and it is found that she is metamorphosing into an alien being, an affliction which begins to strike LaForge as well. (See "Identity Crisis")

LEMEC, GUL : A Cardassian negotiator whom Captain Jellico meets with to discuss the terms of repatriating their prisoner, Jean-Luc Picard. (See "Chain Of Command")

LEMLI: A security guard who appears in several episodes. (See "Return To Tomorrow" and "Turnabout Intruder")

LESLIE, LIEUTENANT: A frequently recurring crew member who manages to survive all landing parties he's involved with. (See "Return Of The Archons", "Conscience Of The King", "The Alternative Factor" and "This Side Of Paradise.")

LESTER, JANICE: Long ago, she was involved with James Kirk. He was in love with her, but her single-minded, almost inhuman devotion to her career drove Kirk away from her. She blames him for abandoning her, unable to see her own responsibility in the situation. Quite out of her mind by the time Kirk meets her again on Camus II, she applies the techniques of consciousness transfer she has obtained to switch bodies with Kirk and take over the command of the *Enterprise*. Her irrational, arbitrary behavior and ignorance of Starfleet protocol soon creates suspicion among the crew, but she is cunning enough to keep them guessing for a while — until she becomes truly mad in her imposture. Kirk is eventually freed, and Lester survives, but only as a broken woman, tended by the sycophantic, weak-willed Dr. Coleman, who loves her. (See "Turnabout Intruder")

LESTRADE, INSPECTOR: A fictional character who appears on the holodeck as part of the Sherlock Holmes program. (See "Elementary, Dear Data")

LETEK: A Ferengi encountered by the *Enterprise* at Delphi Ardu. (See "The Last Outpost")

LETHE: A young woman, an assistant to Tristan Adams — quite brainwashed by her duties. (See "Dagger Of The Mind")

LEYOR: In the matter of the Barzan wormhole negotiations, Leyor is the Caldonian representative. (See "The Price")

LIATOR: One of the Edo, he persecutes Wesley after a minor accident and presses for the death penalty. (See "Justice")

LIKO: The first Mintakan to discover the Federation anthropological station; when he is injured he's brought to the *Enterprise* to have his injuries treated. When Dr. Crusher fails to blank his memories of the incident, Liko tells his people about a god he calls The Picard. Because he believes Picard is a god he wants him to bring his wife back from the dead. (See "Who Watches The Watchers?")

LINCOLN, ABRAHAM: The sixteenth president of the United States of America. Kirk encounters his image, drawn from Kirk's mind and projected by Yarnek; this Lincoln fights with Kirk against Yarnek's champions of evil on the planet Excalbia, and is killed by the Klingon, Kahless. (See "The Savage Curtain")

LINCOLN, ROBERTA: Gary Seven's secretary, a very hip Sixties woman who is drawn into the rocket launch escapade with Seven, Spock and Kirk. (See "Assignment: Earth")

LINDEN, DON: One of the small children mesmerized by the "Good Angel" Gorgan. (See "And The Children Shall Lead")

LINDSTROM, COMMANDER: A presiding officer at James Kirk's court martial for murder. (See "Court Martial")

LINDSTROM: A Federation sociologist who remains on Beta III after the computer Landru destroys itself. (See "Return Of The Archons")

LING: One of Khan Noonian Singh's genetically "superior" followers. (See "Space Seed")

LINKE, DR.: One of the humans the Vians torture in order to test Gem; he dies of his injuries. (See "The Empath")

LIPTON, SERGEANT: A guard at McKinley

Rocket Base, knocked out painlessly by Gary Seven when he infiltrates the base. He has better luck apprehending Spock and Kirk. (See "Assignment: Earth")

LIVA: A member of the Lumerian team that accompanies Ves Alkar to Rekag-Seronia for the peace negotiations. (See "Man Of The People")

LIYANG: One of the Kohm of Omega IV, he is about to kill Cloud William and Sirah when the arrival of James Kirk interrupts the execution. (See "Omega Glory")

L'KOR: An elderly Klingon who has lived in peace for many years at the Romulan prison planet and who knows that to return to the Klingon homeworld would mean disgrace for his family. (See "Birthright")

LOCARNO, NICHOLAS: Wesley Crusher's squad leader at Starfleet Academy in the Nova Squadron. Nicholas ultimately takes the full blame for the accident and is expelled from the Academy. (See "The First Duty")

LOCUTUS: When Jean-Luc Picard is kidnapped by the Borg, he is cybernetically altered and brainwashed into becoming the spokesman for the Borg. He is finally rescued by the *Enterprise* and separated by the Borg collective. (See "The Best Of Both Worlds")

LOGAN, CHIEF ENGINEER: On board the *Enterprise* when it is attacked in orbit around Minos, he recommends that the ship leave in spite of an Away Team still being on the surface. The *Enterprise* leaves and does a saucer separation with Logan put in charge of the saucer section. (See "The Arsenal Of Freedom")

LOJAL: A Vulcan ambassador who visits Deep Space Nine. (See "The Forsaken")

LOKAI: One of the two survivors of the dead planet Cheron: his face is black on the left side, unlike that of his pursuer, Bele. After fifty thousand years, they meet on the *Enterprise* and carry their battle back to the desolate ruins of their ravaged home world. (See "Let That Be Your Last Battlefield")

LORE: The android created right before Data. Dr. Soong created Lore with human emotions, which overwhelmed Lore and caused him to hate all humans. He was deactivated and disassembled by Dr.

Soong, only to be reactivated years later when the pieces are discovered in Dr. Soong's secret laboratory. This android is identical to his "brother" except for a telltale facial twitch (later self-corrected), his more human character, and his downright nasty disposition. Responsible for the destruction of Omicron Theta; cast into space but saved, he was called by the same beacon that reunited Data with Dr. Soong, stole the emotion chip intended for Data, and hastened Soong's death; took command of a group of the Borg after they became confused, defeated by *Enterprise* crew members and dismantled. (See "Datalore", "Brothers" and "Descent")

LORGH: The friend of Worf's father who raised Kurn after his family was killed at the battle of Khitomer. Only when Kurn reached the Age of Ascension was he told that his brother Worf was alive. (See "Sins Of The Fathers")

LOS, TANA: A Bajoran terrorist who continued his activities after the Cardassians left, except that now he wants the Federation off of Bajor. (See "Past Prologue")

LOSIRA: Once the commander of a remote outpost of the now-extinct Kalandan empire, Losira survived for countless years as a projection from the brain room of that outpost on an artificial planet. This image's mission was to explain the death of the outpost to all arriving Kalandans: a new disease wiped out the outpost. Ironically, that disease spread throughout the Kalandan Empire and was the reason for its complete extinction. There are no more Kalandans. More than an image, however, the Losira projection is a protective device, an extension of the powerful subterranean computer that can actually discover the names and histories of members of the *Enterprise* crew. After speaking this pertinent information for any individual, "Losira" can then kill that person with a single touch. This final remnant of the Kalandans vanishes when the *Enterprise* crew destroys the subterranean chamber. (See "That Which Survives")

LOSKENE, COMMANDER: Captain of the Tholian vessel encountered by the *Enterprise*. When the time Spock asks for — just under two hours — is up, Loskene fires; after a brief exchange, another Tholian ship arrives to weave a web around the *Enterprise*. (See "The Tholian Web")

LOUIS: An old friend of Jean-Luc Picard's who offers him an important position when he visits the old homestead in Labarre, France. (See "Family")

LOUISE: A three-hundred-year-old child who reaches puberty, which gives Kirk the chance to explain the real situation to the ancient children. (See "Miri")

LOUVOIS, CAPTAIN PHILIPA: The prosecutor in the *Stargazer* Courtmartial ten years before, then presided in the hearing over Data. Now the senior officer of the Starbase 173 Judge Advocate General's office. (See "The Measure Of A Man")

LOWRY, MS.: One of Alexander's teachers aboard the *Enterprise*. (See "New Ground")

LUMA: The first Eymorg encountered on Sigma Draconis VI, where the *Enterprise* has gone in search of Spock's stolen brain. (See "Spock's Brain")

LUMO: One of the American Indians on the world where Kirk has amnesia; he fishes a boy out of the water and Kirk saves him, making them believe that "Kirok" is a healer. (See "The Paradise Syndrome")

LURRY: He's the manager of Space Station K-7, a thankless job if ever there was one with all those Klingons and tribbles all over the place. (See "The Trouble With Tribbles")

LURSA: The sister of Duras. Along with her sister, B'Etor, they produce a youth, Toral, whom they claim is the illegitimate son of Duras. Through him they hope to gain control of the Klingon High Council. Unknown to the council the sisters are secretly working with the Romulan, Sela, so that the Romulans can gain influence over the Klingons. (See "Redemption")

LUTAN: Leader of the Ligonian people, replaced by his second-in-command after losing favor with his wife due to his abduction of Tasha Yar. (See "Code Of Honor")

LYNCH, LELAND T.: A member of the *Enterprise* engineering staff. (See "Skin Of Evil")

MAAB: A Capellan of Akaar's party who becomes Teer after the Klingon-backed rebellion; he is killed by Kras the Klingon. (See "Friday's Child")

MACDOUGAL, SARAH: Chief Engineer on the *Enterprise* when Picard took command; shared the title and the job with Argyle. (See "The Naked Now")

MACDUFF, COMMANDER KEIRAN: An impostor, he is actually a Satarran, a member of a race long at war with the Lysians. The Satarrans need the *Enterprise* technology to fight the Lysians. (See "Conundrum")

MACET, GUL: A Cardassian who demands to know why the *U.S.S. Phoenix* is attacking Cardassian vessels. (See "The Wounded")

MACKENZIE, ARD'RIAN: On the Tau Cygna V colony, she is a cyberneticist who not only supports Data's instruction for the evacuation of the colony but is also smitten with the android. (See "The Ensigns Of Command")

MADDOX, COMMANDER BRUCE: The only person who opposed Data's entry into Starfleet on the original Starfleet review board. Now the Assistant Chair of Robotics at the Daystrom Technical Institute. A cyberneticist who wants to disassemble Data and download his mind in order to test the positronic brain he has built. His goal is to create more androids for Starfleet use. He is opposed by both Data and Picard, and in a hearing it is proven that Data, as a Starfleet officer, has certain human rights that cannot be wantonly abused. (See "The Measure Of A Man")

MADELINE: In the Dixon Hill holodeck program she is his secretary in this 1941 San Francisco setting. (See "The Big Goodbye" and "Manhunt")

MADRED, GUL: A Cardassian who brutally tortures his prisoner, Jean-Luc Picard. (See "Chain Of Command")

MAGISTRATE: A functionary of the Talosians; it lets Pike and the other humans go when they turn out to be unsuited for Talosian purposes. (See "The Cage")

MAIHAR'DU: A Hupyrian servant of the Grand Nagus. (See "The Nagus")

MAKORA: A male inhabitant of Gamma Trianguli VI, who mates with the female Sayana after the computer Vaal is destroyed. (See "The Apple")

MALENCON, ARTHUR: A member of the ill-fated terraforming project on the planet Velara III; killed by the laser drill. (See "Home Soil")

MALLON: He is left in charge on Hromi by Brull and is given ten days before he is to take any action. ("The Vengeance Factor")

MALLORY, ENSIGN: A crewman who is killed by an exploding rock on Gamma Trianguli VI. (See "The Apple")

MALTZ: A Klingon under the command of Kruge. He dies aboard the boobytrapped Enterprise. (See "Star Trek III: The Search For Spock")

MANDARIN: One of the humanoid simulations providing support to Q in his trial of the Enterprise crew. (See "Encounter At Farpoint")

MANDL, KURT: Chief administrator of the ill-fated terraforming project on Velara III, who tries to cover up problems at the project but only manages to arouse Picard's curiosity. (See "Home Soil")

MANNHEIM, DR. PAUL: A scientist working on experiments involving time distortions, which get out of hand until ultimately Data brings them back under control. (See "We'll Always Have Paris")

MANNHEIM, JANICE: An old flame of Jean-Luc Picard, who later married Dr. Paul Mannheim. She and Picard meet again when her husband's time distortion experiments go awry. (See "We'll Always Have Paris")

MANWAY, DR.: A famous scientist killed in the Malurian solar system by Nomad. (See "The Changeling")

MARA: Probably the first Klingon woman encountered by the Enterprise, she helps Kirk convince Kang to join forces against the hate-feeding entity. (See "Day Of The Dove")

MARCUS, CAROL: A woman whom James Kirk was involved with more than twenty years before. She gave birth to David Marcus, who is actually Kirk's son. She is the co-inventor of the Genesis Device. (See "Star Trek II: The Wrath Of Khan")

MARCUS, DAVID: The son of Carol Marcus and James Kirk, although he doesn't discover who his father is until late in life. David is the co-developer of the Genesis Device, a mechanism which can bring the life matrix to an otherwise dead planet. (See "Star Trek II: The Wrath Of Khan") But because David cut corners and used protomatter in completing the Genesis device, the planet it creates is unstable. David dies on this planet at the hands of a Klingon who wants Admiral Kirk to surrender the Enterprise. (See "Star Trek III: The Search For Spock")

MARGAN: A leader on Ornara who contacts T'Jon and Romas. (See "Symbiosis")

MARISSA: A young girl who is trapped inside a damaged turbolift when the Enterprise hits a cosmic string. (See "Disaster")

MAROUK, SOVEREIGN: The leader of Acamar Three who wants to resolve her world's old problems with the Gatherers. (See "The Vengeance Factor")

MARPLE: A landing party member who is killed on Gamma Trianguli VI. (See "The Apple")

MARPLON: One of the secret anti-Landru underground, but also a technician for the super-computer that bears that name. (See "Return Of The Archons")

MARR, DR. KILA: An expert on the Crystalline Entity; her young son, Renny, was one of its victims and she ultimately manages to destroy the creature at the cost of her own career. (See "Silicon Avatar")

MARRITZA, AAMIN: The name used by a Cardassian who visits Deep Space Nine. Because he has Kalla-Nohra Syndrome, Major Kira believes that he is a war criminal who worked at the Gallitepp forced labor camp. But he claims to have Pottrik Syndrome, a disease similar to Kalla-Nohra Syndrome. He claims he was a military file clerk and was never at Gallitepp. Later he admits being at Gallitepp, but insists he was just a clerk. Then he admits to being Gul Darhe'el, the butcher of Gallitepp but he is really Aamin Marritza, Gul Darhe'el's file clerk. He had cosmetic surgery done so that he would look like Gul Darhe'el in order to force Cardassia to face the responsibility for its war crimes on Bajor. When the truth comes out he winds up being murdered by a Bajoran who hates all Cardassians. (See "Duet")

MARTA: A rather capricious Orion woman, with green skin, encountered as a member of Garth's entourage on the planet Elba II. One of the insane inmates, she flits between the affections of Garth of

Izar and Captain James Kirk. Tired of her vacillations, Garth finally disposes of her in a most explosive fashion. (See "Whom Gods Destroy")

MARTINE, SPECIALIST 2/C ANGELA : A phaser specialist; her fiancé Robert Tomlinson is killed in a Romulan battle. She also takes shore leave on the planet where thoughts become reality. (See "Balance Of Terror")

MARTINEZ: A medical officer on the *Enterprise*. (See "Who Watches The Watchers?")

MARVICK, DR. LAWRENCE: A brilliant scientist involved in warp engine design. In love with Dr. Miranda Jones, he tries to kill the Medusan Ambassador Kollos and is directly responsible for the *Enterprise*'s trip into a bizarre continuum after the sight of Kollos drives him insane. The entire experience proves to be fatal for him. (See "Is There In Truth No Beauty")

MASON: One of the children the Aldeans abduct from the *Enterprise*. (see "When The Bough Breaks")

MASTER OF THE GAMES: He is in charge of making the gladiators fight on 892-IV. (See "Bread And Circuses")

MASTER OF THE UNIVERSE: One of the self-proclaimed titles taken by Garth of Izar. (See "Whom Gods Destroy")

MASTER SURCHID: The title of Falow, one of the Wadi. (See "Move Along Home")

MASTERS, LT. CHARLENE: An engineering officer knocked unconscious by Lazarus A when he steals some dilithium crystals from Engineering. (See "The Alternative Factor")

MATTHEW: A young boy on the *Enterprise*. (See "The Last Outpost")

MATTHEWS: A crew member killed by the large android Ruk when he beams down to Exo III with Captain Kirk and Nurse Chapel. (See "What Are Little Girls Made Of?")

MATTHEWS, TODD: The author of the novel "The Hotel Royale" which aliens use to create an Earth-like setting for Colonel S. Richey, a NASA astronaut who died 283 years before the *Enterprise* encounters the place, which is still functioning. (See "The Royale")

MAURA: The pet dog of Lt. Aquiel Uhnari. It is killed and replaced by a coalescent. (See "Aquiel")

MAVEK: An attendant at the Tilonus Institute for Mental Disorders where Will Riker is imprisoned after being captured on the surface of Tilonus Four. ("Frame Of Mind")

MAVIG: One of Dr. Sevrin's young followers in the ill-fated search for Eden. (See "The Way To Eden")

MAYLOR, RAMID SEV: A woman who arrives aboard the *Enterprise* with Ves Alkar. Everyone thinks that she's his mother, but actually she's an assistant whose life force he is leaching. (See "Man Of The People")

MAXWELL, BEN: The Captain of the *U.S.S. Phoenix* who has a breakdown and declares war on the Cardassians when he determines that they are secretly rearming themselves in defiance of a disarmament accord. (See "The Wounded")

M'BENGA, DR.: Another *Enterprise* doctor, a specialist in Vulcan physiology and medical procedures. He helps Spock on one occasion and is also on hand during the visit to the Kalandan outpost planet. (See "That Which Survives")

McCOY, LT. COMMANDER LEONARD: Ranking medical officer on board the *Enterprise* under Kirk's command. Humane and caring, but acerbic and cynical in outside attitude, he often clashes with Captain Kirk on matters of principle, but is in fact one of Kirk's closest friends. Spock is another matter – McCoy is exasperated by the Vulcan's serene and implacable logic, which seems to him to be cold and heartless. McCoy generally acts from the heart anyway...but he does have a grudging respect for Spock, although he would probably never admit it. Modern technology, to him, is probably an unnecessary evil, especially in the case of the transporters, which he hates to use. [In the mirror universe, **McCoy-Two** is more of a torture expert than a doctor.] A sentimental sort, he took time out of his retirement to visit the *Enterprise-D* before its inaugural mission. (See "Encounter At Farpoint")

McGIVERS, LT. MARLA: The *Enterprise*'s historian, she falls for Khan Noonian Singh when he is awoken, seeing him as some sort of romantic hero from the past. When his plans of renewed conquest are thwarted, she chooses to join him in exile rather than face charges in a Starfleet court martial. (See "Space Seed")

McHURON, EVE: One of Mudd's women. (See "Mudd's Women")

McKINNEY: One of the officers who suspected that there was a conspiracy in Starfleet; killed "accidentally" by that conspiracy. (See "Conspiracy")

McLOWERY, FRANK: In the Melkotian reenactment of the gunfight at the OK Corral, the Clanton sidekick portrayed by Spock. (See "Spectre Of The Gun")

McLOWERY, TOM: The Clanton gang member portrayed by McCoy. (See "Spectre Of The Gun")

McNARY: A police lieutenant, and friend of Dixon Hill, in the holodeck program set in 1941 San Francisco; the first holodeck character to realize that he doesn't really exist. When told he's just a hologram, he asks what will happen to him and his family when they turn the program off? (See "The Big Goodbye")

McNARY, SHARON: Wife of McNary. (See "The Big Goodbye")

McPHERSON: A follower of Khan Noonian Singh. (See "Space Seed")

MEA 3: A woman of Eminiar VII, who "dies" in the war; Kirk keeps her from going to the euthanasia chambers. (See "A Taste Of Armageddon")

MEARS, YEOMAN: She is in the *Galileo* shuttle-craft when it crashes on Taurus II. (See "The Galileo Seven")

MEDIATORS: The two Edo of Rubicam Three who, as the local police, arrest Wesley and sentence him to die for what seems to be a minor infraction. (See "Justice")

MELAKON: The Nazi leader on the planet Ekos, who keeps John Gill prisoner in a permanently drugged state. (See "Patterns Of Force")

MENDAK: The Romulan commander who arranges the phony death of T'Pel, the Vulcan spy who had been working for the Romulans. (See "Data's Day")

MENDEZ, COMMANDER JOSE I. Presiding officer at Spock's court martial as the commandeered *Enterprise* makes its way to the forbidden world of Talos IV. Actually, he remains at his post on Starbase 11; the Mendez on board the *Enterprise* is an illusion created by the Talosians. The real Mendez is able to watch the proceedings, however, and clears Spock once the whole story is made clear. (See "The Menagerie")

MENDON, ENSIGN: As part of the Starfleet Officer Exchange Program, this Benzite is transferred to the *Enterprise*. Mendon is the first one to notice the menace of the extraterrestrial bacteria causing damage to both the Klingon ship the *Pagh* and to the *Enterprise*. (See "A Matter Of Honor")

MENDOZA, SETH: The representative of the United Federation of Planets who goes to the negotiations for the Barzan wormhole and is poisoned for his trouble. (See "The Price")

MENDROSSEN, KI: The chief of staff of Ambassador Sarek who attempts to cover up the fact that Sarek is suffering from a form of Vulcan Alzheimer's disease. (See "Sarek")

MERIK, CAPTAIN R.M.: A commercial spacefarer (commander of the *Beagle*), he crashed his ship on Planet 892-IV, where he and his crew discovered a culture like the Roman Empire — if it had survived into the 20th Century. His men were killed in the gladiatorial contests one by one, but he ascended in this world to become the supreme ruler, or First Citizen. Never a great achiever in the Federation, he has found power and prestige here. At first he hopes that his former Starfleet Academy classmate James Kirk will abandon the Federation and join him, but Kirk would never give up his crew to the cruel and deadly games. After a battle of wills, Merik — known as **Merikus** on this planet — signals the *Enterprise* to take Kirk and his landing party back up. Merik's second-in-command, Proconsul Claudius Marcus, kills him for this act of treason to the state. (See "Bread And Circuses")

MERLIN: Yet another of the historical or legendary characters the immortal Flint claims to have been in his six-thousand-year lifespan. Merlin, of course, was King Arthur's sorcerous ally and mentor. (See "Requiem For Methuselah")

MICKEY D: An android gangster character in the artificial Earth setting of "The Hotel Royale" which aliens created on an otherwise inhospitable world for

Colonel S. Richey, a NASA astronaut who died 283 years before the *Enterprise* encounters the place, which is still functioning. (See "The Royale")

MIDRO: A Troglyte who takes a distinct dislike to Captain Kirk. (See "The Cloud Minders")

MILLER, STEPHEN: The father of Wyatt Miller. His son has been betrothed to Deanna Troi since they were children. (See "Haven")

MILLER, VICTORIA: The mother of Wyatt Miller. Her son has been betrothed to Deanna Troi since they were children. (See "Haven")

MILLER, WYATT: Deanna Troi's betrothed. Wyatt has never met Deanna but has been doing drawings of a dream girl he believed was Deanna, until he actually meets Deanna. (See "Haven")

MINAN: This virotherapist discovers that, in spite of what was believed, humans can survive exposure to hyperonic radiation. (See "The Ensigns Of Command")

MINNERLY, LIEUTENANT.: A martial arts contestant Tasha Yar goes up against. Worf bets that Yar will win. (See "Skin Of Evil")

MINUET: A very beautiful and charming woman who distracts Riker on the holodeck while the Bynars undertake to steal the *Enterprise*; she is actually a hologram simulation created by the Bynars, and Riker tries in vain to find the program after the *Enterprise* is reclaimed. (See "11001001") Later used as a memory implant to fool Riker into thinking that he has forgotten sixteen years of his life; a poor choice, since he couldn't have married a hologram and fathered children with her. (See "Future Imperfect")

MIRAMANEE: The woman Kirk falls in love with and marries on the planet inhabited by American Indians. She dies when the tribe turns on Kirk and stones him and her; she was pregnant with Kirk's child at the time of her death. (See "The Paradise Syndrome")

MIRASTA: The Malkorian Science Minister, she is a forward-looking woman who is largely responsible for her world's great leaps towards warp technology. She chooses to leave her homeworld of Malkor aboard the *Enterprise* when the leader of that world decides that his people are not yet culturally prepared to know about the Federation. (See "First Contact")

MIRI: The centuries-old adolescent girl who helps Kirk find a cure for her people's debilitating disease. Her assistance is diverted by her jealousy of Yeoman Rand but eventually she comes around and helps get back the much-needed communicators taken by her peers. (See "Miri")

MIROK: A Romulan who becomes invisible to normal vision, and intangible, due to an experiment with an Interphase Generator. (See "The Next Phase")

MIRREN, OLIANA: One of the candidates trying out for Starfleet Academy whom Wesley meets on Relba. (See "Coming Of Age")

MIRT: A member of Oxmyx's Chicago-style gang. (See "A Piece Of The Action")

MITCHELL, LT. COMMANDER GARY: Next in command after Spock, Mitchell becomes more and more psionic after contact with the barrier at the edge of the galaxy. As he becomes less human and more destructive, his old friend and captain, James Kirk must combat and destroy him. It's no easy task, either. (See "Where No Man Has Gone Before")

MOGH: The father of Kurn and Worf. He was killed at the Khitomer Massacre and wrongly accused of being a traitor. (See "Sins Of The Fathers")

MONROE: A bridge officer who is killed at her computer console when it explodes. (See "Disaster")

MONTGOMERY: A security guard overpowered by Commodore Decker when the Commodore decides to escape in a shuttlecraft. (See "The Doomsday Machine")

MOORE, ADMIRAL JAMES: The Starfleet officer who contacts Captain Picard and relays the distress call they have received from the Ficus Sector, a region of space where no Earth colonies were previously believed to exist. (See "Up The Long Ladder")

MORAG: A Klingon ship commander who had been trying to intimidate station personnel at a communications relay station near the Klingon border. (See "Aquiel")

MORDOC: One of the Ferengi encountered on Delphi Ardu. (See "The Last Outpost")

MORDOCK: The Benzite student who beats Wesley in the Starfleet Academy admissions test. (See "Coming Of Age")

MOREAU, LT. MARLENA : A chemist on board the *Enterprise*, a post also held by her mirror universe counterpart. Both Marlenas are somewhat interested in the Kirk of our universe. (See "Mirror, Mirror")

MORIARTY, PROF.: The legendary fictional character created by Sir Arthur Conan Doyle in the short story "The Final Problem." During a Sherlock Holmes holodeck recreation, the character of Professor Moriarty is programmed to be as smart as Data, which results in the hologram becoming self-aware. (See "Elementary, Dear Data" and "Ship In A Bottle")

MORLA: Fiancé of Kara, who is killed by the possessed Hengist on Argelia. Jealous of Scotty, he is another suspect in her murder. He lives on Cantaba Street. (See "Wolf In The Fold")

MOSELEY, DR. HAL: A planetary meteorologist consulting on the atmospheric problems afflicting Penthara Four. (See "A Matter Of Time")

MOT: The barber on the *Enterprise*, a fussy character who loves to talk. When Jean-Luc is taken prisoner on the *Enterprise* by raiders, he claims to be Mot to hide his true identity. (See "Starship Mine")

M'RET: The Vice Proconsul of the Romulan Imperial Senate. He defects to the Federation due to his support of Romulan/Vulcan reunification. His two top aides accompany him and they are held in stasis in cargo containers until they can be safely transported to Federation space. (See "Face Of The Enemy")

MUDD, HARCOURT FENTON: A roguish con man and space trader, he's nothing but trouble. Harry Mudd is probably the last person Kirk would want to run into, not because of any danger but because the man is a consummate nuisance. Apparently he's not above a little arranged marriage-brokering, a job barely a step above pimping the way Mudd handles it. Later he narrowly avoids a Denebian death sentence and winds up on a planet peopled by androids looking for someone to serve. This tires Mudd rather quickly, so he tries to get Kirk and the *Enterprise* crew to take his place, only to get stranded there permanently — with five hundred androids reconfigured to look like his hateful wife Stella Mudd. (See "I, Mudd")

MUDD, STELLA: The wife from hell who drove Harcourt Fenton Mudd into space in the first place. (See "I, Mudd")

MULHALL, DR. ANNE: She allows the disembodied Thalassa, wife of Sargon, to borrow her body while android receptacles are built. Thalassa is torn between her husband's integrity and the temptations offered by Henoch, who wants to keep the borrowed humanoid bodies. But Henoch is thwarted and Mulhall, like Spock, is restored to normality. (See "Return To Tomorrow")

MULLIBOK: An unauthorized resident of Jeraddo who refused to evacuate when the government of Bajor ordered it. He is an old farmer who doesn't want to leave his home of 40 years. (See "Progress")

MYERS: A diagnostic engineer aboard the *Enterprise-D*. (See "Hollow Pursuits")

NAGEL, ENSIGN: The Starfleet tactical officer who serves with Riker and Work on the *U.S.S. Hathaway* during wargames. (See "Peak Performance")

NAGILUM: A mysterious alien scientist who lives inside a void in space and studies the reactions of the *Enterprise* when it is lured in there, even killing a crewman. (See "Where Silence Has Lease")

NAGUS: The leader of all major Ferengi business affairs. It is an appointment made for life and a new Nagus is not chosen until the old one dies. (See "The Nagus")

NAKAMURA, ADMIRAL: When Bruce Maddox hatches his plan to disassemble Data, it is authorized by Nakamura, the commander of Starbase 173. (See "Measure Of A Man")

NATIRA: A Yonadan woman who occupies the position of High Priestess. Leonard McCoy marries her when he is dying of an incurable disease. She is unaware that her home world is actually a colony ship en route to a distant planet until proof is rendered incontrovertible. When McCoy's friends help break the power of the Oracle, they also find a cure for McCoy, and he returns to the *Enterprise*. She remains with her people, but hopes that McCoy will rejoin her some day. (See "For The World Is Hollow And I Have Touched The Sky")

NAYROK, PRIME MINISTER: The leader of the planet Angosia who opposes the repatriation of the veterans of the Tarsian War because he considers them a threat to peaceful society. (See "The Hunted")

NECHAYEV, VICE-ADMIRAL: Commander of the starship *Cairo,* he meets with Picard to send him on a secret mission to investigate a secret Cardassian outpost. (See "Chain Of Command") Later he oversees the assembling of a fleet to deal with a new Borg threat. (See "Descent")

NEELA: The Bajoran assistant who works with Chief O'Brien. (See "In The Hands Of the Prophets")

NEIL: An engineer who assists Kelsey in her plot to steal trilithium resin from the *Enterprise.* When Kelsey finds his complaints bothersome, she kills him. (See "Starship Mine")

NERAL: A Romulan Proconsul who has expressed a willingness to meet with Spock and discuss a peace initiative between Vulcan and Romulus. It is all a plot hatched by the Romulans to cover their plan to invade Vulcan. (See "Unification")

NERYS, MAJOR KIRA: First Officer of Deep Space Nine. She is a former Bajoran terrorist who fought against the Cardassian occupation.

NESVIG, COLONEL: Commanding officer of McKinley Air Force base, who has a baffling interrogation session with Spock and Kirk. (See "Tomorrow Is Yesterday")

NIBOR: A Ferengi Riker plays chess with, he uses this as a way to escape from the Krayton. (See "Menage A Troi")

NILREM: A Malkorian who becomes aware that Riker is an "alien" trying to pass as a Malkorian. (See "First Contact")

NOEL, DR. HELEN: Kirk falls in love with this attractive woman psychiatrist on Tantalus V. Not natural, this state is induced by the neural machine of Dr. Adams. (See "Dagger Of The Mind")

NOG: The young Ferengi nephew of Quark, the sharp Ferengi businessman on Deep Space Nine.

NOGURA, ADMIRAL: The head of Starfleet Operations on Earth. Kirk convinces the admiral to give him back the command of the refitted *Enterprise.* (See "Star Trek: The Motion Picture")

NONA: On the planet of Neural, she is the wife of Tyree. She comes from the Kanutu tribe, known for their healing powers. She heals Kirk of his Mugatu bite. She is killed by suspicious villagers, and probably with good reason. (See "A Private Little War")

NOOR: The J'Naii leader who stands in judgment of Soren and condemns her to the psychotreatments which will ensure that she becomes gender neutral like everyone else. (See "The Outcast")

NORESS, DR. SUSAN: The scientist who developed a plasma plague. (See "The Child")

NORMAN: The chief android of Planet Mudd, and the only unique individual among the androids. He is sophisticated enough an android that he is able to pass as human, and he gains access to the *Enterprise.* Norman falls prey to the ancient Empedoclean paradox: "Everything I say is lie." (See "I, Mudd")

NU'DAQ: A Klingon who joins forces with the Enterprise to unlock the mystery of Prof. Galen's quest. He is commander of the Klingon bird of prey the *Maht-H'a.* (See "The Chase")

NUMBER ONE: The First Officer of the *Enterprise* when it was under the command of Captain Christopher Pike. A very logical, emotionless woman, strangely reminiscent of a Vulcan despite the fact that she is human. (See "The Cage")

NURIA: She is the leader of the Mintakan community whom Picard beams up to the *Enterprise* to convince her that he's as mortal as she is in order to prevent the Mintakan culture from stagnating due to wallowing in superstitions. (See "Who Watches The Watchers?")

N'VEK: A Romulan subcommander and part of an underground movement in support of the reunification of the Romulan and Vulcan people. He helps to kidnap Deanna Troi and put her in place aboard the Romulan warbird Kahzara to assist on a dangerous mission. He dies in support of the mission, but his death is not in vain. (See "Face Of The Enemy")

O'BRIAN, LIEUTENANT: An *Enterprise* officer captured by Harcourt Fenton Mudd. (See "I, Mudd")

O'BRIEN, KEIKO: The wife of Miles O'Brien. They were wed in "Data's Day."

O'BRIEN, MILES: Former Transporter Chief aboard the *Enterprise-D* and now Chief of Operations on Deep Space Nine. He is also a cellist.

OCETT, GUL: A treacherous Cardassian commander who is searching for the secret of Prof. Galen's quest. (See "The Chase")

O'CONNEL, STEVE: One of the children bewitched by Gorgan, the so-called "Friendly Angel." (See "And The Children Shall Lead")

ODAN: An emissary who is on his way to negotiate a dispute between two moon colonies when he has an accident which damages his host body. Odan is a Trill, which means that he is a symbiote which can live on and on in a variety of host bodies. Odan's father brought peace to two moons a generation before, and the Governor of the parent world has called Odan in to avert another bitter conflict there. (See "The Host")

O'DELL, BRENNA: The beautiful daughter of Danilo O'Dell and part of a primitive, rural farming community which is rescued and relocated by the *Enterprise*. (See "Up The Long Ladder")

O'DELL, DANILO: In the Bringloidi colony in the Ficus Sector, he is the representative of the leader of a primitive, rural farming community. (See "Up The Long Ladder")

ODO: A shapeshifter from somewhere beyond the wormhole. He works as the Security Officer on Deep Space Nine, just as he did for the Cardassians.

ODONA: Daughter of Hodin of Gideon, she plays "victim" to win Kirk's sympathy in the abandoned *Enterprise*, actually a perfect replica of the *Enterprise* built by the people of Gideon. The real point of all this is for her to contract the latent Vegan choriomeningitis in Kirk's system. She almost dies of it but is cured by McCoy when Spock locates Kirk — but she will still carry the disease to her race as

planned, carrying mortality to Gideon at last. (See "Mark Of Gideon")

O'FERREN, MARTY: A character in a Dixon Hill program on the holodeck. (See "Manhunt")

OFFENHOUSE, RALPH: One of the three 20th Century humans revived from cryogenic freezing on an ancient satellite; he was a very rich man in his first lifetime and seems to expect special treatment from Picard. His wealth cannot be reclaimed in the 24th Century. (See "The Neutral Zone")

OFF-ZEL, MARK: The artisan from Sirrie Four who made a vase which wound up in Fajo's collection. (See "The Most Toys")

OGAWA, NURSE: Dr. Beverly Crusher's chief assistant on the *Enterprise*. (See "Suspicions")

O'HERLIHY, LIEUTENANT: Killed by the Gorns on Cestus III. (See "Arena")

OJI: The daughter of Liko, this child sees her father fall from the secret Federation observation post and supports his story about "The Picard." (See "Who Watches The Watchers?")

OKONA, CAPTAIN THADDIUN: Captain of the freighter the *S.S. Erstwhile*. An intergalactic trader who is on the run after he gets a rich man's daughter pregnant. He is also wanted for the theft of the Jewel of Thesia, a national treasure on the planet Straleb. (See "The Outrageous Okona")

OMAG: A fat Ferengi who was involved with the dead smuggler of the Vulcan shuttle *T'Pau*. (See "Unification")

O'NEIL, ENSIGN: One of the fatalities sustained on Taurus II after the crash of the shuttlecraft *Galileo*. (See "The Galileo Seven")

O'NEIL, LIEUTENANT: A young *Enterprise* officer who sometimes serves as a transporter operator. He is absorbed by Landru on the mission to Beta III, but recovers as soon as the ancient computer ceases to function. (See "Return Of The Archons")

OPAKA: The Bajoran spiritual leader referred to as the Kai. (See "Battle Lines")

ORACLE OF THE PEOPLE: This is the computer that controlled the inhabited asteroid (actually a colony ship) named *Yonada,* built by the Fabrini. A rather autocratic machine, it is a harsh ruler and tolerates no dissension from its people. It kills anyone who crosses its will or tampers with any part of the computer. Actually, it can be accessed through one particular door without any mishap, if one knows how to open it, but ignorant interference is punished. These reactions were designed merely to protect the computer from outside damage or accidental injury, but in the thousands of years since the Yonadans forgot their true origin, they have worshipped this computer as their own wrathful deity, a job the Oracle seems to take quite seriously. (See "For The World Is Hollow And I Have Touched The Sky")

ORIEGA, STAN: The comedian from the 24th Century whose routine includes jokes about quantum mathematics. (See "The Outrageous Okona")

ORTA: A Bajoran terrorist leader at war with the Cardassians, who at the time occupied the world of Bajor. (See "Ensign Ro")

ORTIZ, ENSIGN: An ensign on the *Enterprise-D* who is assigned to play the violin in place of Data at the second ship's concert. (See "The Ensigns Of Command")

ORTON: The administrator of the Arkaria Base. (See "Starship Mine")

OSBORNE, LIEUTENANT: An *Enterprise* officer who takes part in the Horta hunt on Janus VI and who also beams down to Eminiar VII as part of Captain Kirk's guard party. (See "Devil In The Dark" and "A Taste Of Armageddon")

OXMYX, BELA: Head of the largest Iotian gang territory. He wants Kirk to help him out with the firepower to take over the whole planet; Kirk adapts this goal to his own ends, since Iotia doesn't have much of a future unless its warring factions can be unified. (See "A Piece Of The Action")

OZABA, DR.: One of the Federation scientists (on hand to study the nova of the star of the Minaran system) who is tortured and killed by the Vians in their efforts to test the empath whom Dr. McCoy refers to as "Gem." (See "The Empath")

PAINTER: One of the relief navigators who serve on board the *Enterprise.* (See "This Side Of Paradise")

PALAMAS, LT. CAROLYN: The new historical officer on board the *Enterprise,* she is the object of Montgomery Scott's affections but turns her own attention to the god Apollo when the *Enterprise* crew encounters him on Pollux IV. She eventually dumps the deity, provoking his disappearance from view, and perhaps from existence as well. (See "Who Mourns For Adonais?")

PALMER, DR.: The third member of the observation team in the Mintakan station. (See "Who Watches The Watchers?")

PALMER, LIEUTENANT: A communications officer on board the *Enterprise,* seen as relief on occasion. (See "Dagger Of The Mind")

PARDEK: A Romulan senator who is acquainted with Spock. Pardek is supposedly a supporter of the concept of unification between the cultures of Vulcans and Romulans. (See "Unification")

PARMEN: Ruler of the Platonians who won and holds his kingship due to his superior psychokinetic abilities. The *Enterprise* is called to Platonia when the king becomes injured. The Platonians hold Dr. McCoy in high regard after he helps heal Parmen — in such high regard that they will not let him go. Kirk, Spock and the rest of the landing party learn the extent of Platonian cruelty when they go against the will of their hosts. The tide turns after McCoy discovers that the Platonians' mental powers are caused by the effect of kironide, a chemical in their food, on the pituitary gland. With this useful information, Kirk soon becomes the top brainslinger on the planet, and he and his crew are allowed to go, along with the dwarf Alexander. (See "Plato's Stepchildren")

PARKER: A ship's officer aboard the *Enterprise-C.* (See "Yesterday's Enterprise")

PATAKH: An injured Romulan brought aboard the *Enterprise* following his crash in the Galorndon Core. He needs a transfusion of ribosomes and only Worf is the compatible donor. But Worf is against the transfusion as much as Patakh is and eventually the

Romulan dies. (See "The Enemy")

PAVLIK, ENSIGN: An ensign aboard the *Enterprise-D*. (See "Galaxy's Child")

PEDDLER: A holographic salesman who pitches the perfect weapons system to Picard in a cavern on Echo Papa 607. He, or it, is all that remains of that planet's arms-dealing civilization. (See "Arsenal Of Freedom")

PEERS, SELIN: A representative of the Trill who testifies as an expert witness at the trial of Jadzia Dax. (See "Dax")

PENTHOR-MUL: A Gatherer leader of the Lornack clan who was slain 53 years earlier by Yuta using a microvirius. (See "The Vengeance Factor")

PERETOR SAIN: Jameson's secret weapons deal, 45 years before his return to Mordan IV, enabled Karnas to defeat Sain, the political rival who killed Karnas' father. (See "Too Short A Season")

PERRIN: The second human wife of Ambassador Sarek. She knows that he has Bendii Syndrome but attempts to hid it from him until Picard insists she tell him. (See "Sarek")

PETRI, LORD: A member of the diplomatic corps of the planet Troyius, this ambassador is unfortunate enough to land the assignment to escort Elaan of Elas to her arranged marriage with his monarch. His efforts to instruct her in civilized behavior are futile, and come to an abrupt end when she stabs him. After that incident he withdraws from his duties, leaving Captain Kirk to play out "The Taming of the Shrew" with Elaan. He has slightly better luck. (See "Elaan Of Troyius")

PHILANA: A female Platonian, over two thousand years old. She is married to Parmen. When Parmen is injured she requests medical help from the *Enterprise*. The Platonians then decide to keep Dr. McCoy. (See "Plato's Stepchildren")

PHILLIPS: An astrobiologist who is serving on board the *Enterprise* when the M-5 computer is being tested. (See "The Ultimate Computer")

PICARD, CAPTAIN JEAN-LUC: A French guy with an inexplicable British accent. Commander of the *Enterprise*, a highly literate man with strong leadership abilities, superb diplomatic skills and a grudging

tolerance of children. His first command was the *Stargazer*.

PICARD, MAMAN: Picard's mother; an illusion of her appears to him when the Traveler carries the *Enterprise* beyond known space. (See "Where No One Has Gone Before")

PICARD, MARIE: The sister-in-law of Jean-Luc. She is married to Robert Picard. (See "Family")

PICARD, RENE: The young nephew of Jean-Luc Picard and the son of his brother, Robert. Rene hopes to follow in his uncle's footsteps. (See "Family")

PICARD, ROBERT: The older brother of Jean-Luc. The two brothers had been estranged for many years as Robert believed in carrying on family traditions while Jean-Luc preferred to seek his future in Starfleet. (See "Family")

PIKE, CAPTAIN CHRISTOPHER: The second man to command the starship *Enterprise*. Spock was one of his officers for over eleven years. His most famous mission was undoubtedly the one to Talos IV, where he encountered the Talosians and their intergalactic zoo. They tried to make him one of their prisoners and attempted to get him to mate with various women, but his will was too strong and he was able to break free from their illusions. He would have taken the human woman he met there away, but learned that she was hideously scarred from the crash that landed her on Talos IV in the first place. Years later, Pike was crippled and scarred in an accident on a training vessel. Spock, now First Officer of the *Enterprise* under Captain James T. Kirk, violated the standing quarantine of Talos IV to take Pike there, where he would be able to spend the rest of his life enjoying the pain-free illusions generated by the Talosians. (See "The Menagerie") [In the mirror universe, Kirk-Two apparently became the Captain of the *Enterprise-Two* by assassinating Pike-Two.] (See "The Cage" and "The Menagerie")

PINOCCHIO: The main character in an ancient piece of Earth literature, an innocent puppet who wants to become human; an obvious analogy with the android Data. (See "The Measure Of A Man")

PIPER, DR.: The ship's doctor on board the *Enterprise* for a brief period before Dr. Leonard McCoy signed on in that position. (See "Where No Man Has Gone Before")

PIPER, MISS: Assistant to Starbase 11 Commander Mendez. (See "The Menagerie")

PISCOPO, JOE: An obscure 20th Century comedian that Data recreates on the holodeck in an attempt to learn how to laugh. A poor choice, and it is little wonder Data learns nothing. (See "The Outrageous Okona")

PLASUS: Plasus is the ranking governmental official on the planet Ardana, in the city of Stratos: High Adviser of the Planet Council. Although he thinks he's doing the right thing for his planet, he is really an oppressor of the Troglytes who mine Zienite on the planet's surface. (See "The Cloud Minders")

POLA: A young boy on board the *Enterprise*. (See "The Last Outpost")

PORTAL: The ancient guardian of a dead world which was once a part of the T'Kon Empire, located on Delphi Ardu, awakened after many millennia by the arrival of the *Enterprise* and a Ferengi ship. (See "The Last Outpost")

PRESTON, PETER: A Starfleet cadet fresh out of the academy. He is the nephew of Montgomery Scott. Peter is killed during the battle between the *Enterprise* and the *Reliant*. (See "Star Trek II: The Wrath Of Khan")

PRIETO, BEN: Pilot of the shuttlecraft that crashed on Vagra Two with Deanna Troi as passenger; he is seriously injured but survives. (See "Skin Of Evil")

PRIMMIN, LT. GEORGE: A Starfleet security officer who comes aboard Deep Space Nine to oversee security arrangements for a vital shipment of deuridium. (See "The Passenger")

PRIXIS: A member of Wesley Crusher's Selcundi Drema team and a metallurgy and mineralogy specialist. (See "Pen Pals")

PROSECUTOR: A Sarpeidon cast back to his planet's "Restoration" period who has achieved a rather tenuous security by becoming part of his new time's brutal legal system. He lives in complete fear of his superiors, and will only help Kirk when Kirk threatens to make the Prosecutor's true nature and origin known to his contemporaries. (See "All Our Yesterdays")

PROTOCOL MINISTER: He accompanies Compio of Constelaine on board the *Enterprise* when Minister

Compio arrives to prepare for his wedding to Lwaxana Troi. (See "Cost Of Living")

PULASKI, DR. CATHERINE: The temporary replacement for Dr. Crusher when she leaves the *Enterprise* to be the head of Starfleet Medical.

"Q": An omnipotent being who looks down on humans and yet seems strangely drawn to their company. He is Jean-Luc Picard's most relentless nemesis but has also made himself known to Benjamin Sisko, who punched Q out, much to the entity's great surprise. He thinks Jean-Luc is more fun than Sisko. A mischievous and seemingly omnipotent member of an advanced race, he seems to delight in getting under Picard's skin, challenging humanity's beliefs and values at every turn. He interferes with Picard's first mission on the *Enterprise*. (See "Encounter At Farpoint", "Hide And Q," etc.)

QUAICE, DR. DALEN: Dr. Beverly Crusher's former teacher. (See "Remember Me")

QUARK: The Ferengi businessman who runs the bar, gambling room, holosuites and other profitable ventures on Deep Space Nine.

QUINN, ADMIRAL GREGORY: He investigates Captain Picard for possible violations of the Prime Directive. This Starfleet admiral suspects the existence of the conspiracy in Starfleet's upper ranks but is himself infested by the aliens after he tells Picard about the conspiracy. He almost kills Riker but is subdued. (See "Conspiracy")

QUINTEROS: Commander of Starbase 74, the shipyards which orbit Tarsus III. He was involved in the design of the latest *Enterprise* (the Galaxy class). (See "11001001")

QUOL: A Ferengi who gets aboard the *Enterprise* under false pretences so he can attempt to steal a rare, female metamorph. (See "The Perfect Mate")

RABO: A Mentakan hunter who finds Palmer. (See "Who Watches The Watchers?")

RADUE: The political leader of the Aldean people. Picard has a hard time convincing him that radiation has made the Aldeans sterile. (See "When The Bough Breaks")

RAEL: A male Scalosian, one of their top scientists. Because male Scalosians are unable to procreate, Rael must look on from the sidelines as the woman he loves, Deela, tries to seduce Kirk for purposes of reproduction. (See "The Wink Of An Eye")

RAKAL, MAJOR: The false Romulan identity given to Deanna Troi after she was abducted and surgically altered to look like a Romulan. She is supposed to be a member of the Tal Shiar, a type of secret police. (See "Face Of The Enemy")

RAL, DEVINONI: A negotiator who hires out his talents to other races. In the case of the negotiations for the Barzan wormhole he represents the Chrysalians. He is part Betazoid and secretly possesses empathic powers which he uses to aid his negotiating partners. He was born in Brussels in the European Alliance and relocated to Hurkos Three when he was 19. His mother was one-quarter Betazoid. He has four siblings but of them he is the only empath. (See "The Price")

RAMOS: A member of the security detail on duty when the renegade Klingons Koris and Konmil escape; he is killed in the scuffle. (See "Heart Of Glory")

RAMSEY, CAPTAIN: One of the survivors of the U.S.S. Odin who made it to Angel One in an escape pod. He refuses to submit to the female dominated society, but neither does he want to leave that world because he has a woman he's fallen in love with there. (See "Angel One")

RAMSEY, DR.: Chief archeologist of the Deneus Three expedition who gave Donald Varley an Iconian relic. (See "Contagion")

RAND, YEOMAN JANICE: Suffering from an unrequited interest in Captain James Kirk, Yeoman Rand served with the Enterprise for a time but did not stick out the entire five-year mission, perhaps frustrated by her inability to get through to Kirk. She eventually returned to the Enterprise as Transporter Chief and later served as Communications Officer on the U.S.S. Excelsius. (See "Charlie X", "Miri", "Balance Of Terror", "The Enemy Within", "Star Trek: The Motion Picture" and "Star Trek VI: The Undiscovered Country")

RASHELLA: One of the Aldeans who "adopts" an abducted Enterprise child; she doesn't want to give up the human girl Alexandra. (See "When The Bough Breaks")

RASMUSSEN, BERLINGHOFF: He explains that he's a 26th Century historian whose focus of study is the 22nd through the 24th Century. He's actually a fraud who stole the time travel pod from a 26th Century scientist who was visiting the 22nd Century. He killed the scientist and plans to steal 24th Century technology which he can take back to his own time and pretend to invent so that he can make millions off the patents. (See "A Matter of Time")

RATA: Science officer under the command of the Ferengi, Daimon Bok. (See "The Battle")

RAYMOND, CLARE: A 20th Century woman, 35 years of age, put in cryogenic suspension and placed in the ancient Earth satellite discovered by the Enterprise. (See "The Neutral Zone")

RAYMOND, DONALD: Late husband of Clare Raymond. (See "The Neutral Zone")

RAYMOND, EDDIE and TOMMY: Clare Raymond's young sons (8 and 5, respectively), left behind at the time of her death, now long dead. (See "The Neutral Zone")

RAYMOND, THOMAS: A descendant of Clare Raymond, alive in the 24th Century. (See "The Neutral Zone")

REDBLOCK, CYRUS: Fictional villain in the holodeck simulations of Dixon Hill's adventures. Became dangerous due to a holodeck malfunction, but undone when lured outside the holodeck, where he vanishes from sight. (See "The Big Goodbye")

REENA 16: An android created by the immortal Flint. When Kirk and Reena Kapec (serial number unknown) discover the body of this presumably earlier android in Flint's laboratory, they finally begin to suspect that Reena Kapec, Kirk's latest romantic interest, is not really a human being after all — a truth destined to have a dramatic impact on both of them. (See "Requiem For Methuselah")

REGER: A member of the anti-Landru underground movement on the planet Beta III. He runs a boarding house, and has a daughter named Tula. (See "Return Of The Archons")

REGINOD: One of the crew of the Pakled ship the *Mondor*. (See "The Samaritan Snare")

REMMICK, COMMANDER DEXTER: The investigator of Captain Picard's possible violations of the Prime Directive. He is later found to not only be part of a deadly conspiracy against the Federation but is infested with an alien entity controlling it from within Starfleet itself. (See "Coming of Age" and "Conspiracy")

REN, SURMAK: A Bajoran doctor and the head of the Ilvian medical facility. (See "Babel")

RENORA, ELS: A Bajoran arbiter called in when Jadzia Dax is accused of treason and murder. (See "Dax")

REX: In the Dixon Hill 1941 San Francisco holodeck program he is the owner of Rex's Bar. (See "Man Hunt")

REYGA, DR.: A Ferengi scientist who develops a successful metaphasic field but who is killed by a rival who wants to steal the secret of the process and claim it as his own. (See "Suspicions")

RHADA, LIEUTENANT: A relief helmsman on board the *Enterprise*; she covers for Sulu when he beams down to the Kalandan outpost planet, and is the first to realize that the *Enterprise* has been cast light years in a mere moment.

RICE, PAUL: An old friend of Will Riker, and the captain of the *U.S.S. Drake*. He appears to Riker on Minos, but this is only an illusion created by the Echo Papa 607; the real Rice was killed by that highly adaptable weapons system. (See "Arsenal Of Freedom")

RICHEY, COLONEL S.: A NASA astronaut whose 283-year-old corpse is found in a strange recreation of an Earth hotel called The Royale. His personal effects include a second-rate novel entitled *Hotel Royale*, which aliens apparently used to try to recreate an Earth ambiance for the astronaut. The age of the astronaut's corpse is partially determined by the American flag on his uniform which contains only 52 stars. (See "The Royale")

RIKER, COMMANDER WILLIAM THOMAS: Captain Picard's second in command, the First Officer of the *Enterprise*. Musician, ladies' man and old flame of Deanna Troi, Riker is a capable officer destined to have his own command some day. Before serving on the *Enterprise*, he was First Officer to Captain Desoto of the *U.S.S. Hood*. As First Officer, he is the one who heads important Away Teams, and is obligated to deter the Captain from undertaking any hazardous missions. He formerly had a relationship with Deanna Troi when he was a junior officer but his career became more important to him than maintaining that relationship. His quarters are on deck eight. He has rejected three offers to command other ships as he prefers to remain aboard the *Enterprise* and inherit it when Picard either retires or accepts a transfer.

RIKER, KYLE: A Starfleet officer and father of Will Riker. Will and his father were estranged for many years and only reconciled after Will Riker was posted to the *Enterprise*. (See "The Icarus Factor")

RIKER, THOMAS: The identical twin of William Riker. A transporter accident eight years before created a double when an Away Team from the *Potemkin* had rescued the inhabitants of a science station on the planet Nervala-Four. The leader of that team, Lieutenant William Riker, had been the last to beam up, and had almost failed to make it back. The transporter pattern was boosted and the beam split, one going to the *Potemkin* and the other back down to Nervala Four. Each has all of Riker's memories except that one continued on in Starfleet for eight years while the other was marooned in the science station. The second Riker is still in love with Deanna and hopes to marry her one day. The two Rikers make peace with each other and the second Riker, who has a lower rank, chooses to use his middle name, Thomas, and transfer to another ship where he can continue his career in Starfleet. Unlike Will, he has no interest in reconciling with his father. (See "Second Chances")

RILEY, LIEUTENANT KEVIN: When he was four, Kevin Riley's parents were killed by Kodos the Executioner on the planet of Tarsus IV. Later, while serving as a navigator on board the *Enterprise*, Riley attacks Anton Karidian when his true identity is discovered. On another mission, Riley betrays his penchant for sentimental Irish folk songs when the Psi 2000 virus gets hold of him. (See "Conscience Of The King" and "The Naked Time")

RIVA: A famed negotiator who has no gene for hearing, so he uses three companions — the Chorus — to express his thoughts for him. When his Chorus is slain, Riva must learn to negotiate on completely different terms. (See "Loud As A Whisper")

RIVAN: A native of Rubicam Three, one of the Edo, she went on board the *Enterprise* and claimed to see "god." (See "Justice")

RIXX, CAPTAIN: Commanding officer of the *U.S.S. Thomas Paine*. He has a secret meeting with Picard to discuss the threat to the Federation. (See "Conspiracy")

RIZZO, ENSIGN: A crewman killed by the blood-draining cloud on Tycho IV. (See "Obsession")

ROBERTS: An aide to Vanderberg, the ranking engineer on the planet Janus VI. (See "Devil In The Dark")

ROBINSON, LT. J.G.: An *Enterprise* transporter officer whom Okona comes on to after he's beamed aboard. (See "The Outrageous Okona")

ROCHA, LT.: The arrogant comrade of Lt. Aquiel on a communications relay station near the Klingon border. Rocha is killed by a mysterious alien metamorph. (See "Aquiel")

RODENT: A wino on Earth in the 1930s, who steals McCoy's phaser while the doctor is unconscious but only manages to vaporize himself in the process. (See "City On The Edge Of Forever")

RODRIGUEZ: One of Khan Noonian Singh's genetically "superior" followers. (See "Space Seed")

RODRIGUEZ, LT. ESTABAN: An *Enterprise* crew member whose imagination creates a number of threatening manifestations on the shore-leave planet, including a ferocious tiger and an attacking World War Two fighter plane. (See "Shore Leave")

ROGERS, AMANDA: An 18-year-old graduate of Starfleet Academy who joins the crew of the *Enterprise,* only to have to reveal that she has the powers of the Q as she is the human daughter of Q parents. (See "True Q")

ROJAN: The leader of the Kelvans who take over the *Enterprise* in their quest for a new home world to replace their original one. Taking on humanoid bodies proves to be the undoing of Rojan and his fellows, however, as they eventually — with a little help from Kirk and Spock — lose track of their original mission when their new physical existence becomes too distracting. (See "By Any Other Name")

ROJAY: A woman who is the companion of Devinoni Ral. (See "The Price")

ROK-KEL: A Miradorn alien. His brother is Ah-Kel. When Rok-Kel is killed his brother vows vengeance. (See "Vortex")

ROLLMAN, ADMIRAL: The Starfleet officer whom Kira Nerys turns to when Sisko is reluctant to grant asylum to Tana Los. (See "Past Prologue")

ROM: A Ferengi who assists Quark on Deep Space Nine. He is Quark's brother (much to Quark's dismay). Rom's son is Nog. (See "Babel")

ROMAINE, JACQUES: A retired Starfleet engineer and the father of Mira Romaine. (See "The Lights Of Zetar")

ROMAINE, LYDIA: The mother of Mira Romaine. (See "The Lights Of Zetar")

ROMAINE, LT. MIRA: Her first mission into space is quite eventful, for two reasons; she becomes involved with Montgomery Scott, and is possessed by the Lights of Zetar. She almost does in the hapless Scotty under their baleful influence, but is freed when she is placed in an antigravity test area. Increased atmospheric pressure drives the Lights from her body and kills them. She then continues her mission to repair the information banks on Memory Alpha, which was devastated by the attack of the Lights. (See "The Lights Of Zetar")

ROMAS: One of the Ornarans. (See "Symbiosis")

RONDON: A candidate trying out for Starfleet whom Wesley Crusher meets on Relba. An arrogant Zaldan who is rude to Wesley. (See "Coming Of Age")

ROSE: One of the children abducted from the *Enterprise* by the Aldeans. (See "When The Bough Breaks")

ROSS, YEOMAN TERESA: The apparent cause of the duel between Jim Kirk and Trelane. (See "Squire Of Gothos")

ROSSA, ADMIRAL: The grandmother of Jeremiah Rossa, a boy taken by the Tellerians and raised as one of them. She hopes to have the boy returned to her, but Jean-Luc Picard determines that the boy has, for better or worse, become a Tellerian and those are the only people he can relate to now. (See "Suddenly Human")

ROSSA, JEREMIAH: A boy whose parents were killed in the Tellerian war and who was taken and raised by the Tellerians until all he knows is that way of life and now calls himself Jono. (See "Suddenly Human")

ROWE, LIEUTENANT: A member of the *Enterprise* security team who has a run-in with Norman the android in the auxiliary control room. (See "I, Mudd")

ROYKIRK, JACKSON: In the 21st Century, scientist Roykirk created Nomad, the sentient space probe. Roykirk's ego drove him to make the thinking machine venerate him as its creator, which gives Kirk a much-needed edge a few centuries later. (See "The Changeling")

ROZHENKO, HELENA: Worf's human foster mother. (See "Family")

ROZHENKO, SERGI: Worf's human foster father. (See "Family")

RUK: One of the androids of Exo III — not one built by Dr. Roger Korby, but an original, left behind by the extinct "Old Ones." Ruk was undoubtedly one of the androids who turned against their masters countless ages past. James Kirk, a man with a remarkable ability to outwit thinking machines, turns Ruk against Korby. Korby destroys Ruk with a phaser blast when the android attacks him. (See "What Are Little Girls Made Of?")

RUSS: An *Enterprise* crewman in the party which boards the hulk of the *Constellation* after it has encountered the doomsday machine berserker. (See "The Doomsday Machine")

RUSSELL: An engineer on the *Enterprise-D*. (See "Tin Man")

RUSSELL, DR. TOBY: A neuro-geneticist who wants to try an experimental technique of cloning a new spine and transplanting it into Worf even though it is an untested procedure. (See "Ethics")

RUTH: Kirk's girlfriend when he was attending Starfleet Academy. He's a bit surprised when she turns up while he's taking shore leave on a newly discovered planet — but pleasantly surprised. (See "Shore Leave")

RYAN, LIEUTENANT: A relief helmsman who has to be relieved himself when the Psi 2000 virus reduces him to helpless, hysterical laughter. (See "The Naked Time")

SAAVIK, LIEUTENANT: The half-Vulcan, half-Romulan officer on the *Enterprise*. Spock had rescued her as a child from an abandoned Romulan colony world, overseen her education and nominated her for Starfleet Academy. She was sent to study the Genesis Planet with David Marcus, and was an unfortunate witness to his death. (See "Star Trek II: The Wrath Of Khan" and "Star Trek III: The Search For Spock")

SAKKATH: The personal assistant to Ambassador Sarek who has been using his mental abilities to secretly aid Sarek and hide from the ambassador the fact that he has the debilitating disease known as Bendii Syndrome. He finally reveals the truth to Picard. (See "Sarek")

SALIA: An alasomorph and future leader of Daled Four. She travels on the *Enterprise* in the form of an adolescent female along with her guardian, Anya. (See "The Dauphin")

SALISH: The medicine man of the tribe in which Kirk — known here as "Kirok" — spends his time suffering from amnesia and marries Miramanee. The medicine men have long transmitted the secret of the obelisk through the generations, but Salish's father neglected to do so before his death. When "Kurok" saves a boy with mouth-to-mouth resuscitation, the villagers regard this as a miracle and force Salish to turn over his office to "Kurok." Embittered by this, Salish is quick to lead the stoning of "Kurok" and his wife when "Kurok" is unable to operate the obelisk in a crisis. (See "The Paradise Syndrome")

SAM: A crewman cast into some other dimensional reality when he annoys Charlie Evans. The Thasians bring him back when they come to claim Charlie. (See "Charlie X")

SAMURAI: A product of Sulu's imagination on the shore-leave planet; this ancient Japanese warrior threatens quite a few of the vacationing *Enterprise* crew members. (See "Shore Leave")

SANCHEZ, DR.: A medical doctor who serves

directly under Leonard McCoy's command on the *Enterprise*. Sanchez performs the autopsy on the crewman killed by Losira on the Kalandan outpost planet (see **WYATT, ENSIGN**). (See "That Which Survives")

SANDOVAL, ELIAS: Head of the colonists on Omicron Ceti III, Sandoval survives the influence of the spores on that planet and leads the resettlement of the colony elsewhere. (See "This Side Of Paradise")

SAREK, AMBASSADOR: A noted Vulcan diplomat and the father of the half-human Starfleet officer (now ambassador at large), Spock. Just over a hundred years old when first encountered on the *Enterprise*, he is in the prime of Vulcan life despite his heart problems. He is also a leading astrophysicist. He gave the young Spock his first instruction in the sciences, and was bitterly disappointed when Spock went to Starfleet Academy instead of following in his father's footsteps at the Vulcan Academy of Sciences. After eighteen years of not speaking to each other, the two Vulcans made their first efforts at reconciliation after the events surrounding the murder of the Tellarian Ambassador to the Babel Conference. (See "Journey To Babel") His long career had many triumphs including the negotiation of the Klingon Alliance, the Treaty of Alpha Cygnus Nine, and the Coridan admission to the Federation. His last success was the Legaran Treaty. He has had two human wives, Amanda and Perrin. He dies in "Unification."

SAR, GALEK: The captain of the Promellian battle-cruiser *Cleponji*. Galek Sar died at his post a thousand years before the *Enterprise* found the vessel. Sar left a log of his final hours in his computer. (See "Booby Trap")

SARGON: One of the three survivors of the world once known as Arret. Their advanced race managed to destroy their world half a million years ago, through means not revealed to the *Enterprise* team that discovered them. Stored in receptacles for all those years, Sargon, his wife Thalassa and his sometime rival Henoch are revived, but only their mind-forces remain — these once-humanoid people had no means to preserve their bodies, just their mental energies. Three humans lend their bodies to the survivors of Arret in order that they might build androids to house their essences. Sargon borrows Captain Kirk's body. Henoch tries to keep Spock's body, but Sargon helps the humans defeat Henoch, and he and his wife decide not to resume a physical existence after all. (See "Return To Tomorrow")

SARJENKA: The young Dreman girl whom Data becomes friends with by communicating with her via low-level RF waves. In order to save her life Data must bring her aboard the *Enterprise*. Her memories of the encounter are erased by Dr. Crusher but Data leaves the child with a gift of an Alaynan Singerstone. (See "Pen Pals")

SATIE, ADMIRAL: The daughter of an important Federation lawmaker, she comes aboard the *Enterprise* to investigate possible security breaches. She becomes so obsessed with her investigation that she starts persecuting innocent people until Picard puts a stop to it. As a result Satie destroys her own career. (See "The Drumhead")

SAVAR, ADMIRAL: A high-ranking Vulcan Starfleet officer and one of the conspirators who has been taken over by an alien parasite. (See "Conspiracy")

SAYANA: One of the innocent inhabitants of Gamma Trianguli VI, a subject of the all-controlling computer Vaal. She and Makora get into trouble when they imitate humans kissing, but survive to further explore the possibilities of this sort of behavior. (See "The Apple")

SCHMITTER: A miner on Janus VI who is killed by the Horta. (See "Devil In The Dark")

SCOTT, LT. COMMANDER MONTGOMERY: Scott, or "Scotty" is the Chief Engineer of the *Enterprise*. His serial number is SE-197-514. A ladies' man and a fellow fond of drink, he is primarily devoted to his job. A faithful member of the *Enterprise* crew, he's gotten his beloved ship out of more than a few jams, and in record time at that. He's a real technical wizard who has never let his captain down. He is accidentally discovered in the 24th Century, locked in stasis via a transporter beam. Upon release, he explores the *Enterprise-D* and begins a search for his destiny. (See "Relics")

SCOTT, CAPTAIN TRYLA: A Starfleet officer who has a secret meeting with Picard to discuss the threat to the Federation and verify that Picard is not an impostor. A woman Starfleet officer who made Captain faster than anyone in history, thanks in no small part to the fact that she was controlled by the parasitic aliens. (See "Conspiracy")

SECRETARY: Of course Dixon Hill had one. (See "The Big Goodbye")

SELA: The illegitimate daughter of Tasha Yar. When time changed and Tasha Yar went back through the time portal on the *Enterprise-C*, she was taken prisoner by the Romulans. In order to help save her fellow prisoners she agreed to become the consort of a Romulan and had a daughter by him. When Sela attempted to flee with the child, Sela deliberately gave them away because she didn't want to leave Romulus. As a result, Tasha was caught and executed, an action for which Sela apparently feels no regrets. (See "Redemption")

SELAR, DR.: A Vulcan scientist posted to the *Enterprise*. (See "The Schizoid Man")

SEPTIMUS: An old man who once served in the Senate of Planet 892-IV, Septimus is now a member of the neo-Christian underground movement that opposes the cruel Empire there. (See "Bread And Circuses")

SEVEN, GARY: Although Gary Seven is a human of Terran origin, presumably born in the 20th Century where Kirk and crew encounter him, he was raised on an unknown planet by a mysterious race with an interest in protecting Earth culture from its own technological follies and secretly helping it make its way to a more enlightened way of life. As an agent (Supervisor 194) of this agenda, Seven must prevent the launching of a spaceborne bomb by the American space program. Not realizing the situation, Kirk tries to stop him, but Seven succeeds and the Earth survives, to someday create or join the Federation which produced the *Enterprise*. (See "Assignment: Earth")

SEVRIN, DR.: This humanoid scientist from the planet Tiburon is a true genius in several fields: electronics, communication and sound. But when a highly contagious disease limits his access to civilized planets, he starts to go mad, and finally "drops out" like a latter-day Timothy Leary and begins a harebrained scheme to locate the missing planet of Eden, a near-mythical place which he believes to be located somewhere in Romulan space. This does not deter him from assembling a group of like-minded disciples, disaffected human youths who also want to find a pastoral return to their spiritual origins. Their mission leads them to steal a spaceship, but, unfamiliar with its operation, they only manage to blow it up. Luckily for them, the *Enterprise* beams them out in time to save their lives, only to find itself subject to their takeover. Sevrin even tries to kill all the *Enterprise* crew, but fails. Stealing a shuttlecraft, he and his band land on a planet they believe to be Eden.

It is indeed a peaceful, silent, garden of a world, but for a deadly reason: acid in all the plant life there is fatal to all animal life, including humanoids. One of Sevrin's followers is killed, and the rest are injured. Unable to face his failure, Sevrin commits suicide by intentionally eating one of the deadly "apples" of Eden. (See "The Way To Eden")

SHAHNA: One of the thralls of the Gamesters of Triskelion (a.k.a. the Providers), Shahna is assigned to train James Kirk in the gladiatorial "sports," and develops quite an attachment to the good captain, who is, as usual, determined to upset the status quo on Triskelion. (See "The Gamesters Of Triskelion")

SHAPIRO: A famous actor who once portrayed Shakespeare's Henry V. Data believes he can understand the role better by studying Shapiro's recorded performance of it. (See "The Defector")

SHAW, LIEUTENANT AREEL : A lawyer on Starbase 11. She is rather unhappy to be involved in the prosecution of James T. Kirk at his court martial — she used to be involved with him some years earlier. (See "Court Martial")

SHAW, KATIK: When the Ansata attack the Rutian plaza, this man is a waiter there, although he is actually a terrorist in disguise. (See "The High Ground")

SHEA, LIEUTENANT: One of the *Enterprise* crew members on the landing mission that encounters the Kelvans, and one of those turned into a piece of crystal by them. He is eventually restored to his original form by the Kelvan named Rojan. (See "By Any Other Name")

SHELBY, LT. COMMANDER: Starfleet tactical officer assigned to the *Enterprise* because she has been in charge of Borg tactical analysis for six months. (See "Best Of Both Worlds")

SHEL-LA, GOLIN: The warrior leader of the people of Ennis. They are prisoners on a moon surrounded by a satellite defense network capable of returning the dead to life. But once the slain have walked again, they can never leave that planetoid and survive. (See "Battle Lines")

SHIMODA, JIM: A member of the Engineering Department who, affected by the new strain of Psi-2000 disease, takes all the chips from the engineering computer. (See "The Naked Now")

SHRAS: Andorian ambassador to the Babel conference, a distinguished member of his planet's diplomatic corps. (See "Journey To Babel")

SHREK, JAGLOM: The name of the Yridian who approaches Worf when he is visiting Deep Space Nine, claiming to know that Worf's father is still alive on a Romulan prison planet. (See "Birthright")

SHUMAR, BRYCE: Captain of the starship the *U.S.S. Essex*. An alien entity impersonates Bryce Shumar in order to keep the *Enterprise* personnel from determining its true intent and identity. (See "Power Play")

SIGMAN SURVIVOR: An unnamed survivor of the mining accident. (See "Hide And Q")

SINGH, KHAN NOONIAN: One of the conquering "superior" men of the Eugenics Wars, he ruled 25% of the Earth from 1992 to 1996 (!!!) only to be exiled into space when "normal" humanity threw off the yoke of the so-called supermen. He and eighty of his genetically superior followers spent two hundred years adrift in suspended animation on board the *Botany Bay*. After his failed attempt to wrest the *Enterprise* from Captain Kirk, he is exiled once more to Ceti Alpha V, an exile destined to have interesting repercussions years later when he manages to escape and seeks vengeance on Kirk. (See "Space Seed" and "Star Trek II: The Wrath of Khan")

SINGH, LIEUTENANT: The *Enterprise* engineering officer who is given charge of *Nomad* and is quite surprised when it displays signs of auto-locomotion. (See "The Changeling")

SINGH, MR.: An engineer on board the *Enterprise* who is killed by the cloud entity encountered en route to Parliament. (See "Lonely Among Us")

SIRAH: A woman of the Yang tribe on Omega IV. Deprived of his communicator, Spock is able to utilize telepathy to make her contact the *Enterprise* with the communicator instead. (See "Omega Glory")

SIRAH: The Bajoran storyteller. When the Dal'rok threatens a Bajoran tribe each harvest time, only the storyteller, the Sirah, can drive the thing away. (See "The Storyteller")

SISKO, BENJAMIN: Former First Officer of the *U.S.S. Saratoga*. Now commander of the space station designated Deep Space Nine. He fought the Borg in the battle of Wolf 359 where his wife died in combat. (See "Emissary")

SISKO, JAKE: The son of Benjamin Sisko. His mother died in the battle of Wolf 359. He now lives aboard Deep Space Nine with his father.

SISKO, JENNIFER: The wife of Benjamin Sisko and mother of Jake Sisko. She was killed aboard the *U.S.S. Saratoga* at the battle of Wolf 359. (See "Emissary")

SOBI: A representative of the planet Brekka who is providing Felicium for the planet Ornara whose people are hopelessly addicted to the drug while believing that it is actually a plague vaccine they must take on a regular basis to keep them from suffering and dying. (See "Symbiosis")

SOLIS, LIEUTENANT: An officer who joins the bridge crew when LaForge takes command of the *Enterprise* at Minos. (See "Arsenal Of Freedom")

SONAK, COMMANDER: The Vulcan Science Officer aboard the refitted *Enterprise*. He is killed in a transporter accident before the maiden voyage. (See "Star Trek: The Motion Picture")

SOONG, DR. NOONIAN: Creator of Lore and Data, once believed to be a crackpot but now obviously vindicated by the existence of his creations. (See "Datalore") Worked with, and perhaps studied under, Dr. Ira Graves. (See "The Schizoid Man") Presumed dead, he actually survived the destruction of the colony on Omicron Theta Four and settled on a remote planet, where he perfected an emotion chip for Data. Unfortunately, Lore responded to the beacon that called Data there; he stole the chip and killed the ailing Soong. (See "Brothers") Soong programmed Data with various subroutines which enable Soong's image to communicate with Data in dreams. (see "Birthright")

SOREN: One of the race known as the J'Naii. She was "born different" and is a throwback to the time when her people were born with gender and had a tendency to be male or female. But now the J'Naii consider gender to be offensive. The J'Naii feel that by evolving away from gender they have moved onto a higher form of life. (See "The Outcast")

SOVAK: A Ferengi who is also looking for the Tox-Uthat on Risa. (See "Captain's Holiday")

SPOCK, COMMANDER: The Chief Science Officer and First Officer of the *Enterprise* (serial number S179-276-SP). A vegetarian like all his fellow Vulcans, the half-human Spock inherited most of the physical traits of his father Sarek's race: pointed ears, peaked eyebrows, copper-based blood of a greenish coloration (as often noted by Dr. Leonard McCoy) and internal organs of a decidedly non-human configuration. From his mother Amanda Grayson, he inherited such human traits as emotions, but these have been subdued by the Vulcan logic that predominates in his personality. As might well be imagined, his family background has certain inherent internal tensions: his mother is disappointed that Spock chose the Vulcan path over the human, while his father seems to have been let down by the fact that Spock chose to attend Starfleet Academy rather than follow in his footsteps and go to the Vulcan Academy of Sciences. Ultimately, this tension has made Spock a far more uptight individual than the ordinary Vulcan, as may be observed by anyone who has seen Sarek's reserved but gracious treatment of his wife Amanda. When Spock's outer shell of logic crumbles, it is usually with fairly dramatic results, whether the breakdown is the result of a virus, alien spores or the overwhelming onslaught of *pon farr*, the Vulcan mating urge.

After his exemplary record at Starfleet Academy, where he excelled in science but apparently devoted a great deal of his studies to the cultures, philosophies and arts of Earth and perhaps of other worlds as well, Spock joined Starfleet and, having achieved the rank of Lieutenant, was assigned to the *Enterprise* after his first few years of duty. He served as Second Officer and Science Officer under Captain Christopher Pike. He remained with the *Enterprise* when James T. Kirk assumed the captaincy, maintaining his position as Science Officer but rising to the rank of Commander and assuming the post of First Officer. Records are unclear as to whether this promotion took place before or after Kirk's arrival as captain of the *Enterprise*. Perhaps for spiritual reasons, or perhaps for the unvoiced doubts and uncertainties that linger behind his façade of perfect emotional control, Spock seems to have no interest in taking command of his own Starfleet vessel. He seems to be fairly well immersed in Vulcan spiritual practices (see **IDIC**) and his natural telepathic abilities seem undiminished by his diluted Vulcan genetic background. He actually died as a result of radiation he was exposed to while saving the *Enterprise* (see "Star Trek II: The Wrath of Khan"), but was ressurrected when his body was sent to the Genesis Planet. (see "Star Trek III: The Search For Spock"). Spock would ultimately go on to become an ambassador, having his first experience in such matters while promoting peace between the Klingons and the Federation and, later, in his efforts to reunite the Vulcan and Romulan people. (See "Star Trek VI: The Undiscovered Country" and "Unification")

In the mirror universe, Kirk encounters another Spock. Spock-Two is bearded, sinister and a good deal more dangerous than his Federation counterpart — but he's also perhaps the only decent person to be found in that entire universe. Like Kirk's Spock, Spock-Two shies away from top command positions, although his reticence might have more to do with self-preservation than self-effacement. Of some use to the Kirk who replaces his ruthless captain for a short period, Spock-Two is left pondering the possibility that he might somehow be able to effect some much-needed reform in his brutal universe. (See "Mirror, Mirror")

SPOT: Data's cat.

SSESTAR: One of the Selay delegates en route to Parliament. (See "Lonely Among Us")

STARNES, PROFESSOR: One of the "suicides" found on the planet Triacus, Starnes — like the other adults on the expedition — took a fatal dose of cyaladin under the influence of the "Friendly Angel" Gorgan. (See "And The Children Shall Lead")

STARNES, TOMMY: Son of Professor Starnes; one of the children who survived Triacus, Tommy was under the influence of the "Friendly Angel" Gorgan until its destruction. (See "And The Children Shall Lead")

STILES, LT. ANDREW: An *Enterprise* crewman with an anti-Romulan prejudice that probably dates back to his family's involvement in the Romulan War a century earlier. Stiles extends this prejudice towards Spock when he learns of the historical Vulcan/Romulan connection. After Spock saves his life, Stiles is forced to reconsider his illogical dislike of the Vulcan. (See "Balance Of Terror")

STOCKER, COMMODORE GEORGE: Commander of Starbase 10, en route to that command when the chief officers of the *Enterprise* fall prey to the accelerated aging disease. As ranking officer, he is obliged to take command of the *Enterprise* once the disease renders Kirk, McCoy and Spock unfit for command duty. Stocker's lack of field experience almost leads to disaster when Romulans show up and he does not know how to cope; luckily, a cure is found, and Kirk saves the day as usual. (See "The Deadly Years")

STONE, COMMODORE: The port master at Starbase 11. Stone heads the trial board at the court martial of James T. Kirk for negligence in the death of Finney. (See "Court Martial")

STONN: Spock's Vulcan rival for the hand of T'Pring. He is T'Pring's favored lover but she has been betrothed (if not in fact actually married) to Spock since childhood. Stonn is more than willing to combat Spock for the right of marriage, but T'Pring throws a wrench into the works when she chooses Jim Kirk to fight on her behalf — she has no desire to risk Stonn's life, since he is the one she wants. Presumably, she gets him in the end. (See "Amok Time")

STUBBS, DR. PAUL: An astrophysicist who is studying the Kavis Alpha explosion. He is such a controversial figure that even an unauthorized biography has been written about him. Comes on board the *Enterprise* to launch a space probe called "The Egg" which will gather data from a stellar event which happens only once every 192 years as stellar matter builds up to a spectacular explosion. (See "Evolution")

STURGEON: A member of the *Enterprise* crew who is killed by the salt vampire of planet M113. (See "The Man Trap")

SUL, VARIS: The Tetrarch (magistrate) of the Paqu. She is a 15-year-old-girl. (See "The Storyteller")

SULU, HIKARU: The main helmsman serving on board the *Enterprise*, a young man of Asian descent. A dedicated and highly efficient officer, he seems to have a well-balanced life, offsetting the rigors of his official duties with a wide variety of interests. One of his greatest passions is the ancient art of fencing. He is given his own command when he is promoted to Captain of the *U.S.S. Excelsior*. (See "Star Trek VI: The Undiscovered Country")

SUNA, MR.: A Tilonian who appears in Will Riker's hallucination as a Starfleet officer. (See "Frame Of Mind")

SUNAD: The Zalkonian starship commander who threatens the *Enterprise* in an attempt to capture and destroy "John Doe" before his transformation can occur. (See "Transfigurations")

SURAK: A prime mover in the historical period right before the Vulcans embraced logic as their way of life, Surak was the main philosophical architect of the new Vulcan path that carried his planet out of its Dark Age. He — or his image — joins Kirk in his battle against the evil champions chosen by the rock creature Yarnek on the planet Excalbia, where his peace-at-all-costs approach may not be the best way of handling the villains. (See "The Savage Curtain")

SUTTER, CLARA: A little girl on the *Enterprise* who has an imaginary friend named Isabella; an imaginary friend who becomes very real when an alien entity takes on the form of Isabella in order to study human behavior. (See "Imaginary Friend")

SWENSON: An officer who competes with Tasha Yar in a martial arts competition. (See "Skin Of Evil")

SYBO: An empath on the planet Argelius II, married to the prefect, Jaris. Her powers enable her to discover the background of the Jack-the-Ripper being, but she is killed by the possessed Hengist for her troubles. (See "Wolf In The Fold")

SYBOK: Spock's half-brother from Sarek's first marriage (the one nobody ever talks about). Sybok completely rejected his Vulcan heritage. He and his half-brother are estranged until late in Sybok's life. (See "Star Trek V: The Final Frontier")

SYLVIA: 1.) The "witch" encountered by the *Enterprise* crew on Pyris VII, she dominates the more peaceful Korob and torments her new humanoid guests. When she dies she is revealed to be a very small, grotesque creature like a deformed bird embryo. Her appearance as a beautiful human woman was merely an illusion. (See "Catspaw")
2.) A young woman — or illusion of same — the *Enterprise* officers meet in a dance hall in the Melkotian recreation of the gunfight at the OK Corral. (See "Spectre Of The Gun")

SYPE, RYAN: Another suspicious officer killed by the alien conspiracy. (See "Conspiracy")

SYRUS, DR.: One of Will Riker's interrogators when he's captured on Timonus Four. (See "Frame Of Mind")

TAAR, DAIMON: Commander of the Ferengi ship that engages the *Enterprise* at Delphi Ardu. (See "The Last Outpost")

TAGGART, CAPTAIN: The commander of the *U.S.S. Repulse,* which was the vessel Dr. Katherine Pulaski formerly served on. (See "Unnatural Selection")

TAIBAK, COMMANDER: The Klingon in charge of security when Picard and Ambassador Kell visit Governor Vagh of Krios in order to investigate charges that the Federation is supplying arms to Klingon rebels there. (See "The Mind's Eye")

TAL: Subcommander, or second-in-command, of the Romulan ship from which James Kirk steals a cloaking device. (See "The Enterprise Incident")

TALBOT, ST. JOHN: The Federation diplomat stationed on Nimbus III. He is first kidnapped by Sybok and then becomes one of his disciples. (See "Star Trek V: The Final Frontier")

TAMAR: A member of the anti-Landru resistance movement on Beta III, executed by the Lawgivers. (See "Return Of The Archons")

TAMOON: One of the female thralls of Triskelion, she is paired off with a rather reluctant Pavel Chekov. (See "The Gamesters Of Triskelion")

TAMURA, YEOMA: An *Enterprise* crew member of Asian descent who beams down to Eminiar VII with Captain Kirk's party. (See "A Taste Of Armageddon")

TANDRO, GENERAL ARDELON: A military hero on Klaestron Four who was killed. He was actually a victim of the terrorists he gave information to in betrayal of his own people. Curzon Dax was accused of being implcated in the killing until Dax was cleared. Tandro's widow finally revealed the truth about the General's betrayal. Dax had refused to reveal what she knew because Curzon Dax had been involved in an affair with General Tandro's wife at the time of Ardelon Tandro's death. (See "Dax")

TANDRO, ENINA: The widow of General Ardelon Tandro. She had an affair with Curzon Dax, who had been Ardelon's best friend. (See "Dax")

TANDRO, ILON: Special envoy from Klaestron Four. He wants to arrest and prosecute Jadzia Dax for a crime Curzon Dax is accused of. His father was General Ardelon Tandro. (See "Dax")

TANGO: A horse owned by Christopher Pike on Earth, utilized by the Talosians in one of their many illusory scenarios. (See "The Cage" and "The Menagerie")

TANKRIS, YEOMAN: The female *Enterprise* crew member who records the proceedings that clear Scotty, and reveal the real Ripper murderer, on Argelius. (See "Wolf In The Fold")

TAN TSU: A member of one of the warring factions on Tasha Yar's homeworld of Turkana Four. (See "Legacy")

TARAS, SUBCOMMANDER: The captain of the *Harkona,* the Romulan vessel which confronts the *Enterprise* in the Neural Zone in "Contagion."

TARK: Father of Kara, the young Argelian woman who is killed by Hengist. (See "Wolf In The Fold")

TARMIN: The head of the Ullian delegation. He can read memories and enhance a person's own recollections of past events in their life. (See "Violations")

TARSES, SIMON: A medical crewman who comes under suspicion because it is revealed that he has a Romulan grandfather, not a Vulcan one. (See "The Drumhead")

TATAGLIA: A famous concert violinist whose style Data has been programmed to reproduce. (See "Sarek")

TAVA: A Malkorian who becomes aware that Riker is an "alien" trying to pass as a Malkorian. (See "First Contact")

TAXCO: A female Arbazan ambassador who visits Deep Space Nine. (See "The Forsaken")

TAYLOR, DR. GILLIAN: A 20th century scientist whom Jim Kirk befriends in his search for whales to take back to the future. He takes her back to the future with him. (See "Star Trek IV: The Voyage Home")

TAYNA: The assistant to Dr. Apgar. She has a bee-hive hairdo and testifies against Riker at the hearing into Dr. Apgar's "murder." (See "A Matter Of Perspective")

T'BOK: The Romulan commander in charge of a starship which contacts the *Enterprise,* marking the first time the Romulan Empire has initiated contact with the Federation in fifty years. (See "The Neutral Zone")

T'BOK, CAPTAIN: Commander of a Romulan vessel encountered near the Neutral Zone. (See " The Neutral Zone")

TECHNICAL OFFICER, ROMULAN: Rendered unconscious by Kirk as he makes good his escape with the Romulan cloaking device. (See "The Enterprise Incident")

TECHNICIANS: Officers who portray the victims of an accident in Wesley's first entrance test to Starfleet Academy. (See " Coming Of Age")

TELLER: An old friend of James Kirk, whose lack of loyalty is revealed after Kirk is accused of negligence in the death of Finney. Teller snubs Kirk prior to the court martial proceedings on Starbase 11. (See "Court Martial")

TEMAREK: Forced to taste the drink which Marouk offers Brull. (See "The Vengeance Factor")

TEMPLE, NURSE: A nurse on the *Enterprise-D* who assists Dr. Crusher in helping "John Doe." (See "Transfigurations")

TERKIM: The brother of Guinan's mother — the black sheep of the family, according to Guinan, but also the only one with a sense of humor. Guinan liked him. (See "Hollow Pursuits")

TERRELL, CAPTAIN CLARK: The commander of the *U.S.S. Reliant.* When Khan hijacks the starship he puts a ceti eel in Terrell's head to control him. When Khan orders Captain Terrell to kill James Kirk, Terrell resists and kills himself instead. (See "Star Trek II: The Wrath Of Khan")

THALASSA: Wife of Sargon, one of the three survivors of the planet Arett. For a short but action-packed period she borrows the body of Dr. Anne Mulhall. (See "Return To Tomorrow")

THANN: A Vian, involved in the torture/tests on Minara II. (See "The Empath")

THARN: Tharn is a remarkable humanoid: he is exactly the same in our world and in the mirror universe. His reaction to the request/demand of the *Enterprise* for dilithium crystals is constant: he refuses, in order to keep the crystals from military deployment. Kirk has no problem with this in his world, but when he's cast in the role of Kirk-Two the situation suddenly becomes a great deal more complicated. (See "Mirror, Mirror")

THEI: One of the Romulans aboard the vessel which contacts the *Enterprise* after outposts are mysteriously destroyed along the border of the Neutral Zone. Subordinate officer on the Romulan ship commanded by T'Bok. (See "The Neutral Zone")

THELEV: An Orion spy, who disguises himself as an Andorian and joins the Andorian diplomatic team to Babel. Here he pursues his goal: to murder the Tellarian ambassador Gav and somehow cast blame on the Vulcan ambassador, Spock's father, Sarek. The murder is a success; the frame-up is not. Thelev commits suicide when his rescue ship self-destructs. (See "Journey To Babel")

THIRD OF FIVE: What the Borg (dubbed Hugh by Geordi) calls itself when he is initially interrogated aboard the *Enterprise.* (See "I, Borg")

THOLL, KOVA: A Mizarian who demonstrates cowardice when he is captured and imprisoned along with Picard, Esoqq and Mitena. (See "Allegiance")

THOMAS, ENSIGN: Ordered to report to the Combat Information Center on the *Enterprise-D.* (See "Yesterday's Enterprise")

THOMPSON, YEOMAN LESLIE : A casualty of the first Federation contact with the Kelvans, this *Enterprise* crew member is turned into a block of crystal and shattered by the Kelvan leader, Rojan. (See "By Any Other Name")

THULE, TECHNICIAN (1/C): One of the *Enterprise* crew members serving on the bridge when Khan Noonian Singh turns off the atmospheric controls in an effort to kill them. (See "Space Seed")

TIMICIN, DR.: A scientist from Kaelon-2. (See "Half A Life")

TIMOTHY: Another friend of Kirk's who reveals his true colors when he snubs Kirk before his court martial on Starbase 11. (See "Court Martial")

TIMOTHY: A young boy whose parents were killed on the *Vico;* he was the only survivor of the disaster. He blames himself and for a time identifies strongly with Data because androids don't feel pain. (See "Hero Worship")

T'JON: An Ornaran who wants the Felicium for his people because he thinks it is needed to fight a plague. He doesn't realize that his people are addicted to the drug and this is why they begin dying when it runs out. Captain of the Ornaran vessel the *Sanction,* he goes into withdrawal symptoms when his supply of Felicium is cut off. (See "Symbiosis")

TOFF, PALOR: Kivas Fajo's rivals, he has three nostrils. (See "The Most Toys")

TOG, DAIMON: Captain of the Ferengi ship *Krayton* who falls in love with Lwaxana Troi and kidnaps her (along with Riker and Deanna). He says that some females love to give him Oo-mox. (See "Menage A Troi")

TOKATH, COMMANDER: The head of the secret Romulan prison camp where Klingons captured at the Khitomer massacre (and their offspring) live. Tokath took a Klingon woman for a wife and his daughter Ba'el is the result. (See "Birthright")

TOLAKA, CAPTAIN: The Captain of the *U.S.S. Lantree* who falls victim to the strange aging ailment. (See "Unnatural Selection")

TOMALAK: A Romulan commander who leaves the Neutral Zone in order to rescue the survivors of the crash on Galorndon Core. He crosses paths with Picard there and later in the incident involving the Romulan defector. (See "The Enemy" and "The Defector")

TOMAR: One of the Kelvans who take over the *Enterprise,* and the first to fall prey to human wiles: Scotty introduces Tomar to the ancient Earth custom of drinking alcohol to the point of unconsciousness. Tomar likes it. (See "By Any Other Name")

TOMLINSON, ROBERT: A young phaser specialist whose wedding to Angela Martine is permanently disrupted when he is killed in a Romulan attack. (See "Balance Of Terror")

TONGO RAD: The spoiled son of the Catullan ambassador to the Federation, Tongo joins the followers of Dr. Sevrin in their ill-fated search for the mythical planet Eden. (See "The Way To Eden")

TOQ: A Klingon youth in whom Worf engenders excitement for his unknown heritage. (See "Birthright")

TORAK, GOVERNOR: The Klingon governor of the region of space near a Federation communications relay station. He finds Lieutenant Aquiel in a shuttlecraft and returns her to the mysteriously abandoned relay station where she finds herself facing serious charges. (See "Aquiel")

TORAL: The illegitimate son of Duras. Through him the sisters of Duras hope to gain control of the Klingon High Council. Unknown to the council, the sisters are secretly working with the Romulan, Sela, so that the Romulans can gain influence over the Klingons. (See "Redemption")

TORAN: A Bajoran government minister. (See "Progress")

TORAS: The commander of the Romulan vessel which confronts the *Enterprise* in orbit around the planet Iconia. (See "Contagion")

TORETH, COMMANDER: The commander of the Romulan warbird *Khazara*. (See "Face Of The Enemy")

TORG: A Klingon under the command of Kruge. He dies aboard the boobytrapped *Enterprise*. (See "Star Trek III: The Search For Spock")

TORMOLEN, JOE: The first casualty of the Psi 2000 virus, this *Enterprise* crew member tries to commit suicide but is restrained, only to die anyway from the emotional intensity of the experience. (See "The Naked Time")

TORRES: An ensign serving on the *Enterprise* who was frozen by Q. (See "Encounter At Farpoint")

TOSK: A mysterious alien whose ship exits the wormhole and stops at Deep Space Nine. He only needs seventeen minutes of sleep per "rotation", and also has an incredibly effective nutrient storage system in his body, and can go for long periods of time without needing to eat. (See "Captive Pursuit")

TOYA: Mother of Alexandra, one of the *Enterprise* children abducted by the Aldeans. (See "When The Bough Breaks")

T'PAN: Director of the Vulcan Science Academy and a scientist who agrees to visit the *Enterprise* to witness a test of Dr. Reyga's metaphasic field technology. (See "Suspicions")

T'PAU: One of the oldest and most respected pillars of Vulcan society, the woman T'Pau caused quite a stir some years earlier when she refused a position in the Federation Council. Nobody else ever passed up this honor. When she shows up to preside over Spock's wedding, it is a profound honor which reveals the status of Spock's ancestry. A polite request from T'Pau retroactively makes Kirk's disobedience perfectly all right, as far as official records are concerned. (See "Amok Time")

T'PEL: A Vulcan ambassador who is negotiating with the Romulans. She appears to die in a transporter accident but it is actually a cover for the fact that she was a Romulan spy who is returning to the Romulans to be debriefed on all that she has learned. (See "Data's Day")

T'PRING: Spock's betrothed since they were both seven years of age. When Spock goes into *pon farr*, Kirk's only recourse is to take him back to Vulcan, where he is reunited with T'Pring. But she is none too happy about their traditional-style arranged marriage, and prefers another, Stonn. A ritual battle, rendered deadly by Spock's mental state, would free her from this obligation, but instead of sending Stonn into battle she chooses Kirk as her champion, an "honor" the good captain cannot refuse. The result of this devious behavior by T'Pring would have been fatal for Kirk if not for some timely trickery on the part of Dr. McCoy. T'Pau (see above) brings matters to a halt, and Spock, who is no fool, lets Stonn have T'Pring. Stonn's future seems fairly unenviable to everyone but Stonn, who is not the smartest Vulcan around. (See "Amok Time")

TRACEY, CAPTAIN RONALD: Commanding officer of the *Exeter* who breaks the rule of the Prime Directive on the planet Omega IV. He believes that the Kohm longevity, which is actually a function of the planet's eco-system, can be isolated and synthesized. To this end, he interferes in the battles between the Kohms and the Yangs. When Kirk and crew leave Omega IV after their adventure there, they take Tracey back to the *Enterprise* as a prisoner. (See "Omega Glory")

TRACY, LT. KAREN: Another victim of the Ripper-possessed Hengist on Argelius; she is killed when she's alone with Scotty, which strengthens suspicions that he is the brutal murderer. (See "Wolf In The Fold")

THE TRAVELER: The name used by the humanoid alien who accompanies Koszinski, the Federation propulsion expert sent to modify the engines of the *Enterprise-D*. An alien being who is able to travel through time and space via the power of his mind, he informs Captain Picard of the great potential Wesley Crusher has in him. (See "Where No One Has Gone Before")

TRAVERS, COMMODORE: Chief officer of the Federation colony on Cestus III, he is killed in the Gorn attack, but the wily reptilian Gorn mimic his voice to lure the *Enterprise* to Cestus III. (See "Arena")

TREFAYNE: One of the members of the Organian Council, revealed later as an energy being like the rest. (See "Errand Of Mercy")

TRELANE: Creator of the planet Gothos, an immature being who is learning to use his amazing psionic powers. He takes the form of a human in early middle age but this is just a convenient illusion. Kirk's fear of his almost godlike powers is severely undermined by his profound irritation at the fellow's personality. Of course, it turns out he is merely a child of his species, and his parents show up to put an end to his game when he begins to play too rough with his new human toys from the *Enterprise*. (See "Squire Of Gothos")

TRENT: A subservient male resident of Angel One, servant to Beata. (See "Angel One")

TROI, COUNSELOR DEANNA: Half Betazoid, she is an empath, but unlike her mother Lwaxana, she is not a telepath. She is the ship's counselor aboard the *Enterprise-D*. She is a chocoholic, particularly sundaes and especially when she is unhappy about something. She helps personnel deal with various kinds of stress and can sense when someone is telling the truth. She also has an advanced degree in psychology. Once involved with Will Riker, now they are just good friends. Her arranged marriage with Wyatt Miller did not go off as planned. (See "Haven")

TROI, IAN ANDREW: Deanna Troi's father, formerly married to Lwaxana Troi. Deanna names her unusual child Ian after her father. (See "The Child")

TROI, LWAXANA: Emissary from Betazed, daughter of the Fifth House, holder of the sacred Chalice of Rix, heir to the Holy Rings of Betazed. She is a full Betazoid and an excellent telepath. She had another daughter who drowned in an accident before Deanna was born.

T'SAI: The High Master of Vulcan whom Spock goes before as part of the ritual of Kolinahr. (See "Star Trek: The Motion Picture")

T'SHALIK: A female Vulcan student who takes the Academy entrance examination at the same time as Wesley Crusher. (See "Coming Of Age")

TSINGTAO, RAY: One of the children who falls temporarily under the influence of the "Friendly Angel" Gorgan. (See "And The Children Shall Lead")

T'SU, LIAN: An ensign on board the *Enterprise*, who serves under LaForge when he takes command at Minos. (See "Arsenal Of Freedom")

TYLER, JOSE: Captain Christopher Pike's navigator on the *Enterprise*. (See "The Cage" and "The Menagerie")

TYREE: A native of Neural, chief of one of the peaceful hill tribes. Kirk befriended him on a visit to Neural thirteen years earlier. His wife Nona tries to draw Tyree's human friends into a war with the village dwellers. (See "A Private Little War")

UHNARI, LT. AQUIEL: An Hahlilian lieutenant posted to a communications relay station near the Klingon border. (See "Aquiel")

UHURA, LIEUTENANT: A graceful African woman born on Terra in the United States Of Africa, Lieutenant Uhura ("freedom" in Swahili) is the Communications Officer on board the *Enterprise*.

ULETTA: On Ekos, she is engaged to be married to the Zeon, Isak, but is killed by the Nazis and left to die in the street. (See "Patterns Of Force")

UXBRIDGE, KEVIN: A Douwd. There is little known about these immortal aliens except that they are comparable in power to the Q. The Douwd are devout pacifists. Adopting the form of a human, he fell in love with an Earth woman, Rishon, who never knew the truth about him, even after they were married. They were married for 53 years. He went to live with Rishon on Rana IV. When the Husnocks attacked the planet, Rishon went to battle them with the other colonists, but "Kevin" refused. When the Husnocks wiped out all life on the planet (except for himself as he was immune to their attack), he was so overcome with grief over the death of his wife that he destroyed every Husnock in the universe. Ashamed of his action he now lives on Rana IV in self-imposed exile. (See "The Survivors")

UXBRIDGE, RISHON: The 82-year-old wife of Kevin. Killed in an attack on Rana IV, she now exists only as the image of her which Kevin has created. She was married to Kevin for 53 years and never knew that he was one of the immortal aliens known as the Douwd. She was traveling with her parents when she met Kevin and she asked him to marry her two hours after they met. (See "The Survivors")

VADOSIA: A Bolian ambassador who visits Deep Space Nine. For an ambassador he's a bit on the overbearing side. (See "The Forsaken")

VAGH, GOVERNOR: The Klingon governor of the planet Krios who is being manipulated into believing that the Federation is supplying arms to the rebels on his world. He is also targeted for assassination by the Romulans, who hope to use his murder to create a rift between the Federation and the Klingons. (See "The Mind's Eye")

VALERIS: The Vulcan who conspires to prevent an armistice with the Klingon Empire. (See "Star Trek VI: The Undiscovered Country")

VALKRIS: The Klingon lover of Kruge. She manages to steal information about the Genesis Device and pass it on to Kruge. (See "Star Trek III: The Search For Spock")

VALLIS, ELIZABETH: Wilson Granger's aide and Chief of Staff of the Mariposa colony. (See "Up The Long Ladder")

VANDERBERG, CHIEF ENGINEER: Chief Engineer and head administrator of the mining colony on Janus VI, Vanderberg contacts the

Enterprise for help when the Horta begins its attacks on the colonists. (See "Devil In The Dark")

VAN GELDER, DR. SIMON : Assistant head of the experimental penal treatment center on the isolated planet of Tantalus, this psychiatrist is subjected to Dr. Tristan Adams' altered neural neutralizer. Spock touches Van Gelder's mind to discover what's been going on planetside. After the demise of the misguided Adams, Van Gelder becomes head of the program on Tantalus. (See "Dagger Of The Mind")

VANNA: A female Troglyte on the planet Ardana. Employed as a servant in Stratos by Plasus, she is secretly a member of the underground Disruptor movement. She is hard pressed to believe that Kirk is not on hand merely to preserve the unjust and unequal status quo. (See "The Cloud Minders")

VANTIKA, RAO: A brutal serial killer who has been tracked for 20 years by Ty Kajada of Kobliad Security. Vantika is capable of transmitting his mind into the body of whoever is touching him at the moment of his death. (See "The Passenger")

VAREL: A Romulan who is determined to see the *Enterprise* destroyed in order to hide the secret of the Interphase experiments. (See "The Next Phase")

VARLEY, CAPTAIN DONALD: The commander of the Galaxy class vessel the *U.S.S. Yamato*. When the Iconian globe creates a massive computer malfunction and destroys the Yamato, he is killed. (See "Contagion")

VARRIA: A Zibalian who was the aide to Kivas Fajo for fourteen years. When Data risks his life for her she agrees to help the android escape. Fajo catches them and executes Varria as punishment. (See "The Most Toys")

VASH: A con artist who meets Jean-Luc Picard while he's on shore leave on Risa. She'd been the former assistant of Professor Samuel Estragon, who'd spent years searching for the legendary Tox-Uthat. Upon his death she took up the search and Picard becomes involved as well, helping Vash decode the clues. She actually becomes attracted to Picard and following the Tox-Uthat incident visits him on the *Enterprise*. Ultimately she decides to explore the cosmos with Q, before leaving him and arriving on Deep Space Nine from the Gamma Quadrant. (See "Captain's Holiday", "QPid" and "Q-Less")

VEKMA: A Klingon officer aboard the bird of prey the *Pagh*. She is amused when Riker comes aboard under the officer exchange program and taunts him, wondering openly what it would be like to know Riker sexually. (See "A Matter Of Honor")

VENDOR: A newspaper stand operator who gives Picard/Dixon Hill a paper. (See "The Big Goodbye")

V'GER: Actually NASA's Voyager 6 space probe which entered the atmosphere of a machine planet and was joined by that world's inhabitants, allowing Voyager — calling itself V'Ger — to achieve consciousness. Its first task is to seek its creator on the planet Earth, and along the way it absorbs everything that it comes in contact with, including star systems, a trio of Klingon vessels, the Federation's Epsilon 9 space station and nearly the refitted starship *Enterprise*. Earth is saved when Commander Decker and Lieutenant Ilia join with V'Ger, allowing it to evolve to a higher state of existence. (See "Star Trek: The Motion Picture")

VIGO: Starfleet officer who served as Picard's Weapons Officer on board the *U.S.S. Stargazer*. (See "The Battle")

VINA: The only survivor of the ship that crashed on Talos IV years before Captain Christopher Pike was lured there, Vina was terribly disfigured. The Talosians put her back together as best they could, but the other passengers were in no condition to provide a template, and they had to guess how to reconstruct a human being. The result is not pretty, but to Vina and others she appears as a beautiful young woman thanks to the illusory powers of the Talosians. When Pike refuses to remain on Talos, the Talosians create yet another illusion for Vina, letting her believe that Pike has stayed to be her lifelong companion. Years later, Pike actually returns to make that illusion a reality (of sorts). (See "The Cage" and "The Menagerie")

VIXIS: The Klingon lover of Captain Klaa. (See "Star Trek V: The Final Frontier")

VOLNOTH: Killed by Yuta and her microvirius, he was one of the last members of the Lornack clan. (See "The Vengeance Factor")

WAGNOR: The Angosian pilot of the shuttle sent to return Danar to Lunar Five. (See "The Hunted")

WALLACE, DR. JANET: One of James Kirk's seemingly innumerable ex-girlfriends, on hand when the *Enterprise* encounters the accelerated aging disease of Gamma Hydra IV. She helps the nearly senile McCoy create the cure, using adrenaline as its basis. (See "The Deadly Years")

WARREN, DR. MARY: One of the scientists injured when the Federation observation post on Mintaka explodes; she later dies from her injuries aboard the *Enterprise*. (See "Who Watches The Watchers?")

WASHBURN: One of the *Enterprise* crew members who beams over to inspect the condition of the *Constellation* in the aftermath of the doomsday machine's attack on it. (See "The Doomsday Machine")

WATKINS, JOHN B.: A victim of Losira when she appears on board the *Enterprise*, this young black officer was a member of the engineering department. (See "That Which Survives")

WATSON, TECHNICIAN: An *Enterprise* crewman from engineering; he is murdered when he discovers the Elasian Kryton communicating with a Klingon vessel. (See "Elaan Of Troyius")

WESLEY, COMMODORE ROBERT: The captain of the *Lexington*. Wesley receives Starfleet authorization to destroy the *Enterprise* when the M-5 computer, in command of the *Enterprise*, turns war games into a deadly reality. But Wesley withholds the order to fire until he hears from Kirk after the computer relinquishes control, and the *Enterprise* is spared. (See "The Ultimate Computer")

WESTERVLIET, ADMIRAL: A ranking Starfleet officer who denies Kirk his request for permission to follow McCoy while he is on the spaceship/asteroid *Yonada*. (See "For The World Is Hollow And I Have Touched The Sky")

WHALEN: A Federation historian eager to explore the holodeck recreation of 1941 San Francisco; he almost dies when shot by Felix Leech. (See "The Big Goodbye")

WHEALAN: An expert on the 20th Century whom Picard has accompany him into a holodeck recreation of the fictional 1941 realm of detective Dixon Hill. Whelan is wounded when the holodeck malfunctions. (See "The Big Goodbye")

WILKINS, PROFESSOR: One of the adult victims of the "Friendly Angel" Gorgan when that creature is released from its resting place on the planet Triacus. (See "And The Children Shall Lead")

WILLIAMS, ENSIGN: Data remarks that this officer, who is in an art class with Picard, has a style which is obviously influenced by geometric constructivism. (See "A Matter Of Perspective")

WILLIE: A young boy in need of medical attention who is endangered when Data commandeers the *Enterprise* to heed a summons from his creator. (See "Brothers")

WILSON, TECHNICIAN: The transporter officer on duty when the transporter divides Kirk into two warring halves; the evil, aggressive Kirk beats Wilson up and makes off with his hand phaser. (See "The Enemy Within")

WINN, VEDEK: A Bajoran orthodox cleric. She accuses Keiko of heresy and dishonoring the celestial temple for teaching science to Bajoran students. (See "In The Hands Of The Prophets")

WOBAN: The Navot leader. The Navot are a Bajoran faction which is in a territorial dispute with the Paqu, another Bajoran faction. Benjamin Sisko is asked to mediate the dispute. (See "The Storyteller")

WONG, LIEUTENANT: An unseen member of the *Enterprise* engineering staff, mentioned by LaForge. (See "Angel One")

WORF, LIEUTENANT: A full-blooded Klingon, and the only member of his race to serve in Starfleet. Originally Operations Officer, he succeeded Tasha Yar as Chief of Security on the *Enterprise-D*. When he was six his parents were killed in the Romulan Khitomer Massacre and Worf was raised by a Federation officer and his wife on Gault. His father was Mogh and his brother (whom he learned was alive only recently) is Kurn. Worf and his nurse, Kahlest, were the only survivors of the Khitomer Massacre and he later goes to her when he must clear his family name before the Klingon High Council.

WRENN: Chief of the surviving occupants of the Terellian plague ship encountered near Haven. (See "Haven")

WRIGHT, LIEUTENANT: Data remarks that this officer, who is in an art class with Picard, has effectively fused the incongruities of the surrealists with the irrationality of Dadaism. (See "A Matter Of Perspective")

XELO: Mr. Homh's predecessor in the service of Lwaxana Troi; Lwaxana claims to have dismissed him because she could read the lewd thoughts he kept having about her. (See "Haven")

YALE, MIRASTA: A Malkorian scientist who opts to leave her world and go to serve on the *Enterprise*. (See "First Contact")

YANAR: The young woman Okona is accused of getting pregnant. (See "The Outrageous Okona")

YAREENA: Wife of Lutan of Ligon II. She engaged Tasha Yar in a to-the-death, one-on-one combat and lost; revived by Dr. Crusher, she was, having "died", no longer legally married to Lutan, and chose his second-in-command Hagon as her mate. (See "Code Of Honor")

YARI: A Mintakan who is sent to chase down Riker. (See "Who Watches The Watchers?")

YAR, ISHARA: The younger sister of Tasha Yar who remained behind on her planet Turkana Four when Tasha left to enter Starfleet. Ishara is now part of a terrorist underground known as the Coalition. (See "Legacy")

YAR, LT. NATASHA: The former *Enterprise* Chief of Security from the planet Turkana Four. She was killed at Vagra Two by Armus. When the timeline was altered by the presence of the *Enterprise-C*, Tasha Yar lived again, only to return on the *Enterprise-C* into the past after learning that in real time she was not meant to be alive after all.

YARNEK: A rock creature who lives on Excalbia, he studies the notions of good and evil by pitting Kirk, Lincoln and others against some nasty villains from intergalactic history. (See "The Savage Curtain")

YOUNGBLOOD, ENSIGN: A member of the bridge crew.

YUTA: The sole survivor of the Tralesta clan, she is also the chef and food taster for Sovereign Marouk of Acamar III. She is actually very old, even though she looks youthful in order to hide the true facts of her existence. Riker discovers that she is an assassin and has to kill her in order to stop her from killing again. (See "The Vengeance Factor")

YUTAN: An inhabitant of Neural, he is a follower of Tyree. (See "A Private Little War")

ZABO: A follower of the gangster Krako. He abducts Kirk. (See "A Piece Of The Action")

ZARABETH: A young woman exiled to the Ice Age of Sarpeidon by a tyrant several millennia before Spock and McCoy are cast into the same time period. When Spock reverts to an emotional state, he becomes involved with her, but he and McCoy must leave her there when they escape, for her atavachron treatment was, cruelly, only one-way, and to leave her new home would undoubtedly kill her. (See "All Our Yesterdays")

ZAYNER: The aide to Prime Minister Nayrok. (See "The Hunted")

ZEK: The Grand Nagus of the Ferengi. (See "The Nagus")

ZEMBATA, CAPTAIN: The commander of the *U.S.S. Victory,* a vessel Geordi served on when he was an ensign. (See "Elementary, Dear Data")

ZENA: Would have been Alexandra's mother on Aldea if the abduction had been a success. (See "When The Bough Breaks")

ZLANGCO: The warrior leader of the Nol-Ennis. They are prisoners on a moon surrounded by a satellite defense network capable of returning the dead to life. But once the slain have walked again, they can never leave that planetoid and survive because once the biomechanical microbes restore a body to life that body becomes completely dependent on those microbes for survival. (See "Battle Lines")

ZORA: A notorious evil person from the history of the planet Tiburon, she is recreated to fight for evil on the planet Excalbia by the being Yarnek. (See "The Savage Curtain")

ZOR KHAN: The tyrant of ancient Sarpeidon history who exiled Zarabeth to the ice age of their world after her family tried to overthrow him. He killed them all but sent her back in time. (See "All Our Yesterdays")

ZORN, GROPPLER: An Administrator at Farpoint Station who Will Riker meets while waiting for the *Enterprise-D* to come to pick him up. He was the leader of the Bandi, and the man primarily responsible for the captivity of the alien on Deneb IV. (See "Encounter at Farpoint")

ZWELLER, COREY: A close friend of Jean-Luc from his Academy days. (See "Tapestry")

SPACESHIPS

ADELPHI: In the Ghorusda Disaster, Captain Darson of the *U.S.S. Adelphi* was killed. (See "Tin Man")

AJAX, U.S.S.: A ship that took part in some of the scientist Kosinski's experimentation. (See "Where No One Has Gone Before")

ANGOSIAN TRANSPORT: This ship was captured by Roga Danar to escape Lunar Five (See "The Hunted").

ANTARES: A science ship whose crew of twenty is unfortunate enough to rescue Charles Evans from Thasus. (See "Charlie X")

ARCHON, U.S.S.: A Starfleet vessel which was caused to crash on Beta III, a century before the *Enterprise* came along. (See "Return Of The Archons")

ARES, U.S.S.: The captain of this ship is retiring and the command is offered to Will Riker, who turns it down. (See "The Icarus Factor")

ARTEMIS: This colony ship landed on Tau Cygna V, although when it had been launched 92 years before, its destination was Septimus Minor. (See "The Ensigns Of Command")

ASTRAL QUEEN: The ship transporting the Karidian Players to their destination, Benicia. Intercepted by the *Enterprise*. (See "Conscience Of The King")

ATLEK: A ship captured by Debin which is a class 7 vessel containing a crew of 26. (See "The Outrageous Okona")

AURORA, U.S.S.: The space vessel stolen by Dr. Sevrin and his youthful followers. Overtaxed by its untrained crew, it blows up; Kirk beams its occupants over to the *Enterprise* just in the nick of time. (See "The Way To Eden")

BATRIS: The renegade Klingons led by Koris take over this Telarian ship and make it their own. The *Enterprise* meets it in the Neutral Zone. (See "Heart Of Glory")

BEAGLE, U.S.S.: A Starfleet ship (named after the ship in Charles Darwin's famous scientific voyage) helmed by Captain Melik. Its wreckage is discovered by the *Enterprise* at planet 892-IV six years after its destruction. (See "Bread and Circuses")

BERLIN, U.S.S.: A Starfleet vessel on duty patrolling the Neutral Zone. The *Enterprise* is en route to join the *Berlin* when illness causes it to stop over at the planet Angel One. (See "Angel One")

BOTANY BAY, S.S.: The ship (of the Dy-100 class) in which Khan and his followers lie in suspended animation until their discovery by the crew of the *Enterprise*. (See "Space Seed")

BOZEMAN, U.S.S.: A 23rd Century starship under the command of Captain Bateson which is caught in a time loop and emerges in the 24th Century. (See "Cause And Effect")

BRADBURY, U.S.S.: The Starfleet ship which Wesley is originally slated to travel to Starfleet Academy on, although he misses the flight due to an emergency aboard the *Enterprise*. (See "Menage A Troi")

BRATTAIN, U.S.S.: A starship which becomes disabled and its crew suffers a strange fate (See "Night Terrors")

CAPTAIN'S RUNABOUT: A slightly larger than normal shuttlecraft maintained primarily for the use of a starship captain. (See "Timescape")

CAROLINA, U.S.S.: A Federation ship, in the area

of Capella IV. (See "The Cloud Minders")

CHARLESTON, U.S.S.: The ship that was unable to meet the *Enterprise* and take its 20th Century passengers to Earth. (See "The Neutral Zone")

CHARYBDIS: This was a NASA exploratory vessel launched July 23, 2037 which was the third attempt by an Earth ship to leave the solar system. It was under the command of Colonel Richey. Earth lost contact with the vessel when its telemetry failed. (See "The Royale")

CLASS J CARGO SHIP: A small space transport ship.

CLASS J STARSHIP: An earlier classification of starship; Christopher Pike's crippling injuries occurred as the result of an accident on a class J starship. (See "The Menagerie")

CLEPONJI: A millennium-old Promellian battlecruiser. Its commander was Galek Dar. (See "Booby Trap")

COLONY SHIP: A Starfleet transport vessel carrying a large number of personnel shuttles.

CONSTANTINOPLE, U.S.S.: A Starfleet liner with 2012 colonists aboard. The ship becomes disabled and its crew begins to suffer from hypoxia until the *Enterprise* comes to its assistance. (See "The Schizoid Man")

CONSTELLATION, U.S.S.: Commander Decker's ship, the crew of which is killed by the doomsday machine from beyond our galaxy. (See "The Doomsday Machine")

COPERNICUS: An *Enterprise* shuttlecraft; like the *Galileo*, named after a famous Earth astronomer.

CORVALLEN FREIGHTER: The ship which is supposed to accept the "cargo" of Romulan defectors from the *Kahzara*. When Troi detects treachery, N'Vek destroys the Corvallen ship. (See "Face Of The Enemy")

D'DARIDEX CLASS: A type of Romulan warbird.

DEFIANT, U.S.S.: The starship trapped between dimensions in the Tholian region of space; James Kirk becomes trapped on it as it drifts between universes. Its crew is dead, driven mad by the new dimension; Kirk risks the same trouble if he isn't rescued soon enough. (See "The Tholian Web")

DEVO: A Ferengi ship; the *Enterprise* meets it near Zendi Sabu. (See "The Last Outpost")

DRAKE, U.S.S.: A Federation starship which is lost when it visits the planet Minos, an automated world which demonstrates deadly weapons on any who come near. Its captain, Paul Rice, was a friend of Will Riker. (See "The Arsenal Of Freedom")

DY-500: Class of 21st Century spacecraft, like Khan's *Botany Bay*. (See "Space Seed")

EL-BAZ: Shuttlepod five of the *Enterprise*.

ENTERPRISE, U.S.S.: Federation starship NCC-1701, most famous for its exploits under the command of James T. Kirk. Previous Captains were Robert April and Christopher Pike. A Constellation class vessel, this *Enterprise* — the latest in a line stretching back to early American nautical history — carries a crew of over four hundred people of mixed racial, sexual and planetary background. This *Enterprise,* like those to follow it, is essentially the lead ship in Starfleet, the most advanced space vessel currently in commission. Two replicas have been encountered: **I.S.S. Enterprise,** the equivalent vessel in the alternate mirror universe, and another **Enterprise**, a mock-up created by the people of Gideon to fool Kirk into thinking that his crew has vanished.

ENTERPRISE-C, U.S.S. (NCC-1701-C): Ambassador class starship which sacrifices itself to save the Klingon outpost on Narendra Three. (See "Yesterday's Enterprise")

ENTERPRISE-D, U.S.S. (NCC-1701-D): The Federation flagship under the command of Jean-Luc Picard. The first Galaxy class starship. Contains 42 decks and 1,000 people. The fifth Starfleet vessel to bear the name, serial number NCC-1701-D. Its first Captain is Jean-Luc Picard, whose command has been fairly continuous over a seven-year period. Like the *Enterprise* commanded by James Kirk in the previous century, this *Enterprise* is on a mission of exploration.

ERSTWHILE, S.S.: A class 9 vessel and interplanetary cargo freighter under the command of Captain Thaddiun Okona. (See "The Outrageous Okona")

ESSEX, U.S.S.: A starship lost years before on the unexplored M class moon of Mabu Six. (See "Power Play")

EXCALIBUR, U.S.S.: The Federation ship whose crew is utterly destroyed by the M-5 computer when it controls the *Enterprise* in a war game. The computer failed to understand that it was only a practice exercise. (See "The Ultimate Computer")

EXCELSIOR: The latest wave in starship technology featuring trans-warp drive. (See "Star Trek III: The Search For Spock", "Star Trek VI: The Undiscovered Country")

EXETER, U.S.S.: The Starfleet vessel whose crew succumbs to a virus from the planet Omega IV. Only the *Exeter*'s captain, Captain Tracey, survives, on the planet rather than on his ship. (See "Omega Glory")

FARRAGUT, U.S.S.: The ship on which James Kirk, then a young lieutenant, did his first tour of duty in space. Half the crew died near Tycho IV after an attack by a vampiric cloud. Kirk has always been haunted by his hesitation at the phaser controls that day, although phasers would have been useless anyway. (See "Obsession")

FEARLESS, U.S.S.: The scientist Kosinski and his silent assistant (The Traveler) are brought to the *Enterprise* by this vessel. (See "Where No One Has Gone Before")

FESARIUS: Balok's gigantic, and, it turns out, somewhat oversized space ship. (See "The Corbomite Maneuver")

GAGE, U.S.S.: A Starfleet vessel which is part of the fleet deployed against the Borg at the battle of Wolf

359. (See "Emissary")

GALILEO: A shuttlecraft on board the *Enterprise*, craft number NCC-1701/7. The original was destroyed in the crash on Taurus II, but its replacement managed to put in quite a bit of duty. (See "The Galileo Seven")

GANDHI, U.S.S.: The Starfleet vessel which Thomas Riker is posted to following his rescue from the world of Nervala Four. (See "Second Chances")

GANGES: The name of one of the runabouts used on Deep Space Nine. (See "Past Prologue")

GETTYSBURG, U.S.S: The ship commanded by Admiral Jameson earlier in his career. (See "Too Short A Season")

GODDARD, U.S.S.: The starship which the *Enterprise* was on its way to rendezvous with in "The Vengeance Factor."

GRISSOM, U.S.S.: The 23rd Century incarnation of this vessel was under the command of Captain J. T. Esteban. The Grissom is sent to survey the Genesis planet, where it is destroyed by a Klingon vessel whose commander is determined to steal the secret of the Genesis Device for himself. (See "Star Trek III: The Search For Spock")

GRISSOM, U.S.S.: Federation starship referred to in the episode "The Most Toys".

HARKONA: A Romulan ship which attacks the *Enterprise* until it falls victim to the Iconian computer virus. (See "Contagion")

HATHAWAY, U.S.S.: For 80 years this old Constellation class vessel lay in orbit around Braslota Three as a derelict. Riker is put in temporary command of the starship as part of some wargames, but the simulations turn real when he is attacked by the Ferengi ship the *Krik'ta*. (See "Peak Performance")

HOOD, U.S.S.: One of the Starfleet ships that takes part in the wargames with the M-5 computer. (See "The Ultimate Computer")

HOOD, U.S.S.: An Excelsior class Federation starship which Will Riker served on before his transfer to the *Enterprise*. On the *Hood*, Riker was the First Officer under Captain Robert DeSoto. The *Hood* brings the Crushers and LaForge to Farpoint as well. (See "Encounter At Farpoint")

HORATIO, U.S.S.: Captain Walker Keel's ship, which is blown up in Sector 63 after Keel clues Picard in to a conspiracy in Starfleet Command. (See "Conspiracy")

HORIZON, U.S.S.: The ship that left the book *Chicago Mobs of the Twenties* on the planet Iotia, a mistake that produced the strange culture encountered by Kirk and crew a century later. (See "A Piece Of The Action")

HUSNOCK STARSHIP: A starship five times the mass of the *Enterprise* which fires jacketed streams of positrons and antiprotons and could pulverize a planet. Since the Husnock no longer exist as a race, neither do their starships. (See "The Survivors")

INTREPID, U.S.S.: A Vulcan-manned Starfleet vessel whose crew of four hundred is killed by the giant space amoeba. Spock is able to sense their deaths across great reaches of space. (See "The Immunity Syndrome")

INTREPID, U.S.S.: The first Federation ship to arrive on the scene following the Khitomer Massacre; it rescued the survivors Kahlest and Worf. (See "Sins Of The Fathers")

JENOLAN: A space shuttle which disappeared in the 23rd Century and which is found in the 24th Century crashed in the exterior of a Dyson Sphere. (See "Relics")

JOVIS: The private ship of the Zibalian trader Kivas Fajo. (See "The Most Toys")

KAHZARA: A Romulan warbird infiltrated by sup-

porters of the reunification movement. (See "Face Of The Enemy")

KARTAG: A Klingon vessel, the one which pursues the renegade Klingons who stole the *Batris*. (See "Heart of Glory")

KLINGON BIRD OF PREY: The type of Klingon starship used late in Kirk's command of the *Enterprise* and which is still used in the 24th Century.

KOBAYASKI MARU: The name of a starship in distress in a Starfleet battle simulation. A third class neutronic fuel carrier, crew of 81 with 300 passengers. The test also bears this ship's name as it is considered a no-win situation. Responding to the distress call from the vessel leads the cadets into a trap in which everything they try fails. James T. Kirk is the only cadet who ever beat the simulation. (See "Star Trek II: The Wrath Of Khan")

KRAYTON: The Ferengi starship under the command of Tog (see "Menage A Troi").

KRIK'TA: The Ferengi ship commanded by Daimon Bractor which attacks the *Enterprise* and the *Hathaway* while they are engaged in wargames. (See "Peak Performance")

K'VORT-CLASS BATTLECRUISER: A type of Klingon bird of prey seen in "Yesterday's Enterprise."

KYUSHU, U.S.S.: A Starfleet vessel which is part of the fleet deployed against the Borg at the battle of Wolf 359. (See "Emissary")

LALLO, S.S.: A commercial vessel affected by the time distortion generated by Mannheim's experiments. (See "We'll Always Have Paris")

LALO, U.S.S.: A Federation freighter which is between Zeta Alpha Two and Sentinel Minor Four when it is attacked by the Borg. (See "The Best Of Both Worlds")

LANTREE, U.S.S.: This is a class 6 supply ship under the command of Captain L. Iso Tolaka. This Federation starship is found by the *Enterprise* with its entire crew dead of natural causes — if old age striking the entire crew at once can be called natural. (See "Unnatural Selection")

LEXINGTON, U.S.S.: Another ship involved in the wargames against the *Enterprise* while it was under the command of the M-5 computer, it sustained heavy casualties thanks to the computer's poor understanding of the situation: it believed that the wargames were a real battle situation. (See "The Ultimate Computer")

MAGELLAN: This vessel traveled to Andromeda and made the first close-range observation of a supernova. (See "Star Trek III: The Search For Spock")

MARIPOSA, S.S: This Earth vessel, under the command of Captain Walter Granger, crashes on a planet in the Ficus System. The five survivors establish a scientific colony there by cloning themselves. (See "Up The Long Ladder")

MELBOURNE, U.S.S.: Another ship docked at Starbase 74. (See "11001001") A Starfleet vessel which is part of the fleet deployed against the Borg at the battle of Wolf 359. (See "Emissary") In "The Best of Both Worlds", Riker is offered command of this starship.

MERRIMAC, U.S.S.: This vessel arrives at Legara Four to return Sarek, his wife Perrin and the rest of their party to Vulcan. (See "Sarek")

MONDOR: A Pakled vessel under the command of Grebnedlog. (See "The Samaritan Snare")

MONITOR, U.S.S.: Referred to in "The Defector" as a Federation ship which is on its way to the Neutral Zone to help Picard, but which will arrive too late to provide immediate assistance.

NCC-1701: Official serial number for the *U.S.S. Enterprise.*

NOMAD: An early 21st Century space probe that collided with an alien space probe, the *Tan Ru.* After this it achieves sentience, but its mission — to find

life — and that of the *Tan Ru* — to sterilize biological samples — became confused, and it now kills all life forms, including the billions of people in the Malurian system. It believes that James Kirk is its creator, Jackson Roykirk, which gives Kirk the opening he needs to get Nomad to destroy itself. (See "The Changeling")

NORKOVA: A starship transporting deuridium to the Kobliad. (See "The Passenger")

ODIN, U.S.S.: A derelict freighter, found by the *Enterprise* on Asphia, which had been reported lost seven years earlier. Three escape pods had been jettisoned, leading to the belief that there may have been survivors. Indeed its captain, Ramsey, and several crew members survived, and escaped to Angel One in the pods. (See "Angel One")

ONIZUKA: Another *Enterprise* shuttlepod, this one named after Ellison Onizuka, one of the crew members of the space shuttle Challenger.

OTHER: *Nomad*'s name for the *Tan Ru*, the alien space probe with which *Nomad* merged. (See "The Changeling")

PAGH: The Klingon vessel which Riker was temporarily assigned to. A Bird-of-Prey class Imperial Klingon ship under the command of Captain Kargan. (See "A Matter Of Honor")

PHOENIX, U.S.S.: The Federation starship commanded by Ben Maxwell which breaks the treaty with the Cardassians and begins attacking Cardassian ships because he believes that they are secretly rearming for war. (See "The Wounded")

PI: The code name employed by a Romulan scout vessel which crashes in the Galorndon Core. (See "The Enemy")

PIKE: An *Enterprise* shuttle named after former *Enterprise* captain Christopher Pike. The shuttlepod *Pike* explodes in "The Most Toys."

POTEMKIN, U.S.S.: One of the Starfleet vessels involved in the ill-fated war games simulation with the *Enterprise* under the command of the M-5 computer. (See "The Ultimate Computer")

POTEMKIN, U.S.S.: This ship was a former posting of Will Riker when he was a lieutenant. He once saved the vessel by hiding it from an opponent's sensors by using a planet's magnetic poles. (See "Peak Performance")

PR'ANG: When the *Enterprise* is en route to meet the *T'Ong,* the Klingon ship the *Pr'ang* is following at a careful distance. (See "The Emissary")

PROBE: The gigantic mechanism which enters our solar system in the 23rd Century and attempts to make contact with ceacean life forms on Earth — none of which still exists then. Only by going back to the 20th Century and bringing two whales back to the future to begin the repopulation of the species is Earth saved from the wrath of the alien device. (See "Star Trek IV: The Voyage Home")

REKLAR: A Cardassian ship under the command of Gul Lemec. (See "Chain Of Command")

RELIANT, U.S.S.: The vessel under command of Captain Clark Terrell. It is hijacked by Khan Noonian Singh and used to attack the *Enterprise*. (See "Star Trek II: The Wrath Of Khan")

RENEGADE, U.S.S.: A Starfleet vessel whose captain, Tryla Scott, was infested with the alien parasites. (See "Conspiracy")

REPUBLIC, U.S.S.: A Starfleet vessel (NCC-1373). James Kirk served on this ship as an ensign. Kirk's friend Finney also served on the *Republic*. Kirk was obliged to report Finney for an error, which led to Finney being held back. This was the birth of Finney's secret hatred of Kirk, which ultimately led him to fake his own death in a mad attempt to destroy Kirk's career. This scheme didn't work — but it came very close. (See "Court Martial")

REPULSE, U.S.S.: An Excelsior class starship, under the command of Captain Taggart, which transfers Dr. Katherine Pulaski to the *Enterprise*. Dr. Pulaski's transporter records are later retrieved from there. (See

"The Child" and "Unnatural Selection")

RIO GRANDE: The name of one of the runabouts used on Deep Space Nine. In "Battle Lines" O'Brien and Dax use this shuttle to search for the Yangtze Kiang when it becomes overdue.

ROMULAN SCOUT SHIP: A small vessel seen in "The Enemy" and "The Defector".

ROMULAN WARBIRD: Also called Romulan B-Type warbirds. The large warships used by the Romulan empire.

SAKHAROV: The name of *Enterprise* shuttle number two. Named after the 20th Century scientist and Russian dissident Andrei Sakharov.

SANCTION: One of the last Ornaran freighters, destroyed due to equipment malfunction. It carried a shipment of Felicium, which Beverly Crusher discovers to be an addictive narcotic with no medical benefits. (See "Symbiosis")

SARATOGA, U.S.S.: The Federation vessel whose first officer was Benjamin Sisko at the time of the battle with the Borg at Wolf 359. (See "Emissary")

SARATOGA, U.S.S.: A Reliant class starship which was the first Federation vessel to be impacted upon by the Probe. (See "Star Trek IV: The Voyage Home")

SHUTTLECRAFT: Small craft with impulse power only, these can generally carry up to seven passengers comfortably. For use in planetary systems only, highly unsuited to deep space transportation.

SHUTTLE 10: From the *U.S.S. Repulse*. Dr. Katherine Pulaski is transferred from the *Repulse* to the *Enterprise* on this shuttle. (See "The Child")

SHUTTLE 13: This shuttlecraft crashes on Vagra Two with a pilot and one passenger, Deanna Troi. They were rescued but the shuttle was wrecked. (See "Skin Of Evil")

SOYUZ CLASS: A type of Federation starship used in the 23rd Century. The *U.S.S. Bozeman* is such a vessel. (See "Cause And Effect")

STARGAZER, U.S.S.: The vessel Jean-Luc Picard commanded for 22 years prior to his command of the *Enterprise*. Lost in a battle with the Ferengi (the Battle of Maxia), it led to Picard's court martial. He was cleared. Years later, a Ferengi captain returned the ship to Picard as part of his plan to get vengeance for his son's death at Maxia. (See "The Battle" and "The Measure Of A Man")

STRELEB SHIP: A class 7 vessel under the command of Kushell. (See "The Outrageous Okona")

SUTHERLAND, U.S.S.: A Federation starship which Data is assigned to command when a Tachyon Grid is organized to detect Romulan ships running supplies to the Duras sisters during the war of succession for the Klingon High Council. (See "Redemption")

T'ACOG: A ship destroyed by the Klingon-commandeered *Batris*.

TAN RU: Originating from some unknown planetary culture, the *Tan Ru* was a space probe designed to seek soil samples from other worlds. When it collided with Nomad, the two probes achieved a strange synthesis of purpose. Unfortunately, the *Tan Ru's* sample sterilization program created Nomad's need to destroy biological beings that did not live up to its impossibly exacting standards. (See "The Changeling")

TERELLIAN PLAGUE SHIP: The last such ship, containing survivors of the biological war that destroyed Terella, was encountered near Haven, and is now somewhere in deep space, where Dr. Wyatt Miller is trying to cure its people — or perhaps he has already succeeded. (See "Haven")

THOMAS PAINE, U.S.S.: A Starfleet vessel under the command of Captain Rixx. (See "Conspiracy")

TOH'KHAT: A Klingon bird of prey which returns through the Bajoran wormhole a month ahead of schedule and then mysteriously explodes. They were supposedly just on a bio-survey mission to the Gamma Quadrant. (See "Dramatis Personae")

T'ONG: A D-7 class Klingon vessel under the command of K'Temoc. It was placed in cryogenic sus-

pension and the crew awakened 75 years later in the 24th Century, when the Klingons and the Federation are no longer at war. It is near the Boratis system and the *Enterprise* has to deal with this potential threat before the *T'Ong* attacks any Federation vessels. (See "The Emissary")

TRANSPORT SHIP: Similar to a shuttlecraft. (See "Manhunt")

TRIESTE, U.S.S.: The closest Federation ship to Starbase 74 when the Bynars steal the *Enterprise*, but it is not fast enough to catch up. (See "11001001")

TRIPOLI, U.S.S.: The Starfleet vessel that first found Data on Omicron Theta IV. (See "Datalore")

TSILKOVSKY, S.S.: A Federation ship which is lost when its crew goes insane under the influence of a new variant of the Psi 2000 virus; they all kill themselves or each other, leaving a real mess for the *Enterprise* Away Team that investigates. (See "The Naked Now")

VALIANT, U.S.S.: 1.) An early Federation survey ship. Two hundred years before Kirk commanded the *Enterprise*, the *Valiant* reached the galactic barrier and had problems similar to those Kirk had with Gary Mitchell — except the commander of the *Valiant* destroyed the entire ship as the resolution to his crisis. Kirk learns this from a recorder marker found in the area. (See "Where No Man Has Gone Before") 2.) Another vessel named *Valiant* was destroyed when it wandered into the "war" between Vendikar and Eminiar VII, fifty years before the *Enterprise* arrived there. (See "A Taste Of Armageddon")

VICO: A disabled exploratory vessel found drifting in a strange black cluster by the *Enterprise*. The Away Team finds everyone aboard the *Vico* is dead except for a young boy, Timothy, who they beam back with them after Data frees the child from debris. (See "Hero Worship")

VICTORY, U.S.S.: A Constellation class starship named for an ancient Earth sailing vessel. The starship which Geordi LaForge was previously posted to. During an Away Team mission while with that vessel, Geordi and his crewmates were exposed to some strange aliens which infect other beings in order to reproduce. (See "Identity Crisis")

VORTIS: A Klingon vessel contacted by Worf in "The Defector."

WELLINGTON, U.S.S.: The docked vessel that the Bynars were working on before they tried to steal the *Enterprise*. (See "11001001")

YAMATO, U.S.S.: A Federation vessel which explodes, killing all one thousand personnel aboard. The ship's logs reveal that the captain believed he had discovered the planet of Iconia, home of a race that could travel through space without use of vessels. A Galaxy class vessel, NCC-1305-E, under the command of Captain Donald Varley. (See "Contagion")

YANGTZE KIANG: The name of one of the runabouts used on Deep Space Nine. (See "Past Prologue")

YONADA: An atomic-powered space ship disguised as an asteroid. Those who live on it do not realize that they are on a space vessel, but think it is their world. Astray from its original course, *Yonada* threatens the planet of Daran V. (See "For The World Is Hollow And I Have Touched The Sky")

YORKTOWN, U.S.S.: Kirk delays an important rendezvous with this vessel in order to pursue the deadly vampiric cloud that obsesses him. (See "Obsession")

YOSEMITE, U.S.S.: When this vessel is reported lost, the *Enterprise* is dispatched to the Igo sector to search for it. (See "Realm Of Fear")

ZALKONIAN SHIP: Seen in "Transfigurations", it is the equal of the *Enterprise*.

ZAPATA, U.S.S.: In "Menage A Troi", this Starfleet vessel is assigned to rendezvous with the *Enterprise*.

ZHUKOV, U.S.S.: Lieutenant Barclay's previous posting; the ship was commanded by Captain Gleason.

ARTIFACTS, PLANTS, PLAGUES, PHRASES, PROCEDURES, SUBSTANCES, BELIEFS, DESIGNATIONS & DEVICES

ACCESS TUBE: The only — and highly dangerous — access to the anti-matter/matter chamber.

ACETON ASSIMILATORS: These devices feed on power, convert it into radiation and broadcast it at its original source. These booby traps were created a millennium ago by the Menthars. A Promellian ship, the *Cleponji*, fell victim to it a thousand years ago and that derelict ship lured the *Enterprise* into the same trap. (See "Booby Trap")

ACETYLOCHOLINE TEST: One of the tests Spock performs on the giant space amoeba. (See "The Immunity Syndrome")

ACTS OF CUMBERLAND: The precedent in law which Starfleet uses to attempt to prove that Data is in fact Starfleet property. (See "The Measure Of A Man")

ADVANCED GENETICS: This course is being taken by Wesley Crusher and a study of nanites is the final project in the course. But the nanites get away from him. (See "Evolution")

AFT STATION: A station at the rear, or aft, end of a starship. Riker is transported to the aft station of the *U.S.S. Yamato*. (See "Where Silence Has Lease")

AGE OF ASCENSION: An important Klingon ritual. (See "The Icarus Factor")

AGE OF INCLUSION: An important Klingon rite of passage; Worf seems to have missed his thanks to the massacre at Khitomer and his subsequent adoption by humans on Gault. (See "Heart Of Glory")

AGE OF THE RESOLUTION: On Kaelon-2 this is when a person reaches the age of 60 and must commit ritual suicide. (See "Half A Life")

AGONIZER: In "Mirror, Mirror" a pain-inducing instrument for low-level punishment. Standard crew issue in that brutal alternative universe. The Klingons have a similar device in the "real" universe.

AGONY BOOTH: Yet another charming punishment from "Mirror, Mirror", which can be used for capital punishment. The mirror-world Chekov gets a taste of it when he tries to kill Kirk.

AHN-WOON: A Vulcan weapon of ancient design,

with which Spock strangles Kirk in "Amok Time" — a long piece of leather with grips at each end.

AIRLOCKS: Standard spacefaring equipment, a safety buffer between the ship's inner atmosphere and the vacuum of space.

ALAYNAN SINGERSTONE: The gift Data gives to the Dreman girl Sarjenka. It is a stone which emits a different tone, or "song", for each person who holds it. (See "Pen Pals")

ALBENI MEDITATION CRYSTAL: Beata gives Riker one of these as gift. (See "Angel One")

ALDABREN EXCHANGE: A chess move employed by Riker against Nibor during a game in Ten Forward. (See "Menage A Troi")

ALDEBARAN SERPENT: A fearsome beast, mythical or real; Q takes the form of one when he disturbs the *Enterprise* the second time around. (See "Hide and Q")

ALERT B-2: Order to seal off the main areas of the Enterprise.

ALGOLIAN CEREMONIAL RHYTHMS: During the closing ceremonies of the Trade Agreements Conference, these chimes are played. Later they are duplicated on subspace static in order to signal the *Enterprise*. (See "Menage A Troi")

ALTARIAN CONFERENCE: Picard first met Rixx at this conference, some years before the events surrounding the alien conspiracy. (See "Conspiracy")

ANASTAZINE: An anti-personnel gas. Data floods the cargo bays with this gas at 70 parts per million in order to put Danar to sleep. (See "The Hunted")

ANBO-JYUTSO: In the 24th Century this system is described as the "ultimate evolution of martial arts". On deck 12 the gymnasium of the *Enterprise* includes an anbo-jyutsu ring; it is a sport played with long sticks between two players inside a large circle. (See "The Icarus Factor")

ANCHILLES FEVER: An epidemic disease that breaks out on Styris Four; the *Enterprise* has to go to Ligon II for the cure. (See "Code Of Honor")

ANDONESIAN ENCEPHALITIS: A disease which is not contagious, but Anya is so concerned about the safety of the Dauphin that she attempts to kill Hennessy, the crewman who has the disease. (See "The Dauphin")

ANDONIAN TEA: The alien-infested conspirators offer Picard this tea as part of their hospitality before their true nature is revealed; Picard prefers Earl Grey anyway. (See "Conspiracy")

ANDROID: An artificial being designed to resemble a human being. While humanity has encountered humanoid androids created by other races in the past, Data is the creation of Dr. Noonian Soong, perhaps the first human since Flint to create successfully a fully functional android (see "Datalore"). To date, only two creations of Soong have been encountered, the other being Lore (see "Datalore", "Brothers", "Descent" and "Inheritance"). The rights of androids still generate controversy (see "The Measure Of A Man" and "The Offspring"), but the Federation seems inclined to treat them like any other sentient beings.

ANGOSIAN ALTERATION: This is the process the Angosians used to create their super soldiers. It involves employing such chemicals as tricienidil, cryptobiolin, macrospentol and other substances combined with additional biochemical conditioning and psychological manipulation. (See "The Hunted")

ANIMATION CONTROL: The technique that allows McCoy to keep Spock's body going until Kirk can locate the Vulcan's missing brain. (See "Spock's Brain")

ANTAREAN BRANDY: The blue drink so often seen on board the *Enterprise*.

ANTAREAN GLOW-WATER: One of the many items for sale from Cyrano Jones. (See "The Trouble With Tribbles")

ANTHROPOLOGICAL STATION: These exist on some primitive worlds so that a small anthropological field team can observe the inhabitants of the planet. They are not allowed to interact with the inhabitants or make them aware of the field team in any way as this would violate the Prime Directive. When there is an accident at the station on Mintaka Three, the society there is put in danger of serious sociological contamination. (See "Who Watches The Watchers?")

ANTIGRAVITY TEST UNIT: Useful in getting rid of the Lights of Zetar.

ANTIGRAVS: As the name suggests, small anti-gravity units.

ANTI-MATTER: A crucial component in the warp drive of the *Enterprise* and similarly-outfitted Starfleet vessels: combined with positive matter (a tricky procedure) it helps create the warp fields that make faster-than-light travel possible. When wargames between the *Enterprise* and the *Hathaway* get complicated by alien intervention, Wesley's expertise (and his science project) gives LaForge the anti-matter needed to go to warp speed and save the *Hathaway*. (See "Peak Performance")

ANTI-MATTER CONVERTER: A device which can be used in conjunction with Bi-Dyttrium to create a powerful explosive device. (See "Past Prologue")

ANTI-MATTER INPUT VALVES: Important controls for the deadly anti-matter in the warp engines.

ANTI-MATTER MINES: Weapons distributed by Riker via an *Enterprise* shuttle which cause the surrender of the Cardassian battle fleet. (See "Chain Of Command")

A & P PARISIAN GRAND PREMIER: Lore proposed a toast to Data using this champagne; it was drugged and incapacitated Data, enabling Lore to impersonate him. (See "Datalore")

ARCH: The combined exit/control panel for the holodeck. (See "The Big Goodbye", "Elementary, Dear Data", and others) The arch can be summoned by vocal commands directed at the ship's computer.

ARCTIRUAN FIZZ: A drink which contains pleasure-enhancing qualities. (See "Menage A Troi")

AREA 39: The *Enterprise's* recreational area.

A-7: Spock's rating as a computer specialist.

ATAVACHRON: A time travel device used by the Sarpeids to escape into their past before their planet is destroyed by their sun's nova explosion. More than a travel device, it also helps the mind and body adjust to their new temporal location. (See "All Our Yesterdays")

ATLANTA BRAVES: Sonny Clemons was a fan of this 20th Century baseball team, just one more thing he won't find on Earth in the 24th Century. (See "The

Neutral Zone")

AUXILIARY CONTROL CENTER: A backup bridge on board Starfleet vessels. The ACC for the *Enterprise* is on the eighth deck.

AWAY TEAM: The new designation for a Landing Party begun in "The Next Generation".

BARYON PARTICLES: Particles which collect on a spacecraft over time and which must be neutralized every few years to prevent baryon contamination. The *Enterprise-D* undergoes a baryon sweep to clear them, a process which requires that all personnel be evacuated from the starship. (See "Starship Mine")

BARYON SWEEP: The process by which baryon particle buildup is removed from a starship. All personnel must be evacuated from a vessel undergoing this sweep as the process is deadly to all life forms. (See "Starship Mine")

BASOTILE: A rare and priceless artifact, the first one was created centuries ago. One is owned by Fajo. (See "The Most Toys")

BAT'LETH SWORD: A weapon forged by the legendary Klingon warrior Kahless. The tale of how the bat'leth sword was made is known only to the High Clerics of Boreth. (See "Rightful Heir")

BATTLE BRIDGE: This is used to control the lower portion of the starship whenever the *Enterprise* undergoes a saucer separation. It is located on deck eight.

BATTLE OF MAXIA: The site of the first encounter between a Federation ship and the Ferengi. A famous battle between Picard's *Stargazer* and an unknown alien vessel, later discovered to be a Ferengi ship. Although Picard got the better of his opponent, he and his crew had to abandon their damaged ship. (See "The Battle")

BENDII SYNDROME: The Vulcan version of Alzheimer's disease, it is nonetheless rare and only afflicts some Vulcans over the age of two hundred. The disease leads to a complete loss of emotional control and is so rare that Sarek is the first Vulcan to be afflicted with it in generations. (See "Sarek")

BENJISIDRINE: The medicine Sarek must take for his vascular problems. (See "Journey To Babel")

BERTHOLD RAYS: Deadly radiation that destroys human cells. (See "This Side Of Paradise")

BESSEL FUNCTIONS: One of the apparently meaningless mathematical/scientific processes that Koszinski tries out on the *Enterprise*. (See "Where No One Has Gone Before")

BETA 5 COMPUTER: Gary Seven's super-computer, conveniently located in his Manhattan apartment. (See "Assignment: Earth")

BI-DYTTRIUM: A very powerful energy source. When used in conjunction with an anti-matter converter, it becomes an explosive device of incredible power. (See "Past Prologue")

BIO-BEDS: Standard life-support and medical monitoring beds in sickbay. (See "Contagion")

BIOFILTER: A standard component of the transporter system, the biofilter prevents alien diseases and microscopic life forms from beaming up in humanoids by using the original trace of the person to filter out the unwanted organisms. (See "Shades of Gray")

BIOPLAST SHEETING: This is the substance which forms Data's exterior shell. (See "The Most Toys")

BLUEJAY 4: The 20th Century code name for the American jet intercepted by the *Enterprise* in the 20th Century. (See "Tomorrow Is Yesterday")

BONDING GIFTS: The ceremonial wedding gifts that the Millers bring for Deannna Troi. (See "Haven")

BORGIA PLANT: When the Salt Vampire kills Darnell, it puts this extremely toxic plant in his hands to give his death the appearance of a poisoning. (See "The Man Trap")

BOTANICAL GARDENS: An area on the Enterprise where a variety of plant life is grown in a controlled environment. (See "Imaginary Friend")

BRAIN ROOM: A computer chamber located on the long-dead world of the Kalandans, where the deadly image of the beautiful Losira is generated. (See "That Which Survives")

BRIDGE: Command center of the *Enterprise,* dominated by a large viewscreen. This is where much of the action takes place.

BRIDGE MONITOR SCREEN: A screen in the transporter room that can monitor the bridge, if need be.

BUFFERS: These are information processors that the Bynars wear on their waists. (See "11001001")

C-335 CARGO MANAGEMENT UNIT: A new addition to standard cargo processing programs. (See "The Battle")

CABINET: The central government of the evil mirror universe. (See "Mirror, Mirror")

CAPTAIN'S WOMAN: Official mistress of the captain on board ships in the evil mirror universe. Kirk-Two's woman was Marlena-Two. (See "Mirror, Mirror")

CARDIOSTIMULATOR: One of McCoy's medical devices, it can restart heart activity as needed.

CARGO BAYS: The section of the *Enterprise* where cargo is unloaded and stored.

CARREL: The part of the Sarpeid library where time travelers are made ready for their trip. (See "All Our Yesterdays")

CELEBIUM: A deadly radiation of the planet Camus II, used by Dr. Janice Lester to kill off her fellow archeologists. (See "Turnabout Intruder")

CEREBRAN YOUTH DRUG: A drug which, if administered properly over a long period of time, can reverse aging in humanoids; Jameson tries to hurry the process, which turns out to be a very bad idea. (See "Too Short A Season")

CETACEAN OPS: "Cetacean" pertains to an order (Cetacea) of marine animals consisting of whales, dolphins, porpoises, narwhals, etc., having a large head, a fishlike hairless body and paddlelike forelimbs. What this consists of on the *Enterprise-D* is uncertain, except that in "Yesterday's Enterprise" Dr. Joshua Kim is heard being ordered to go to Cetacean

ARTIFACTS, PLANTS, PLAGUES...

Ops on the loudspeaker, so one does exist, at least in the altered timeline.

CHA'DLCH: When a Klingon is accused of something, a defender is appointed to fight for him. This defender is called the cha'Dlch. (See "Sins Of The Fathers")

CHALICE OF RIXX: Something which Lwaxana Troi was awarded, although she describes it as being just "an old clay pot with mold growing inside it." (See "Menage A Troi")

CHAMBER OF THE AGES: The egg-chamber of the Hortas on Janus VI; Spock discovers this name when he melds with the Horta. (See "Devil In The Dark")

CHAMELEON ROSE: A mood-sensitive flower that alters its hue in response to its holder's feelings. Deanna receives one from Wyatt Miller when they first meet. (See "Haven")

CHANDRA: One of the moves made in the Wadi game Chula. (See "Move Alone Home")

CHARNOCK'S COMEDY CABARET: The holodeck establishment where Data tests his ill-fated attempt to become a comedian. (See "The Outrageous Okona")

CHART 14A: The space chart which the sentient space probe *Nomad* recognizes as showing its point of origin: Earth. (See "The Changeling")

CHECH'TLUTH: An alcoholic beverage of Klingon origin. (See "Up The Long Ladder")

CHICAGO MOBS OF THE TWENTIES: A 1992 Terran book which served as the basis for the culture of Iotia. (See "A Piece Of The Action")

CHIEF OFFICER, COMMISSION OF POLITICAL TRAITORS: The Cheron Bele's job description. (See "Let That Be Your Last Battlefield")

CHIME, BETAZOIDS': The Betazoids ritually sound this chime during meals in order to express thanks; Deanna seems to have given up this potentially annoying habit. Lwaxana, true to form, has not. (See "Haven")

CHULA: A game the Wadi bring to Deep Space Nine and which involves using people as game pieces.

(See "Move Along Home")

CLOAKING DEVICE: The Romulans' most insidious device, capable of concealing an entire ship from view. It takes some improvement to make it sensor-resistant, as well. Even though James Kirk successfully steals such a device, the Federation apparently never adopts the use of cloaking devices. (See "Balance Of Terror") Originally developed by the Klingons, but used by Klingons and Romulans alike for purposes of stealth and strategy. Cloaked ships cannot fire their weapons, and must risk revealing themselves to do so. (See "Star Trek III: The Search For Spock", "Contagion")

COALITION: One of the warring factions on Tasha Yar's homeworld. (See "Legacy")

COCO-NO-NO: Guinan offers this exotic drink to Christy, although the contents of the drink are unknown. (See "Booby Trap")

CODE 1: Indicates impending attack on a massive scale.

CODE 2: A defunct code, already broken by the Romulans.

CODE 47: A coded transmission from Starfleet, a high-priority message intended for the captain alone. (See "Conspiracy")

CODE 710: The warning to stay away from the planet Eminiar VII. (See "A Taste Of Armageddon")

COLONY OPERATIONS: The source of the distress call received from Rana Four which summons the *Enterprise* to that world. (See "The Survivors")

COMBAT INFORMATION CENTER: Ensign Thomas is ordered by the intercom to go to this location, presumably a part of the *Enterprise* in the altered universe. (See "Yesterday's Enterprise")

COMMUNICATOR: Those palm-sized and portable communication devices that make keeping in touch with the ship and with each other easy for Starfleet personnel. As far as range goes, the transporters and the communicators cover about the same distances at optimum performance levels. Feedback from a communicator can be put to good use in extenuating circumstances.

COMPLETE KLINGON CULTURE INDEX: The

most exhaustive text on Klingon cultural practices available to the Federation; Wesley finds it useful on at least one occasion. (See "The Icarus Factor")

COMPTRONICS: Dr. Richard Daystrom's own brand of computer science. (See "The Ultimate Computer")

COMPUTER: The brains of the *Enterprise,* this amazing computer maintains all shipboard systems: navigation, life-support and climate, tactics, and science. An incredible repository of information, it carries everything there is to know about Earth history and culture, as well as a similar wealth of information on other Federation worlds, and as much as is known about enemies like the Klingons and the Romulans. The primary interface with the computer is at Spock's science station on the bridge. The computer is voice activated, and speaks in response to questions and queries. For a while, a prank played by technicians caused the computer to address James Kirk as "dear."

COMPUTER VIRUS: Any program that disrupts a computer's normal functioning. The *Enterprise* encounters an ancient computer virus from the planet Iconia. This virus was responsible for the fate of the *USS Yamato.* The *Enterprise* and a Romulan ship nearly succumb but Data discovers — quite dramatically — how to get rid of it with little ill effect. (See "Contagion")

COMSOL: Standard Starfleet abbreviation for "Commander, Solar Forces".

CON: Standard abbreviation for "console". representing the position of bridge command.

CONDITION GREEN: Communicator code: "I'm in trouble, but don't do anything— just stand by."

CONFERENCE ROOM: On the Enterprise this can be arranged to accommodate a variety of species, including a tank which can hold a Legaran.

CONTAINMENT FIELD: A force field placed around something when there is a danger of either an explosion or some sort of contamination from whatever is inside the protective field. The portion of the matter/anti-matter engines which contains the anti-matter. (See "Realm Of Fear")

CONTAINMENT UNITS: Standard safety devices for the transportation of dangerous substances.

Geordi LaForge designs a new variety of containment unit to deal with deadly plague samples. (See "The Child")

CONTROL BOOTH: Located above the shuttlebay, it can be used to control the shuttlebay and launch shuttles.

CONTROL CENTRAL: Under the control of Norman the android, this computer maintains all functions of Mudd's planet. (See "I, Mudd")

CONTROL COILS: The component of the Ornaran ships that fails; Picard makes two, but realizes that helping them continue trade with Brekka would be a disaster, and refuses to hand them over. (See "Symbiosis")

CONTROLLER: Another name for the brain generally in the use and possession of Spock, used by the Eymorgs when they "borrow" that organ to keep their central computer on line. Returned to Spock in reasonably good condition. (See "Spock's Brain")

CONVERTER ASSEMBLY: An important piece of equipment, it converts dilithium crystals to energy to power warp engines and weapons systems.

CORBOMITE: A fictional substance, devised by James Kirk in a fit of inspiration when confronted by Balok. It worked pretty well on the Romulans, too. If corbomite was a real component of the *Enterprise* hull, it would deflect any assault back on the attacker, destroying the *Enterprise* and the attacker all at once. This is enough to give pause to anyone who doesn't know better. (See "The Corbomite Maneuver")

CORDRAZINE: The drug that drives Leonard McCoy out of his mind and leads him to leap through the time portal to the 1930s. That was the result of an extreme overdose; in small, measured amounts it is a useful stimulant, and is used as such in other episodes. (See "City On The Edge Of Forever")

CORRELLIUM FEVER: When an epidemic of this disease breaks out on Nahmi Four, the Mikulaks donate tissue which aids in curing it. (See "Hollow Pursuits")

CORTICAL STIMULATOR: When Worf goes into cardiac arrest, this is used to attempt to get his heart beating again. (See "Ethics")

CRIMSON FORCE FIELD: The deadly weapon

which frightens the Pakleds into giving their prisoner Geordi back to the *Enterprise*; they don't know that it is only a visually spectacular but harmless discharge of hydrogen, passed off as a weapon by Riker. (See "Samaritan Snare")

CRYONETRIUM: This substance in its gaseous form can be used to lower drastically the temperature to minus 200 degrees Celsius and make an invidium contamination inert. (See "Hollow Pursuits")

CUSTODIAN: The name of a computer used by the Aldeans. The ancestors of the Aldeans built this computer, which shields their planet with a cloaking shield, defends the planet and acts as a transporter. (See "When The Bough Breaks")

CYBERNETICS CONFERENCE: This influenced Data to create Lal because he attended a conference where a submicron transfer technology was introduced. Data discovered that this new transfer technology could be used to create a complex series of neural net pathways. Thus he learned a way to advance Dr. Soong's own discoveries. (See "The Offspring")

CYALODIN: A deadly poison that leaves a blue-spotted corpse, used by several of Gorgan's adult victims. (See "And The Children Shall Lead")

CYCLING STATION: One component of a starship drive.

DABO WHEEL: A game in Quark's gambling den. (See "Move Along Home")

DAMAGE CONTROL TEAM ALPHA: In the altered timeline they are ordered to report to the engineering level. (See "Yesterday's Enterprise")

DARK MATTER: The preponderance of this in space can cause gaps in normal space. When a ship encounters one of these regions of dark matter, portions of the ship can fade out and cause explosive decompression. (See "In Theory")

"DARMOK AT TANAGRA, WHEN THE WALLS FELL.": Through cross-referencing the *Enterprise* personnel determine that Darmok was a warrior leader and Tanagra an island. This phrase is one of the metaphors used by the Children of Tama to communicate. (See "Darmok")

DARNAY'S DISEASE: A deadly degenerative disease that Ira Graves dies from. (See "The Schizoid Man")

DEACTION SHIFT: Dropping out of warp speed due to rapid de-acceleration.

DECK TWO: High security living area, where prisoners are kept.

DECONTAMINATION FIELD: When this is increased by Data to combat the kroniton particles he detected, it also enables him to detect the presence of Geordi and Ensign Ro. (See "The Next Phase")

DEFLECTORS: An array of force fields surrounding Federation ships like the *Enterprise;* other cultures (Romulan, Klingon, etc.) have variations of the same thing. While deflectors are up, transporters are useless. Controlled by the ship's computer, the deflectors keep objects from damaging the ship; maximum deflection usually comes into play in severe crises, such as enemy attack or intense radiation. They cannot, however, defend against photon devices (torpedoes, etc.).

DELTA RAYS: The form of radiation that crippled Christopher Pike. (See "The Menagerie")

DENASIAN: A language related to Iconian, spoken on Deneus Three, that enables a rough translation of the controls to the Iconian computer. (See "Contagion")

DENKIRS: A unit of measurement employed by Fajo to measure a finoplay. (See "The Most Toys")

DERMATIRAELIAN PLASTICINE: A drug taken by a person following cosmetic surgery in order to maintain skin resilience. (See "Duet")

DESTRUCT SEQUENCE: A sequence of vocal commands (spoken by the Captain, the First Officer and the Chief Engineer in turn) which begins the auto-destruct sequence which no one but the Captain can countermand. (See "Let That Be Your Last Battlefield", "Star Trek III: The Search For Spock")

DEURIDIUM: A valuable element, a shipment of which is passing through Deep Space Nine when Rao Vantika, a notorious killer, attempts to hijack it. (See "The Passenger")

DEWAN: Another Iconian-type language, used to correlate the translation attempt. (See "Contagion")

DIAGNOSTIC PANEL: 23rd Century medical monitors, which chart a patient's vital functions in sickbay; located over sickbay beds.

DIBURNIUM-OSMIUM: An alloy devised by the Kalandans; their outpost is obviously on a created world, since this alloy does not occur in nature, and the planet is made completely of this substance.

DICOSILIUM: This substance is delivered to Dr. Apgar at the Tanuga Research Station. (See "A Matter Of Perspective")

DI-KIRONIUM: An element that can only be found in the deadly cloud of Tycho IV, or under specially controlled laboratory conditions.

DILITHIUM: A key element in warp drive technology, dilithium crystals focus the energies produced in the matter/anti-matter chamber. Without them, warp drive is next to impossible, and so dilithium crystals are often the focus of difficulties; they are highly abundant on Troyius, however. The world of Coridian is also another vital source of the crystals, and is often subject to piracy as a result. It is a crystalline mineral with some metallic properties. There isn't much dilithium available on the *Hathaway* during wargames, so the ship at first seems limited to impulse power. (See "Peak Performance")

DILITHIUM CHAMBER: Within this area the dilithium crystals can be reoriented by adjusting their lattice structure direction. By making this alteration Geordi is able to strengthen the ship's shields. (See "Booby Trap")

DIMENSIONAL SHIFTER: A dangerous device employing a technology abandoned for being unsafe. It enables an individual to invert themselves and transport instantaneously by employing dimensional shifting. The side effects of multiple transports using this technique include warped DNA, genetic breakdown and eventual death. It was employed by the Ansata terrorist group on Rutia in order to prevent their movements from being traced by traditional means. The *Enterprise* determines a way to trace the dimensional shifters. (See "The High Ground")

DIRECTIONAL CONTROLS: As the name suggests, the controls of speed and direction.

DIRECTOR: On a Sheliak vessel, this title corresponds roughly to Captain or Commander. (See "The Ensigns Of Command")

DISKS: The medium on which Sarpeidan history is recorded; played back in the atavachron. (See "All Our Yesterdays")

DISCOMMENDATION: A Klingon ritual of disgrace which involves being banished from the Empire. Worf accepts Discommendation in order to preserve stability in the Klingon High Council and thereby in the Klingon Empire. When the time arises for him to clear his family name publicly, he takes advantage of it. (See "Sins Of The Fathers" and "Redemption")

DISPERSAL PATTERN SIERRA: A targeting pattern for photon torpedoes employed by the *Enterprise-D* during a battle engagement. (See "Yesterday's Enterprise")

DISRUPTORS:
a: A disintegration weapon, used on Eminiar VII.
b: Photon-type weapons fired by Klingon vessels.
c: Troglyte freedom fighters.
d: The types of weapons used by Romulans.

DISTORTION FIELD: The planet Nervala Four is ringed by such a field which prevents the use of transporter beams or other equipment in the atmosphere except during certain periods of field inactivity. (See "Second Chances")

DISTRESS BEACON: Standard distress broadcast device. However, the SOS transmitted from the Ficus Sector is fairly archaic and takes some figuring out, as it is a type of beacon used primarily during the 22nd Century.

DISTRIBUTION NODES: The points in a Borg vessel which distribute power equally so that it won't lose power to a specific point. (See "The Best Of Both Worlds")

DOLAMIDE: A substance used in producing weapons. During the Cardassian occupation of Bajor, Valerians provided weapons grade dolamide to the Cardassians. (See "Dramatis Personae")

DOM-JOT: A game which Jean-Luc Picard almost loses his life over when he and his friends catch some Nausicaans cheating. (See "Tapestry")

DOOMSDAY MACHINE: Also known as a

Berserker, this is an incredibly huge vessel, a super-destructive weapon from ancient, forgotten wars which still roams the galaxies feeding on entire planetary systems. Federation starships are barely a match for it: before the *Enterprise* meets it, it destroys another Federation vessel, the *Constellation*.

DRAG COEFFICIENT: The force which acts on an object to slow it down. (See "Imaginary Friend")

DREAM OF FIRE: A book highly regarded in Klingon literary circles; although not written by a Klingon, it apparently became popular once translated into their language. Typically, the Klingons — Worf among them — regard the translation as an improvement upon the original, as Worf tells Data when presenting the book as a gift. (See "The Measure Of A Man")

DUOTRONICS: Dr. Daystrom's original breakthrough in computer technology, the basis for Starfleet ships' computers. (See "The Ultimate Computer")

DURANIUM: This metallic alloy was used to line the interior of the *Enterprise* hull. It is susceptible to Krieger radiation. (See "Hollow Pursuits")

DURANIUM SHADOWS: These register on sensors as indications of photon torpedoes. (See "Emissary")

DYTALIX MINING CORPORATION: The company that runs the mines on the planets of the Mira System. (See "Conspiracy")

EARL GREY TEA: Jean-Luc Picard's personal favorite. (See "The Best Of Both Worlds")

EARTH-SATURN PROBE: The important space mission that was (or will be) led by Captain John Christopher's son Shaun Gregory Christopher. It is for this reason that James Kirk returns John Christopher to his rightful place in the 20th Century. (See "Tomorrow Is Yesterday")

E-BAND WAVELENGTH: The wavelength used by Ambassador Kell to manipulate Geordi in his plan to kill Governor Vagh and thereby create an interplanetary incident between the Federation and the Klingons. (See "The Mind's Eye")

ECHO PAPA 607: Top-of-the line weapons system once available from the people of Minos. Still operable long after the destruction of its creators, it tries to sell itself to Picard while demonstrating its lethal adaptability on the *Enterprise* and its Away Team. (See "The Arsenal Of Freedom")

EGG: The nickname which Dr. Paul Stubbs gives to the pod which the *Enterprise* will launch to study the Kavis Alpha explosion. (See "Evolution")

EICHNER RADIATION: A rare variety of radiation. The child Ian, born to Deanna Troi, produces it; although not directly harmful to humanoids, it stimulates growth of the plague virus in the hold, and Ian discorporates to save the *Enterprise*. (See "The Child")

ELECTED ONE: The female ruler of the planet Angel One. (See "Angel One")

ELECTROMAGNETIC SYNTHOMOMETER: A device utilized in the reconstruction of the android Lore. (See "Datalore")

ELEVATOR: A somewhat baffling and archaic turbolift, encountered in the simulated Royale Hotel. (See "The Royale")

ELWAY THEOREM: This is the theory behind the dimensional shifters used by the Ansata. It involves the use of an isolated field coil and was abandoned as being unworkable back in the 23rd Century. (See "The High Ground")

EMERGENCY MANUAL MONITOR: As the name suggests, controls which allow for the monitoring of active systems as the need arises.

EMERGENCY TRANSPONDER: A concealable signaling device, which Worf gives to Will Riker right before he transfers to the Klingon ship *Pagh* as an exchange officer. (See "A Matter Of Honor")

EMITTER BEAM: Used by Data to lure parasites off the Enterprise when the parasites' appetite for nitrium endangers the ship. (See "Cost Of Living")

ENERGY TRANSFER DEVICE: A nonmechanical, mentally-operated transport device on Minara II, which Spock learns to use in order to rescue McCoy from the Vians. (See "The Empath")

ENERGY VORTEX: A distortion that creates the

time loop that brings Jean-Luc Picard face-to-face with his unspeaking self from the very near future. (See "Time Squared")

ENGINEERING: The deck level on the Enterprise which contains the engineering department, Scotty's domain. All engines and related systems are operated from here, although controlled from the bridge.

ENGINEERING STATION: The station where Scotty commands engineering while he's on the bridge.

ENGRAMS: Mental patterns that have been placed in a computer. Dr. Daystrom's new theory is that human patterns will enhance a computer's capacities — but when Daystrom, not realizing his mental problems, places his own engrams in the new M-5 computer, the result is a complete disaster. (See "The Ultimate Computer")

EPIDERMAL MOLD: The mold used by Dr. Soong to shape the face and skin of his two android creations, Lore and Data. As his "sons", they were made with his face. (See "Datalore", "Brothers")

ERSALOPE WARS: A recent historical conflict which was fueled by weapons supplied to both sides by the arms dealers of the planet Minos. (See "The Arsenal Of Freedom")

EUGENICS WAR: A global war on Earth in the late 20th Century, circa 1990. Genetically "superior" humans, including Khan, took over the planet for a time until the rest of humanity overthrew them and exiled the survivors into space. (See "Space Seed")

EUROPEAN ALLIANCE: The single nation which the countries of Europe have formed on Earth by the 24th Century. (See "The Price")

EUROPEAN HEGEMONY: The 22nd Century government of Earth (or of most of it). (See "Up The Long Ladder")

EXCEIVER: A device Gary Seven uses to render the bomb in space harmless; an extension of his Beta 5 computer. (See "Assignment: Earth")

EXOCOMPS: Small maintenance robots invented by Dr. Farallon, the scientist in charge of the Tyan Particle Fountain on Tyrus 7-A. Data determines that these robots exhibit characteristics which qualify them for being considered as living, intelligent

begins. (See "Quality Of Life")

EXTRADITION: The Federation regulations regarding extradition state that if an officer is within the jurisdiction of the planet demanding extradition of a subject, then whether the extradition will take place is up to the captain of the ship the officer is on. (See "A Matter Of Perspective")

FACTOR SEVEN: The level of artificial power that Spock's sensors detect on Excalbia. This indicates that this is not really the lifeless world it appears to be. (See "The Savage Curtain")

FAL TOR PAN: The refusion of a Vulcan's katra with a physical body. (See "Star Trek III: The Search For Spock")

FEDERATION: More properly, the United Federation of Planets.

FEINBERGER: Technical name for McCoy's hand-held medical scanners and other similar devices of the 23rd Century.

FELICIUM: An addictive drug. Two centuries before the *Enterprise* stumbled across the situation, the Brekkans created Felicium to cure a disease that ravaged their world and nearby Ornara. They allowed the Ornarans to believe that they still needed the drug, in order to drain Ornaran resources for themselves; in effect, the Ornarans are all junkies and the Brekkans are all pushers. (See "Symbiosis")

FELODESINE CHIP: A suicide wafer, orange in color, which is ingested by Jarok after he learns that he was manipulated into defecting by the Romulan high command as part of a plot to attempt to trap the *Enterprise*. (See "The Defector")

FINOPLAK: One hundred denkirs of this solvent are employed by Fajo to dissolve Data's uniform. (See "The Most Toys")

FIRST ONE: The title given to the primary wife of the leader of Ligon II. (See "Code Of Honor")

FIVE CARD DRAW: A variant of the ancient Earth game known as poker. Data is beaten by the playing technique known as bluffing until he figures it out, which leads to the creation of a truly great android poker player. (See "Peak Performance")

FIZZBIN: Another one of Jim Kirk's inspired, off-the-cuff inventions. If you're inclined to believe Kirk, fizzbin is a game that originated on Beta Antares IV. Its complicated and self-contradictory rules serve to confuse Oxmyx's gangster flunkies and enables Kirk and "Spocko" to get the drop on their inept captors. (See "A Piece Of The Action")

FLU VIRUS: Still kicking round in the 24th Century, along with an ancient remedy: chicken soup. (See "The Icarus Factor")

FLUX CAPACITOR: A technical system on the *Enterprise* also called a Flow Capacitor. (The term is actually an in-joke borrowed from "Back to the Future" where a "flux capacitor" operates the Delorean time machine.)

FOOD DISK: The type of nourishment supplied to Picard, Haro, Esoqq and Tholl when they are kidnapped. Picard describes it as being shaped "like a hockey puck." (see "Allegiance")

FOOTPRINT: The magnetic resonance, or trace, left after a Borg attack. This trace is found in the blasted remains of the Jouret Four colony.

FORMATION L: Defensive formation used in dangerous situations by landing parties on a strange planet.

FRAME OF MIND: The name of the play Will Riker is performing in aboard the *Enterprise* and which becomes mixed up with the mind probe being forced on him when he is captured and imprisoned on Tilonus Four. (See "Frame Of Mind")

FUSION BOMBS: The weapons of choice in the Eminiar VII/Vendikar war — even though these weapons do not actually exist, the populace turns over its "casualties" to euthanasia centers. (See "A Taste Of Armageddon")

GAKH: A high point of Klingon cuisine. Riker learns to eat these worms in preparation for his exchange duty on the *Pagh,* but is alarmed to discover that Klingons eat them alive. He copes. (See "A Matter Of Honor")

GALACTIC CULTURAL EXCHANGE PROJECT: As the name suggests, a cultural organization. This is the group that backed the interplanetary tour of the Karidian Players. (See "Conscience Of The King")

GALACTIC ZOOLOGICAL CATALOG: The standard reference work on the many species inhabiting the worlds of known space. (See "The Dauphin")

GAMBLING: Although the financial aspects of gambling are fairly abstract by the 24th Century, games like poker survive. An *Enterprise* Away Team discovers gambling in its unadulterated form at the simulated Royale Hotel. (See "The Royale")

THE GAME: A mind control device concocted by the Kitarians in order to capture the *Enterprise*. Wesley and Data save the crew when Wesley reactivates Data and the android flashes a hand-held light whose pulses cancel out the hypnotic effects of the Game. He has programmed lights in computer consoles throughout the ship to do the same and free the rest of the *Enterprise* crew. (See "The Game")

GAMMA FIELD: When the nanites escape from Wesley Crusher's lab experiment, a low-level gamma field is used to reduce their processing speed. When Dr. Paul Stubbs employs a much larger burst in an attempt to eradicate the nanites, they respond with hostility directed at Stubbs. (See "Evolution")

GAMMA SEQUENCE: A battle tactic employing an evasive maneuver used by the *Enterprise* when it is attacked by Klingon ships in the altered timeline. (See "Yesterday's Enterprise")

GARDENERS OF EDEN: The title given to the terraforming project on the planet Velara. (See "Home Soil")

GATEWAY: The ancient Iconian version of the transporter, the gateway apparently effects instantaneous transportation across distances undreamed of by any race still alive; the source of the Iconians' power and influence. (See "Contagion")

GENERAL ORDER ONE: The Prime Directive.

GENERAL ORDER SEVEN: The warning to stay away from Talos under any condition. This is the only Federation law whose violation can be punished by the death penalty. (See "The Menagerie")

GENERAL ORDER TWENTY-FOUR: James Kirk's orders to Scotty to destroy Eminiar VII within a certain time frame....a bluff, since destroying planets is a bit outside of Kirk's authority. (See "A Taste Of Armageddon")

GENERAL QUARTERS: A general state of alert: battle stations.

GENERAL QUARTERS THREE: General alert: intruder aboard.

GESTAPO: The 20th Century Nazi police, revived, after a fashion, on Ekos after John Gill interferes in its culture. (See "Patterns Of Force")

GHORUSDA DISASTER: Because the captain of the *Adelphi* ignored the recommendations of Tam Elbrun regarding cultural differences, 47 people, including the Adelphi Captain, were slain. The killed included two of Riker's friends from Starfleet Academy and he harbors ill will towards Tam Elbrun over this. (See "Tin Man")

GIN'TAK: A Klingon weapon which resembles a spear. Worf is shocked when he sees Toq, a Klingon youth, using the Gin'tak spear as though it were a garden hoe. (See "Birthright")

GI'RAL: A Klingon woman who married a Romulan man and gave birth to a half-Klingon, half-Romulan daughter named Ba'el. (See "Birthright")

GLAVYN: A Ligonian hand weapon. (See "Code Of Honor")

THE GLOBE ILLUSTRATED SHAKESPEARE: A prime piece of Earth literature prized by Picard; he owns a copy in book form, being a purist at heart. (See "Hide And Q")

GRATITUDE FESTIVAL: The biggest Bajoran holiday of the year. (See "The Nagus")

GRAVITON EMISSIONS: These are used to attract the Crystalline Entity to the *Enterprise*. Once there, Dr. Lila Marr alters the wavelength and destroys the entity. (See "Silicon Avatar")

GUILE: A basic Klingon virtue: a true Klingon should be able to draw upon it as a weapon even when deprived of any other defense. The Ferengi, wily as they are, are no match for it.(See "Peak Performance")

GULLIVER'S TRAVELS: An ancient work of satiric Earth literature, cited by Riker when faced with the absurd situation between Atlek and Streleb. (See "The Outrageous Okona")

HANGAR DECK: The large deck area which holds the *Enterprise*'s contingent of shuttlecrafts.

HEISENBERG COMPENSATORS: Captain Picard tells the Countess Batholomew that by uncoupling these the *Enterprise* personnel would be able to beam an object out of the holodeck and maintain its integrity. But it is just a ruse to trick Moriarty. (See "Ship In A Bottle")

HOLODECK: Virtual reality taken to its utmost limit, a chamber where the computer creates totally immersive locations, characters and scenarios. A device used for both recreation and research which can be programmed to create holograms of virtually anything. For amusement purposes, programs have been run featuring the fictional detectives Sherlock Holmes and Dixon Hill. Geordi has used it for research, such as when created the design rooms of the Utopia Planitia shipyards and a facsimile of Dr. Leah Brahms, the designer of the *Enterprise-D*. Montgomery Scott utilized it to recreate the bridge from the original *Enterprise* he had served on nearly a century earlier. (See "Encounter At Farpoint", "The Big Goodbye", "Relics", etc.)

HOLODICTION: An addiction to the fantasy worlds which the holodeck can create. Barclay exhibits symptoms of this as he uses the holodeck to create holograms of his superior officers whom he belittles. (See "Hollow Pursuits") Although Barclay's symptoms are not too extreme, the holodeck carries with it the same dangers attributed to the hallucination powers of the inhabitants of Talos Four. (See "The Menagerie")

HONOR: In its various forms, this concept plays an important role in many cultures throughout space and history. Its meaning can vary widely. For the Klingons, death in battle is the highest honor; Klingons who are taken prisoner have none left, and so might as well be dead. (See "A Matter Of Honor")

HORGA'HN: A large round stone idol from Risa which is a symbol of sexuality. To display a Horga'hn is to announce that one is seeking Jamaharohn, and to own one is to summon forth its mythical powers. (See "Captain's Holiday")

HOT CHOCOLATE: Still popular centuries after the Aztecs invented it; Picard responds graciously after Sonya Gomez accidentally spills some on him. (See "Q Who")

HOTEL ROYALE: A cheap potboiler of a book dating from the early part of the 21st Century, about a troubled casino and the passions, intrigue and crime that take place there. Apparently, astronaut Stephen Richey had a copy with him when his ship was accidentally destroyed by aliens; to make up for the death of his comrades, they kept him alive and used the book to create a backdrop for him to live out his existence. It keeps going long after he dies, leaving Riker to figure out the plot of the book in order to escape. (See "The Royale")

HOVERBALL: A game which involves, naturally, a ball which hovers. (See "Captain's Holiday")

HUMOR: One of the main stumbling-blocks in Data's quest to understand humanity, and to become more human himself. For a while, he becomes almost obsessed with it, but eventually learns enough to let it drop. (See "The Outrageous Okona")

HYDROGEN COLLECTORS: Located to the front of the warp nacelles, these do just what their name suggests, although they can also project the gas as well. (See "Samaritan Snare")

HYPERONIC RADIATION: A type of radiation ordinarily dangerous to human life; although the Tau Cygnan colony has survived, one-third of the colony was lost before they learned how to adapt to the radiation. (See "The Ensigns Of Command")

HYPERSPACE PHYSICS TEST: A test taken by Wesley when he is trying out for his initial attempt to enter Starfleet Academy. He aces this test. (See "Coming Of Age")

HYTRITIUM: When Beta Agni Two experiences tricyanate water contamination, the rare element hytritium is the only way to treat it. (See "The Most Toys")

ICOBAR: Another Iconian-type language. (See "Contagion")

IDIC: "Infinite Diversity in Infinite Combinations": an English translation of a concept central to Vulcan philosophy, it is represented by a small pin that Spock sometimes wears, a piece of jewelry that embodies this concept visually. (See "Is There In Truth No Beauty")

ILIUM 629: An isotopic byproduct of dilithium crystals. (See "Pen Pals")

IMPULSE ION TRAIL: An energy trace left by the *Enterprise* which can be detected with sensors. (See "Relics")

IMPULSE POWER: Sublight propulsion system on Starfleet vessels, for use as a backup system or in planetary systems where warp drive cannot be used safely.

IMPULSE VENT: Exit path for impulse ions from the impulse engines.

IMZADI: A Betazoid term meaning a true love, or the love of one's life. (See "Second Chances", "Shade of Gray")

INOPROVALINE: A drug which Dr. Crusher administers to prevent massive infection in "John Doe". (See "Transfigurations")

INSPECTOR GENERAL'S OFFICE: The internal investigative branch of Starfleet; Dexter Remmick worked there. (See "Coming of Age", "Conspiracy")

INSTRUMENT OF OBEDIENCE: The Oracle of *Yonada* uses these tiny implants to monitor the thoughts of the Yonadans, and to punish or kill its subjects with them as well. (See "For The World Is Hollow And I Have Touched The Sky")

INTELLIGENCE FILES: The sum total of information amassed by the Fabrini, stored in their computers, destined to be handed over to their descendants the Yonada when they reach the planet they are on course to. (See "For The World Is Hollow And I Have Touched The Sky")

INTERMIX CHAMBER: A component part of the warp drive engines.

INTERPHASE: The sort of space/time distortion that claims the *Defiant* and almost claims Kirk as well, who risks madness in it while Spock strives to outwit the Tholians. (See "The Tholian Web")

INTERPHASE GENERATOR: A Romulan device designed to enable a living thing to be cloaked by invisibility and move through walls. (See "The Next Phase")

INVIDIUM: A substance used in medical containment fields. In case of a leak it can be stopped by temperatures of minus 200 degrees Celsius. (See "Hollow Pursuits")

ION ENGINE: Another term for impulse engines.

ION POWER: The power source of the Eymorgs of Sigma Draconis VI.

ION PROPULSION: Not to be confused with impulse-style ion engines, this is a radically different form of propulsion used by the Draconians, who use it to reach extremely high speeds in space. Although this far outstrips Federation technology, it leaves a distinctive trail that allows the *Enterprise* to track the Draconians in its search to reclaim Spock's brain. (See "Spock's Brain")

IRESINE SYNDROME: A rare neurological disorder. When Troi and Riker fall into comas they are tentatively diagnosed as having this disorder. (See "Violations")

IRISH UNIFICATION OF 2024: The Ansata movement is compared to this by Data. (See "The High Ground")

ISOLATION FIELD: A type of force field Geordi develops which enables someone to beam inside a time distortion field without being affected by the time distortions. (See "Timescape")

ISOLINEAR OPTICAL CHIPS: Storage devices employed by the *Enterprise*. On the ancient starship the *Cleponji*, Data finds mechanisms which are similar to these. (See "Booby Trap")

IVERSON'S DISEASE: The affliction which Admiral Mark Jameson is suffering from until he takes an illegal alien youth drug. The Cerebran rejuvenation treatment undoes this illness for Admiral Jameson, but the cure is worse than the illness. (See "Too Short A Season")

JAKMANITE: A substance with a half-life of fifteen seconds; it can alter glass. (See "Hollow Pursuits")

JAMAHAROHN: A word which approximately translates as sexual contact. Displaying the Horga'hn (a Risian fertility statuette) is the same as announcing that one is seeking Jamaharohn. (See "Captain's Holiday")

JAZZ: Earth music genre, Riker's favorite. He plays jazz trombone. (See "11001001")

JEFFRIES TUBES: Standard equipment-access tubes that crisscross the *Enterprise* and other Starfleet vessels, in which technicians can reach manual controls and out-of-reach equipment.

JINAG: A Klingon amulet given to a daughter when she becomes old enough to choose a mate. (See "Birthright")

JOINING: A process, mysterious in nature, which Bele wants to subject Lokai to. Lokai is frightened of this prospect, but Kirk prevents it — whatever it is — from happening. (See "Let That Be Your Last Battlefield")

JOINING: The traditional Betazoid wedding ritual. Lwaxana Troi favors it; the Wyatts, perhaps put off by the fact that the ceremony requires the total nudity of all participants, prefer an Earth-style wedding for Deanna and Wyatt. (See "Haven")

JUDGE ADVOCATE GENERAL'S OFFICE: The legal arm of Starfleet. (See "The Measure Of A Man")

KAH-IF-FARR: The words that begin the Vulcan mating rituals. (See "Amok Time")

KAHS-WAN: A test of maturity which Vulcan boys voluntarily undertake at age seven. (See "Yesteryear")

KALANDAN COMPUTER: The defense mechanism at an outpost of the extinct Kalandan empire, which uses the image of its commanding officer Losira to kill intruders. (See "That Which Survives")

KAL-IF-FEE: The Vulcan challenge to hand-to-hand combat, as seen at Spock's disastrous wedding. Kirk knows it all too well. (See "Amok Time")

KALLA-NOHRA SYNDROME: A disease which resulted from a mining accident at a Bajoran forced labor camp called Gallitepp during the Cardassian occupation. (See "Duet")

KARST TOPOGRAPHY: A reference to underground rivers and caverns which confuse the Enterprise sensors. (See "Who Watches The Watchers?")

KATRA: A Vulcan's soul or persona. Spock gives his to McCoy for safe keeping until the *fal tor pan* can take place. (See "Star Trek III: The Search For Spock")

KAVIS TEKE ELUSIVE MANEUVER: A tactic first employed by the Menthars. (See "Booby Trap")

KENZIE REBELLION: The Ansata terrorist movement is compared to the Kenzie Rebellion. (See "The High Ground")

KERR LOOP: This is formed from superstring material and requires high-energy interactions. A Kerr Loop is a phenomenon capable of creating a temporal rift. (See "Yesterday's Enterprise")

KHITOMER MASSACRE: A Romulan attack on the Klingon outpost at Khitomer which was accomplished via the betrayal of the Klingon Duras, a fact covered up years later to prevent the Klingon High Council from being undermined. Duras sent defense access codes to the Romulans. Thousands died with only the small child named Worf and his nurse, Kahlest, as survivors. (See "The Sins Of The Fathers")

KIROIDE: The chemical in the food of the planet Platonius that gives most of its people psychokinetic abilities by altering the pituitary gland. (See "Plato's Stepchildren")

KLIGAT: A triple-bladed, hand-wielded weapon, used with deadly results by the inhabitants of the planet Capella IV. (See "Friday's Child")

KLINGON DEATH RITUAL: In which a warrior howls over the body of a dead warrior as a warning to the netherworld that a Klingon is on his way there. (See "Heart Of Glory")

KNIFE OF KIROM: A sacred knife which is stained with the blood of Kahless, the legendary Klingon warrior. (See "Rightful Heir")

KNITTER: A standard medical tool that speeds up natural bone repair. (See "Contagion")

KOINONIAN MINES: Subspace proximity detonators which cannot be detected by a tricorder. Six of these had been left buried from an ancient war. One of them exploded, killing Marla Aster. The other five were subsequently found and disarmed by the Koinonian energy beings. (See "The Bonding")

KOLINAHR: The Vulcan ritual performed with the Masters on the high plateau of Gol which purges the last vestige of emotion from a Vulcan's soul. (See "Star Trek: The Motion Picture")

KOON-UT KAL-IF-FEE: A Vulcan phrase referring to marriage. Remarkably similar to the word for "challenge". (See "Amok Time")

KOSINSKI THEOREMS: When Wesley Crusher experiments with these, his mother is accidentally thrown into a pocket universe containing a duplicate *Enterprise* where things keep changing as the pocket universe grows smaller. (See "Remember Me")

KRIEGER WAVES: Dr. Nel Apgar has developed this new power source in conjunction with a Lambda Field generator. He has been working on this with Federation support but plans to secretly sell the discovery to the highest bidder. (See "A Matter Of Perspective")

KRONITON PARTICLES: These are found aboard a disabled Romulan vessel after a phase converter and a Romulan cloaking device are combined. When Geordi and Ro Laren become victims of this device, Data is able to detect them because they leave kroniton particles wherever they go. (See "The Next Phase")

KUMA MANEUVER: A standard starship battle maneuver. (See "Peak Performance")

KROYKAH: A strong imperative in the Vulcan language. Spoken by T'Pau, it brings Spock to a halt in time to save Kirk, although it at first seems otherwise. (See "Amok Time")

KUT'LUCH: A Klingon ceremonial weapon of assassination. (See "The Sins Of The Fathers")

LAMBDA FIELD GENERATOR: Located on the planet below the orbiting science station, it requires a minimum of five thousand kilometers for the field to collimate. (See "A Matter Of Perspective")

LANG CYCLE FUSION ENGINES: The ancient Promellian vessel the *Cleponji* was thus powered. (See "Booby Trap")

LAWMIM GALACTOPEDIA: An exquisitely rare object in the collection of Kivas Fajo. (See "The Most Toys")

LEFT-HANDED SPANNER: A phony name for a tool. Calling a tool this name is a trick played on young cadets. (See "Star Trek II: The Wrath Of Khan")

LENARIAN COMPRESSED TERYON BEAM: Jean-Luc Picard is shot in the chest with this weapon during an assassination attempt. (See "Tapestry")

LEPTON: In combination with mesons, a buildup of these in the accretion disk of the Barzan wormhole enables Geordi LaForge to determine that the wormhole is unstable after all. (See "The Price")

LEUTSCHER VIRUS: The nanites are similar to this. (See "Evolution")

LEVEL ONE DIAGNOSTIC SERIES: A computer diagnostic. Picard orders this when the food unit in sickbay malfunctions and the inertia dampeners fail. (See "Evolution")

LEVEL TWO QUERY: This is what Riker sends out (although coded) when he is searching for the vessel the *Jovis*, owned by Kivas Fajo. (See "The Most Toys")

LIFE-ENTITY TRANSFER: As the name suggests, a means of switching consciousnesses between bodies. The ancient civilization on the planet Camus II developed a machine that could accomplish this; Janice Lester discovered it and used it on James Kirk. (See "Turnabout Intruder")

LIFE-FORM READINGS: Ship's scanners and tricorders are both able to detect the presence of life forms under most circumstances; for example, they cannot detect the carbon-based race of the evil Yarnek on Excalbia, but are generally effective. (See "The Savage Curtain")

LIFE SCIENCES: Data is assigned to this duty when the *Enterprise* is headed for Beta Stromgren. (See "Tin Man")

LINEAR MODELS OF VIRAL PROPAGATION: Dr. Catherine Pulaski's important contribution to 24th Century medical literature. (See "Unnatural Selection")

LITTLE ONE: A pet name Deanna's mother had for her. Deanna hates it and wants Lwaxana to stop calling her that. (See "Menage A Troi")

LOCATOR BOMB: A Ferengi assassination device which locks onto its target's pheromones. (See "The Nagus")

LUCROVEXITRIN: A toxic substance which can alter glass. Investigated as the cause of mysterious breakdowns on the *Enterprise*. (See "Hollow Pursuits")

LYZOMES: The lyzome levels in the Mintakans are lower than that normally found in humanoids. (See "Who Watches The Watchers?")

MAGNETIC PROBE: One of Montgomery Scott's engineering tools, of variable polarity.

MAGNETIC SWEEP: A standard proceedure for a landing party. Sulu is taking such a reading on the Kalandan outpost world when the projection of Losira makes its first appearance. (See "That Which Survives")

MAGNETOMETRIC GUIDED CHARGES: When the *Enterprise* seeks refuge in the Paulson Nebula, the Borg launch these explosive devices. (See "The Best Of Both Worlds")

MAIN BATTERIES: The primary array of starship weaponry.

MAJQA: A Klingon ritual in which one strives to achieve visions, particularly revelations about one's father. (See "Birthright")

MAKO ROOT: A root used in healing by the Kanutu; when Kirk is poisoned by a Mugatu, Nona employs mako root to save his life. (See "A Private Little War")

MALIAMANDA TAPESTRY: An exquisitely rare item in the collection of Kivas Fajo. (See "The Most Toys")

MANITOBA JOURNAL OF INTERPLANETARY PSYCHOLOGY: At the time of the negotiations for the commercial rights to the Barzan wormhole, a representative of this journal asks Deanna Troi about a research inquiry. (See "The Price")

MANNHEIM EFFECT: The temporal distortion created by Paul Mannheim on Vandor IV. (See "We'll Always Have Paris")

MARALTIAN SEEV-ALE: An alcoholic beverage sold by Quark on Deep Space Nine. (See "Duet")

MARTINI: An alcoholic concoction (made with gin or vodka, and vermouth) originating on Earth in the 20th Century. Sonny Clemons is surprised to discover that they are still made in the 24th Century. (See "The Neutral Zone")

MASIFORM D: The drug McCoy uses to save Spock from a poisonous plant on Gamma Trianguli VI. (See "The Apple")

MATTER/ANTI-MATTER INTEGRATOR: Where matter and anti-matter are mixed for use in the warp drive engines.

MATTER/ENERGY SCRAMBLER: An alien variety of transporter used on Minara II.

MAXIMUM SHIELDING: Top crisis situation, when the shields are 100% in use while under severe attack.

THE MEDIATORS: Those who carry out the orders of execution for the Edo. (See "Justice")

MEK'BA: This is the Klingon trial which Worf undergoes when his father is posthumously accused of being the traitor behind the Khitomer Massacre. (See "The Sins Of The Fathers")

MELKOTIAN BUOY: The device that warns the Enterprise away from Melkotian space. Kirk ignores its advice — not a smooth move. (See "Spectre Of The Gun")

MEMORY ERASURE: Developed by Dr. Pulaski; her technique dates the recent chemical linkages that form memories and removes them. (See "Pen Pals")

M-4: A small spheroid robot created by the immortal human Flint as his household servant. It can also be very deadly. Spock destroys one but another identical device immediately replaces it. (See "Requiem For Methuselah")

M-5 COMPUTER (MULTITRONIC UNIT): A new computer created by Dr. Richard Daystrom. Its purpose is to take over all the activities of a starship, including tactics and command. The ship chosen to test the M-5 is the Enterprise, which doesn't sit very well with Kirk. Things go from bad to worse when the computer mistakes war games for real attacks and kills everyone on board the Excalibur as well as inflicting heavy casualties on some other ships. Kirk must convince the computer that it has committed murder; programmed with a moral sense, the M-5 decides that it must be destroyed, and gives up command of the ship. (See "The Ultimate Computer")

MERCULITE ROCKETS: Three renegade Klingons led by Koris use these to fend off their Ferengi attackers. (See "Heart of Glory")

MESON: In combination with leptons, a buildup of these in the accretion disk of the Barzan wormhole enables Geordi LaForge to determine that the wormhole is unstable after all. (See "The Price")

METAGENIC WEAPONS: Weapons being developed by the Cardassians; Jean-Luc Picard has a great deal of experience working with them. (See "Chain Of Command")

METAPHASIC FIELD TECHNOLOGY: Developed by the Ferengi scientist Dr. Reyga, this technology is capable of generating a force field powerful enough to protect a shuttlecraft from the fury of the corona of a star. (See "Suspicions")

METATHALMUS: This is examined in order to detect the rare Vulcan disorder Bendii syndrome. (See "Sarek")

MICROSCOPIC DRILL: This is used above Ten

Forward by Geordi in order to shock the entities which have possessed Troi, Data and Ro and then trap them in a containment field. (See "Power Play")

MICROVIRIUS: This rare type of virus is genetically engineered. Yuta carries this in her body and uses it to assassinate members of rival clans. (See "The Vengeance Factor")

MILITARY LOG: In the normal timeline this is called the "Captain's Log", but in the altered timeline where the Klingons have been at war with the Federation for 20 years (and are winning) it is called the Military Log. (See "Yesterday's Enterprise")

MIND-ERASING TECHNIQUE: A procedure to selectively remove memories, generally applied to beings from worlds not in the Federation in order to protect races from cultural contamination. (See "Who Watches The Watchers?")

MIND LINK: Telepathic communion as practiced by Vulcans, Medusans and other telepathic races.

MIND-SIFTER: A Klingon device that attacks the minds of humanoids. Bad news for humans, but Vulcans can fight its effects. (See "Errand Of Mercy")

MIND-SPHERE: A highly dangerous device, outlawed galaxy-wide. Daimon Bock used one to drive Picard mad and create illusions in his mind. (See "The Battle")

MINTAKAN CLOTH: An ornament given as a gift to Jean-Luc by Haki and Nuria, two Mintakans. (See "Who Watches The Watchers?") The same cloth is later seen in Picard's quarters when Sarek mindmelds with him. (See "Sarek")

MODULE L-73: One of the plague virus containment units in the *Enterprise* – the one affected by the Eichner radiation generated by the child Ian. (See "The Child")

MOEBIUS LOOP: A mathematical description of a twisted loop, which also describes a time loop encountered by the *Enterprise*.(See "Time Squared")

MOK'BARA: A Klingon exercise ritual which centers the mind and body. (See "Birthright")

MOLECULAR CYBERNETICS: A scientific field that was taken to its limit by Dr. Ira Graves, and then

by his student Dr. Noonian Soong. Molecular cybernetics probably contributed directly to the creation of Data. (See "The Schizoid Man")

MOLYBDENUM COBALT ALLOYS: One of the metals of which the android Data is made. (See "The Most Toys")

MOROPA: The Bolians have an uneasy truce with this race. (See "Allegiance")

MORTAE: A manual mining device used on Ardana by the suppressed Troglyte; it also doubles as a crude weapon. (See "The Cloud Minders")

MOTOR ASSIST BANDS: The medical personnel on the *Enterprise* can use these to stimulate electrically a person's arms and legs in order to help a person to walk. (See "Transfigurations")

M-RAYS: A radiation form that Spock uses to undo Apollo's force field. (See "Who Mourns For Adonais?")

MUKTOK PLANTS: These plants live for centuries and are known to emit music. When Will Riker and Deanna Troi were involved they planted a Muktok Plant in a clearing on Betazed and years later find that it is still there.

MURINITE: The hilt of the knife used in the Ripper murders on Argelia is made of this mineral, found on Rigel IV. (See "Wolf In The Fold")

NACELLES: The two tubelike structures on the back of the *Enterprise* and similar Starfleet vessels. They are positioned so that they can be separated from the ship if the matter/anti-matter containment is compromised.

NAISKOS: A small Buddha-like statue from the third Kurlan dynasty. (See "The Chase")

NAME THE WINNER: A popular television series broadcast on Planet 892-IV, presenting gladiatorial battles for public amusement. Spock and McCoy are lucky enough to be selected as contestants. (See "Bread And Circuses")

NANITES: Microscopic robots which nonetheless

have gigabytes of mechanical memory. Normally employed in genetic systems in order to enter living cells to make repairs on a cellular level. They were developed on Earth at Dakar, Senegal. Wesley experiments with nanites and they get away from his control. (See "Evolution")

NEURAL FIELD: The device the Kelvans use to overpower the *Enterprise* crew. (See "By Any Other Name")

NEURAL NEUTRALIZER: Dr. Tristan Adams' deadly mind control device, which he used to evil effect on Tantalus V. (See "Dagger Of The Mind")

NEURAL PARALYZER: This drug induces a state of unconsciousness so severe it can appear like death. McCoy uses it on Kirk to trick Spock into thinking that he has killed the captain. (See "Amok Time")

NEUROCHEMICAL DRAIN: The mind probe process being employed against Will Riker when he is captured on the surface of Tilonus Four and taken to the Tilonus Institute for Mental Disorders. (See "Frame Of Mind")

NEUROTRANSMITTERS: This part of Reginald Barclay's brain is increased by 500 per cent, causing the two hemispheres of his brain to act as a single unit. The result is that his IQ increases to a level between 1200 and 1450, and for a time he becomes the smartest human who ever lived. (See "The Nth Degree")

NEUTRINO BEACON: A neutrino source set up on the surface of a world ravaged by electromagnetic storms. Geordi is lost on the surface and Wesley knows that if Geordi can find this then he will modify it in order to contact the *Enterprise*. (See "The Enemy")

NITRIUM: This element is in many components in the *Enterprise* and a strange space parasite which absorbs nitrium gets aboard the vessel. The *Enterprise* is taken into an asteroid field where Data uses as emitter beam to lure the parasites off the ship. (See "Cost Of Living")

NOH-JAY CONSORTIUM: The phony company Jake Sisko and Nog use in order to make business deals with adults via the computer. (See "Progress")

NORANIUM ALLOY: This alloy vaporizes at 2314 degrees under a phaser setting of 7. It was found at the Gatherer encampment on Gamma Hromi II. (See "The Vengeance Factor")

NOREPH: Dr. Crusher uses this drug on the fatally wounded Tasha Yar but is unable to save her. (See "Skin of Evil") She uses it on Warren after she is injured in the explosion of the Federation observation post. (See "Who Watches The Watchers?")

NORKAN MASSACRE: A Romulan attack led by Admiral Jarok, who later defects to the Federation. The Romulans describe this attack as the Norkan Campaign. (See "The Defector")

NOVA SQUADRON: This is the squadron Wesley Crusher belongs to at Starfleet Academy. His Squadron leader is Nicholas. (See "The First Duty")

NUCLEO-SYNTHESIS: When invidium leaks from tissue sample containers it creates this affliction. (See "Hollow Pursuits")

NULL-G WARD: We hear Dr. Selar summoned here over the intercom. (See "Yesterday's Enterprise")

NUMBER FOUR SHIELD: The starboard deflector shield.

OFFICER EXCHANGE PROGRAM: The exchange of personnel between Federation members and allies. The Benzite, Ensign Mendoc, is part of this program; William Riker is the first human to serve on board a Klingon ship. (See "A Matter Of Honor")

ONKIANS: A Romulan system of temperature measurement. (See "The Defector")

OO-MOX: A Ferengi erogenous zone on their ears. A Ferengi likes it very much when one gives them Oo-mox. (See "Menage A Troi")

OPTI-CABLE: Standard cable used for transfer of information and power on board Starfleet vessels. (See "Peak Performance")

ORGANIAN PEACE TREATY: A remarkable feat of diplomacy, if the term can really be applied in this instance, this treaty involved no negotiations whatsoever but was thought up and put into effect by the authority of the Organians — whether the two parties affected by the treaty liked it or not. Its primary feature, beyond the enforced peace, is the fact that in the case of contested worlds the world goes to the side better equipped to develop it. The treaty also casts Klingons and humans together at unusual spots, like Space Station K-7. (See "The Trouble With Tribbles") The occasional off-duty fisticuffs (as seen there) do not seem to count against either side as far as the Organians are concerned. (See "Errand Of Mercy")

ORNARAN PLAGUE: The long-dead disease that led to the mass addiction of the Ornarans. (See "Symbiosis")

OSKOID: A type of Betazoid food kept warm by sap. (See "Menage A Troi")

OVERSEER: A being of Mintakan mythology whose worship had faded until Liko's encounter with "The Picard" renewed their belief in a superior being. According to myth, the "Overseer" was an entity who could provide plentiful hunting, fertile crops and gentle winters. (See "Who Watches The Watchers?")

OWAN EGGS: A difficult recipe that Riker doesn't quite manage to pull off; his human guests don't like them, but Worf finds them quite to his Klingon tastes. (See "Time Squared")

PARROT'S CLAW CASE: A Dixon Hill adventure referred to in passing. (See "Manhunt")

PARSTEEL: A very strong metallic alloy; Data twists a bar of it in court to demonstrate his incredible strength. (See "The Measure Of A Man")

PARTHUS: This is a plant indigenous to Acamar Three. It is a vegetable with fleshy roots which can be prepared in a spiced parthus dish. (See "The Vengeance Factor")

PASSIVE LURE STRATAGEM: This is a military maneuver used by the Menthars to lure Promellian warships in to be trapped by Aceton Assimilators. (See "Booby Trap")

PATCHES: Jeremy Aster's calico cat. (See "The Bonding")

PATTERN ENHANCERS: Used to strengthen the pattern of any object being sent via a transport beam. (See "Ship In A Bottle")

PERGIUM: A fissionable material found on Janus VI and used in the old-style nuclear reactors that power that world. (See "Devil In The Dark")

PERICULES: A Ferengi flower, species Zan Periculi, indigenous to Lappa IV. (See "Menage A Troi")

THE PHASE: The period during which Betazoid women quadruple their sex drive, but the Phase also impairs their telepathic powers, at least with men. (See "Manhunt")

PHASE ONE SEARCH: Standard Starfleet code describing a search for someone who is probably injured, sick or otherwise incapacitated and unable to communicate — as in the case of Finney (although he doesn't want to be located; he wants to be presumed dead). (See "Court Martial")

PHASERS: 1.): Handheld: Standard-issue Starfleet weaponry of variable range and intensity. Generally small enough to fit into the palm of the hand, they can be used to stun in varying degrees, from the inducement of confusion to complete unconsciousness. On higher settings they can kill and even disintegrate their target. Different settings can adapt it to excavation work, and other non-violent applications. Pistol and rifle style grips with built-in power sources are often used to increase the distance and strength of the phaser's range.
2.): Ship's: Located in the saucer section of the *Enterprise* and comparable Starfleet vessels, these are extremely powerful phaser weapons that can direct considerable firepower against other space ships, planets and the occasional oversized space creature.

PHASER COOLANT: A toxic gas, pink in color, which serves to keep down the temperature of the *Enterprise*'s main phaser banks.

PHASER ONE: An earlier form of less effective phaser power, used on backwater worlds like the mining planet of Janus VI.

PHASER TWO: The currently used form of phaser power, utilized by the *Enterprise*.

PHASER RANGE: The onboard practice range on the *Enterprise*. (See "A Matter Of Honor")

PHASING: The mysterious technique by which the Traveler moves from place to place and time to time. (See "Where No One Has Gone Before")

PHOTON TORPEDOES: A matter/anti-matter weapon, originally developed by the Romulan Empire but subsequently adapted and employed by the Federation. Photon torpedoes can follow a target at low warp speeds for a considerable distance.

PHYROX PLAGUE: Cor Caroli Five was ravaged by this deadly epidemic. (See "Allegiance")

PHYSIO STASIS: The ability of Takarans to control their physiology at a cellular level. (See "Suspicions")

PICARD MANEUVER: The strategy Picard used to defeat his foes at the Battle of Maxia; by using a very short burst of warp speed, he created the illusion that the Stargazer was in two places at once — just long enough to confuse the Ferengi. (See "The Battle")

PITUITARY GLAND: The organ, located in the brain area, that regulates the endocrine system in humans and humanoids. The substance kironide, found on the planet Platonius, interacts with this gland to create psychokinetic powers. The Platonian Alexander is a dwarf due to a pituitary failing, which also prevented him from developing the mental powers shared by most of his fellow Platonians. (See "Plato's Stepchildren")

PLAK TOW: A Vulcan term: the worst phase of pon farr, when the subject is so out of control that he could, potentially, kill even his closest friend, so intent is he on mating. (See "Amok Time")

PLASMA INFECTION: Caused when plasma microbes infect a human body. (See "Realm Of Fear")

PLASMA PLAGUE: A deadly disease. Strains created in antidote research exist in storage, and the Enterprise must transport these to Racheis when the plague breaks out on that planet. (See "The Child")

PLASMA STREAMER: The U.S.S. Yosemite was sent to observe these in the Igo Sector and was then reported lost. (See "Realm Of Fear")

PLASMA TRAILS: The ships in the Nova Squadron attempt a stunt in which they ignite their plasma trails in order to create a spectacular effect, but this is a dangerous stunt and while practicing for it one of the squadron members, Josh Albert, is killed. (See "The First Duty")

POD: Attached to the outside of the Enterprise hull, these are used to observe and monitor unusual cosmic activity. In the case of Lieutenant Commander Finney, he was observing an ion storm, and apparently was unable to get back inside the Enterprise before the pod was jettisoned for safety reasons. This leads to Captain Kirk's court martial for negligence and murder, but it turns out that Finney, who is really alive, set the whole thing up to ruin Kirk's career. (See "Court Martial")

POD PLANT: A deadly thorned plant on the planet Gamma Trianguli VI. It seems to possess some sort of rudimentary sensory apparatus, if not intelligence, because it is able to aim its poisoned thorns at its victims. This is how crewman Hendorf is killed. Spock is also attacked, but Dr. McCoy is able to save his life. (See "The Apple")

POKER: An ancient Earth card game of skill and strategy. In time, even Data and Worf become good at it, but Riker is probably the best all-around poker player on board the Enterprise.

PON FARR: The culmination of the seven-year Vulcan mating cycle. Most of the time, the Vulcan sexual drive is dormant, thanks to their incredible emotional control, but when pon farr hits, its effect can be quite devastating — not just for the Vulcan affected, but to those around him as well. A Vulcan in the grip of pon farr can be quite violent, as Captain Kirk learns the hard way. (See "Amok Time")

POSITRONIC BRAIN: The form of artificial intelligence that Data possesses, perfected by Dr. Noonian Soong after many failures. (See "Datalore", "The Measure Of A Man")

POTEEN: An alcoholic drink originating in Ireland, on Earth; still brewed by the Bringloidi. (See "Up The Long Ladder")

POTTRIK SYNDROME: A disease similar to the Kalla-Nohra syndrome. (See "Duet")

POWER: The Platonians' term for their psychokinetic, or telekinetic, mental abilities. (See "Plato's Stepchildren")

POWER GENERATOR: The power source for the

library and atavachron on the planet Sarpeidon. This power source tells the *Enterprise* sensors that there are still people alive on Sarpeidon. (See "All Our Yesterdays")

POWER SURGE: What happens when Losira, the projection of the long-dead commander of the Kalandan outpost planet, appears on board the *Enterprise*. The planet below quakes, while the *Enterprise* is cast nearly a thousand light years away from the planet. (See "That Which Survives")

PRIME DIRECTIVE: In Starfleet regulations, this is the all-important General Order One. The Prime Directive stipulates that Starfleet personnel visiting or observing cultures on other planets — specifically less technologically developed cultures— may not interfere in any way whatsoever with the natural evolution of other cultures and peoples. Thus John Gill clearly violates this order on Ekos, and Melik, the captain of the *Beagle*, does the same on Planet 892-IV. Kirk has been known to bend the rules a bit himself, but then the Prime Directive is somewhat more flexible when it comes to cultures that are either completely messed up, like the culture ruled by the computer Landru on Beta III, or ones that have already been tampered with and need to be set back on track, like Ekos, Iotia and numerous others. It is the foremost rule of the Federation, decreeing a policy of noninterference with cultures that are technologically behind the Federation. Called into question during the events concerning Drema Four. (See "Pen Pals")

PRIME ORDER: This is the mirror universe equivalent to the Prime Directive, although it has — as might be expected — a somewhat different focus: absolute punishment for any culture that defies the evil Empire. Kirk's violation of this rule will probably prove fatal — or worse — for his mirror universe counterpart after he is restored to his own world.

PRIORITY A-1: Top priority danger alert on the Quadrant level; high-level alert throughout a Quadrant is established by this message.

PROBE, ICONIAN: A blue sphere that serves as a sentry for Iconia. Not specifically a weapon, it nevertheless wreaks havoc on the systems of Federation and Romulan ships because its programming is so radically different. It has survived its creators by 200, 000 years. (See "Contagion")

PROBE, CLASS 1: One of these is launched by Picard to monitor Nelvana Three, which is supposed-ly the site of a Romulan war base just inside the Neutral Zone. (See "The Defector") A basic sensor/telemetry probe. One vanishes without effect into a strange vortex. (See "Time Squared") They can also be altered to function as resonators. (See "Pen Pals")

PROBE, CLASS 2: In order to deliver hytritium to the site of the tricyanate water contamination, it is loaded on a class 2 probe and launched from the *Enterprise*. (See "The Most Toys")

PROBE, CLASS 3: A neutrino beacon is placed aboard a class 3 probe and sent down into the Galorndon Core. (See "The Enemy")

PROBE, CLASS 8: A long-distance probe, which can travel at speeds up to Warp Factor 9. Stripped of its usual contents and outfitted with a basic life support system, a class 8 probe can serve as a rather cramped mode of transportation, as used by K'Ehleyr. (See "The Emissary")

PROCEDURE Q: Standard procedure where there is the possibility of hostility; under this procedure in such situations, all landing parties must be armed and prepared prior to beaming down.

PROGRAM PICARD DELTA ONE: This program stored in active memory in the *Enterprise* computer is the holodeck program which maintains the illusion for Moriarty that he has escaped from the *Enterprise* and is exploring known space. (See "Ship In A Bottle")

PROMENADE: The level of Deep Space Nine where all of the businesses are located.

PROMETHEAN QUARTZ: A rare gemstone from the Gamma Quadrant. (See "Q Less")

PROTECTORS: A term for the gas filtration masks which Dr. McCoy introduces to the planet Ardana. These will protect the Troglytes from the Zienite gas in the mines and restore their intelligence, thus undermining the cloud dwellers' claims of advanced evolutionary and intellectual status. (See "The Cloud Minders")

PROTODYNOPLASER: Dr. Crusher uses this medical device when she needs to stabilize the immune system of "John Doe". (See "Transfigurations")

PSI-2000 VIRUS: An inhibition-releasing disease

encountered by Kirk's *Enterprise* and Picard's also; the new variety does not respond to the cure created by Dr. Leonard McCoy. (See "The Naked Now")

PSYCH TEST: A mental test taken by Wesley the first time he tries out for entrance into the Starfleet Academy. It tests how someone would react in a life-or-death situation as well as using the person's own personal fears as part of the test. A dramatized psychological test placing the subject in a crisis situation to measure his or her response. (See "Coming Of Age")

PSYCHOKINESIS: A mental, or psychic, power to move objects from a distance. The strongest instances of psychokinesis encountered to date were among the Platonians. (See "Plato's Stepchildren")

PSYCHOTECH: Personnel trained specifically in the use of the psychotricorder.

PSYCHOTRICORDER: A variety of tricorder with specific psychological applications. It can read mental states and brain conditions, and can even be used to uncover memories if necessary.

PSYCHOTRONIC STABILITY EXAMINATION: The psychological test that lets Deanna Troi investigate Data's strange behavior after he has been taken over by the dying scientist Ira Graves. (See "The Schizoid Man")

PXK REACTOR: A fairly obsolete variety of fission reactor, still found in more isolated backwater regions such as on the mining planet of Janus VI. When the Horta, protecting its young, makes off with part of this reactor, Scotty can only jury-rig a temporary solution. (See "Devil In The Dark")

PYROCYTES: A blood extract which can be used to create an allergic reaction in people. During the Barzan negotiations, Arridor uses pyrocytes from Goss to incapacitate Mendoza. (See "The Price")

Q'APLA: The Klingon word for farewell.

QA'VAK: A type of Klingon target practice employing the Gin'tak. It is supposed to sharpen a warrior's skills in preparation for a hunt. (See "Birthright")

QUADRATANIUM: One of the elements used in the construction of the androids Lore and Data. (See "Datalore")

QUADROTRITICALE: A grain hybrid (a mixture of wheat and rye) that is crucial to avert a famine on Sherman's Planet. Tribbles are rather fond of it. Klingons poison the shipment for Sherman's Planet, but the hungry tribbles unveil the problem. This is good news for everyone except the tribbles. (See "The Trouble With Tribbles")

QUANTUM FILAMENT: A stellar particle not detectable by ordinary sensor probes and which can cause serious damage if one comes into contact with a starship. (See "Disaster")

QUATLOOS: The currency used for gambling and exchange on the planet Triskelion. (See "The Gamesters Of Triskelion")

RADANS: Raw dilithium crystals in an unprocessed form, found on Troyius and used there as good-luck charms and jewelry. Elaan's necklace, a wedding present, enables Scotty to power the *Enterprise*'s warp engines in a crisis. (See "Elaan Of Troyius")

RAPAKH UNGUHR: A Klingon disease similar to measles. Although it is not particularly dangerous, Worf is embarrassed to catch it, as it is a childhood disease. Pulaski helps him keep it secret. (See "Up The Long Ladder")

RECEPTACLES: The *Enterprise* landing party on Arret discovers many spherical receptacles deep beneath that planet's surface. Only three of them still hold the life forces of Arret's survivors: Sargon, Thalassa and the evil Henoch. Kirk, Spock and Mulhall occupy these receptacles when they lend the alien life forces their bodies for a temporary period. (See "Return To Tomorrow")

RECORDER-MARKER: In a crisis when the *Enterprise* is threatened, this is an object launched from the ship with a record of the events and related messages, so that if the ship is destroyed some record of the situation can be found by Starfleet. The *Enterprise* finds a recorder-marker left by the *Valiant* two centuries earlier, and has occasion to leave one when faced by Balok and his ship, the *Fesarius*. (See "The Corbomite Maneuver")

RED HOUR: Not the best time to arrive on Beta III, the planet ruled by the computer Landru: the Red Hour marks the start of the Festival, a no-holds-barred bacchanalia when all citizens go quite out of control, a reign of violence and abandon. (See "Return Of The Archons")

RED ZONE PROXIMITY: A situation in which the warp containment shielding fails, bringing the ship closer to the "Red Zone" in which the warp engines are more than slightly likely to explode, taking the ship and everyone on it with them.

REFRIGERATION UNIT: A device engineered by the Scalosians for the express purpose of putting the *Enterprise* crew in suspended animation until they are needed for procreative purposes. Basically, this would turn the *Enterprise* into one large, orbiting sperm bank — an idea Kirk does his best to defeat. (See "The Wink Of An Eye")

REGENERATION: The Gideonite ability to regenerate body cells, prolonging their lives to lengths which almost approach immortality, in human terms. (See "Mark Of Gideon")

REHABILITATION CHAIR: A once-useful, beneficial mind-restoration device that Garth of Izar adapts to purposes of torture and uses on James Kirk, among others. (See "Whom Gods Destroy")

REJAC CRYSTAL: An exquisitely rare item in the collection of Kivas Fajo. (See "The Most Toys")

REPLICATIVE FADING: The tendency of succeeding generations of duplicates to lose the form of their original pattern; particularly disastrous is the case of excessive generations of clones. (See "Up The Long Ladder")

REPLICATOR: A variation of transporter technology, the replicator can create things — food, clothing, tools and weapons — as if out of thin air. (See "Samaritan Snare")

REPULSOR BEAM: Basically, a tractor beam reversed to repel objects. (See "The Naked Now")

RESSIKAN FLUTE: The musical instrument Jean-Luc Picard plays. He learned how to play it when he lived a lifetime in a few moments after being hit by a beam from a thousand-year-old alien probe. (See "Inner Light" and "Lessons")

RIBOSOMES: A blood extract that the Romulan, Patakh, needs to survive. Worf is the only person on the *Enterprise* who has compatible ribosomes but he refuses to agree to a transfusion since Romulans were responsible for the death of his parents. Ribosomes are too complex to be reproduced in the *Enterprise* replicator. (See "The Enemy")

RIGELLIAN FEVER: A plague-like disease that affects the *Enterprise* crew; the *Enterprise* has to go to Holberg 917G to obtain ryetalyn, the only known antidote. (See "Requiem For Methuselah")

RIGELLIAN KASSABA FEVER: An illness McCoy invents to trick the Kelvans into leaving the *Enterprise*. He claims that Spock is a victim of this highly contagious disease. (See "By Any Other Name")

RIGELLIAN PHASER RIFLES: These weapons are used by the Gatherers on Gamma Hromi II to attack an Away Team. (See "The Vengeance Factor")

RIGHT OF STATEMENT: Romulan and Vulcan law share this ancient right which allows a convicted criminal to explain his crime and the reasons behind it. Spock takes full advantage of this technicality when he is captured by Romulans, in order to give Scotty time to outfit the *Enterprise* with the cloaking device that James Kirk has "liberated" from the Romulan ship. (See "The Enterprise Incident")

RIGHT OF VENGEANCE: A Romulan claim made when Tin Man destroys one of the Romulan ships which attack it. (See "Tin Man")

RITTER SCALE: Standard scale for measuring levels of interstellar radiation.

ROBBIANI DERMAL-OPTIC TEST: Similar to the Voight-Kampff test used in the early 21st Century, but a great deal more advanced, this test measures psychological states with readings of skin reactions and retinal responses to various stimuli.

RODINIUM: Despite the fact that rodinium is the most adamant material available to Federation technology, it is not strong enough to keep Outposts 1, 3, 4 and 8 from being destroyed by Romulan photon torpedo attacks. (See "Balance Of Terror")

ROMULAN ALE: A potent alcoholic drink that the Federation has prohibited. (See "Star Trek II: The Wrath of Khan" and "Star Trek VI: The Undiscovered Country")

ROSTRUM: An interrogation area, with torturing rays attendant, used in Stratos to question Troglytes from the surface of Ardana. (See "The Cloud Minders")

RUBINDIUM: Crystals used in simple electronics on Ekos. Spock is able to use them to build a simple phaser — just strong enough to help him escape. (See "Patterns Of Force")

R'UUSTA: The Klingon ritual known as "The Bonding" which creates ties of brotherhood between two people who are unrelated by blood. During the ceremony a candle is extinguished to represent the passing of a loved one. (See "The Bonding")

RVN: The portion of cell chemistry which changes with adolescence. When some *Enterprise* crew members lose some specific viroxic sequences in their RVN they physically revert to adolescence. (See "Rascals")

RYETALYN: Located in abundance on the planet Holberg 917G, this is the only known cure for Rigellian fever. The *Enterprise* goes to Holberg 917G when the disease ravages its crew. (See "Requiem For Methuselah")

SAHSEER: Crystals used by the Kelvans for some unknown purpose. (See "By Any Other Name")

SAKURO'S DISEASE: Found on the planet Epsilon Canaris III, this is a potentially lethal disease that is a great deal like leukemia in its symptoms and effects. There is a cure, but it cannot be administered on an isolated planet with simple medical supplies; treatment in a fully-equipped sickbay is necessary to save someone suffering from Sakuro's Disease. (See "Metamorphosis")

SALTZGADUM: An ancient substance which can alter glass. (See "Hollow Pursuits")

SAPLIN: A poison that affects the functioning of the heart. The thorns of the pod plant on Gamma Trianguli VI use a poison that is a much more potent version of saplin. (See "The Apple")

SATELLITE FLARES: Trimagnesium flares producing bright light which includes the ultraviolet range. Deployed on satellites orbiting Deneva, these destroy the ultraviolet-sensitive flying parasites that have ravaged many worlds. (See "Operation: Annihilate")

SAURIAN BRANDY: A flavorful and strong liqueur favored by Dr. McCoy. The immortal human Flynn offers some fine hundred-year-old Saurian brandy to the *Enterprise* landing party; even Spock accepts a glass. (See "Requiem For Methuselah")

SCIENCE GROUP HEADQUARTERS: The room on Camus II where Janice Lester lures Kirk in order to subject him to the concealed life-entity transfer mechanism and steal his body. (See "Turnabout Intruder")

SECOND EYELID: Vulcans have a second, or nictitating, eyelid which allows light through but protects the eye; felines native to Earth have a similar second eyelid. (See "Operation: Annihilate")

SECURITY BOARD: A warning light that reveals any interference with the controls of the *Enterprise*.

SECURITY STATION: Located on deck nine of the *Enterprise*. (See "The Defector")

SELGNINAEM: A toxic substance which can alter glass. (See "Hollow Pursuits")

SENSOR SHADOWS: A method of detecting a cloaked starship, but only under unusual circumstances can these sensor shadows be detected. (See "Face Of The Enemy")

SENSOR WEB: A fine web of silver that forms a sensory apparatus, presumably attuned, somehow, to the wearer's mind. Useful for those lacking the sense of sight, such as Dr. Miranda Jones. The fact that she is a telepath is undoubtedly useful in accenting the usefulness of the web, which in her case is concealed in plain view as part of the design of her black dress. (See "Is There In Truth No Beauty?")

SENTRY PODS: Unmanned mechanisms around Lysian Central Command. When the *Enterprise* crew are tricked into believing that they are at war with the Lysians, the fact that the Central Command is not well armed is a tip-off that something is wrong. Riker wonders how their enemy could be one hundred years behind them in weapons technology. (See "Conundrum")

SERVO: A small hand-held device that, depending on its design and function, can be used in a variety of settings — a sort of portable 23rd Century tool kit. (See "Assignment: Earth")

SEVENTH GUARANTEE: The Federation equivalent of the Fifth Amendment. (See "The Drumhead")

"SHAKA, WHEN THE WALLS FELL": This phrase is one of the metaphors used by the Children of Tama to communicate. (See "Darmok")

SHAP TWO: One of the moves made in the Wadi game Chula. (See "Move Alone Home")

SHAP FOUR: Another of the moves made in the Wadi game Chula. (See "Move Alone Home")

SHIELD: Rudimentary sunglasses worn by the Troglytes of Ardana, who are not used to the bright light on the surface of their world. (See "The Cloud Minders")

SHIELD MUTATION: This defensive method is used to protect the *Enterprise* from the weapons employed by the Borg. (See "The Best Of Both Worlds")

SICKBAY: The main medical facility on board spacefaring vessels like the *Enterprise*; in sickbay, Dr. McCoy's word is absolute.

SIGN LANGUAGE: Data learns at least five forms of signing in his efforts to communicate with Riva. (See "Loud As A Whisper")

SLINGSHOT EFFECT: The time travel technique used several times by James Kirk's *Enterprise* (See "Tomorrow is Yesterday", "Assignment Earth", "Star Trek IV: The Voyage Home"); Picard gives it some thought when faced with a most vexing time loop — and a duplicate of himself. (See "Time Squared")

SOLAR HELIUM FUSION ENHANCEMENT: The life work of Dr. Timicin that involved experiments in the use of modified photon torpedoes to revitalize his solar system's sun. (See "Half A Life")

SOLITON WAVE: This wave will be generated on a planet's surface and then propel an unmanned test ship waiting in its path. It will be able to achieve warp speeds without the use of warp engines. (See "New Ground")

SONIC DISRUPTOR FIELD: A Klingon device used on Romulan ships, this is a force field of sorts which serves as an impenetrable door for prisoners' cells in the brig area. (See "The Enterprise Incident")

SONIC SEPARATOR: A medical device for very close surgical procedures.

SPACE BUOY: A buoy left by Balok's ship the *Fesarius*. This large spinning cube holds up the *Enterprise* until Balok can arrive and check out the Federation starship and its crew. When it starts to put out potentially dangerous levels of radiation, the *Enterprise* fires on it and destroys it. (See "The Corbomite Maneuver")

SPINNING WHEEL: Antiquated Earth device for producing fabric, still used by the Bringloidi settlers. (See "Up The Long Ladder")

SPLINT: A simple but effective means of setting broken bones, although the patient must wait for the break to heal naturally; Pulaski uses splints when the knitters don't work anymore. (See "Contagion")

S'SMARITH: When Troi and Picard are discussing the precision needed in the communication between races, Deanna employs this test. While holding a cup of coffee she asks if the word "coffee" refers to the cup, what it's made of or the liquid in the cup. (See "The Ensigns Of Command")

STACIUS TRADE GUILD: An organization which Kivas Fajo, the insane collector, belongs to. (See "The Most Toys")

STAFF, LAWGIVER'S: On Beta II, the Lawgivers — the enforcers of the computer Landru's will — used these staffs, which emit deadly beams, to punish or kill dissenters. (See "Return Of The Archons")

STARDATE: Standard timekeeping system for spacebound Starfleet vessels. A rather complicated procedure makes this a fairly flexible approach to time; warp speeds and distances traveled can affect the Stardate considerably. The first four numerals indicate the date; the numeral after the decimal point indicates the time of "day."

STARFLEET: The command structure of the Federation's spacefaring branch, military in hierarchy and function despite the Federation's lofty, peaceful goals.

STARFLEET EMERGENCY COMMUNIQUÉ: A communication dispatched for the eyes of Captain Picard only. Jean-Luc receives the message from his old friend Walker Keel, who warns Picard that Starfleet is in danger, but he can't be more specific. Picard is told to meet Walker for a face-to-face conference on a remote planet. (See "Conspiracy")

STARFLEET EXCHANGE PROGRAM: A temporary exchange of primary duty officers between Federation and Klingon vessels. Riker served aboard the *Pagh* for a time. (See "A Matter Of Honor") In exchange, Commander Kurn temporarily serves on the *Enterprise*. (See "The Sins Of The Fathers")

STARFLEET PRIORITY ONE SIGNAL: Employed by Admiral Haftel when he wants the *Enterprise* to come to him so that he can meet Lal. (See "The Offspring")

STARFLEET TACTICAL: The branch of Starfleet which examines the Borg threat and makes plans on how to deal with this looming menace. (See "The Best Of Both Worlds")

STARITHIUM ORE: A substance found on Risa. It interferes with sensor readings. (See "Captain's Holiday")

STARRY NIGHT: A painting by 19th Century Earth artist Vincent van Gogh which ends up in the collection of Kivas Fajo. (See "The Most Toys")

STELLAR CARTOGRAPHY: A department aboard the *Enterprise-D*. (See "Lessons")

STELLAR CORE FRAGMENT: This threatens the Genome Colony on the world of Moab Four. (See "The Masterpiece Society")

STELLAR SCIENCES LAB: A department aboard the *Enterprise-D*. Captain Picard becomes involved with the head of the department, Nella Daren. Because of the disruptions this ultimately creates in their professional lives Nella decides to transfer to another vessel. (See "Lessons")

STERILITE: An anti-infection medication used in various forms of surgery.

STOKALINE: A combination of vitamins used as a dietary health supplement. McCoy uses this to fool the Kelvans into thinking its a cure for a rare disease, the imaginary Rigellian Cassaba Fever. (See "By Any Other Name")

STORAGE CAPSULE: A biochemical storage medium with RNA memory. (See "Transfigurations")

STO-VO-KOR: The Klingon belief in life after death. (See "Rightful Heir")

STRATEGBREY: A very difficult strategy game. Riker is quickly beaten by the master strategist Kohlrami. So is Data. But when Data devises a strategy not to win but to hold his opponent in a state of balance, Kohlrami cannot beat him. (See "Peak Performance")

SUBCUTANEOUS COMMUNICATIONS: Involves implants so that transmissions from the *Enterprise* will be inaudible to anyone near the person who has the communications implant. (See "Who Watches The Watchers?")

SUBDIMENSIONAL PHYSICS: A branch of physics which the Vulcans seem to have made their own special scientific province. The immortal Flint certainly seems to think so. (See "Requiem For Methuselah")

SUBHADAR: A rank which Danar earned during the Tarsian War. (See "The Hunted")

SUBLIGHT SPEED: Speeds below warp one. Provided by the impulse engines. Travel inside planetary systems, and sometimes between nearby systems, is generally done at sublight speed. Going to warp speeds near planetary masses is not a particularly good idea.

SUBSPACE RADIO: A form of long-distance communication that uses a subspace warp to significantly reduce the time of radio transmission across large reaches of space.

SUBSURFACE CHARTS: Charts showing the mining tunnels on the planet Janus VI. New passageways not documented on these charts are probably the work of the Horta. (See "Devil In The Dark")

SUSPENDED ANIMATION: Techniques used to

keep human beings and humanoids alive in a state of reduced metabolic activity. Khan Noonian Singh and his followers are found in suspended animation on board the drifting *Botany Bay*, and the Scalosians seem to have devised a means of putting the *Enterprise* crew on ice until the males are needed for breeding purposes — but this plan is never put into effect. (See "Space Seed" and "The Wink Of An Eye")

SUSPENSION: A variety of stasis field which the immortal Flint has invented. He "freezes" the *Enterprise* in time to keep his ancient secret from spreading across the galaxy. He assures Kirk that the effect will wear off in a millennium or so, restoring the crew to normality without damage. (See "Requiem For Methuselah")

SWEEP: A diffused phaser firing pattern that can be used at different levels; useful in confronting large groups or areas.

SYMBALENE BLOOD BURN: A deadly plague, but one which moves slowly through a population.

SYNTHEHOL: The alcohol substitute used in Ten Forward. It produces an agreeable sensation but has no effect on the motor system or the mind; its mild effects can be shaken off easily. For purists, the galaxy still provides a wide variety of real booze, including good old-fashioned whiskey. (See "Up The Long Ladder") Scotty can immediately tell the difference when he tastes his first drink in 75 years. (See "Relics")

SYTHOCOCCUS NOVAE: A dangerous, fast-spreading disease. Most people have been immunized against it, but carriers, like Dr. Sevrin, are of necessity treated as a health hazard and subjected to travel restrictions that prevent them from going to planets that do not have medical technology advanced enough to fight the bacillus that causes it. (See "The Way To Eden")

TACHYON GRID: An organized arrangement of starships done so as to create a pattern of triangulation to enable them to detect any cloaked ships in the vicinity. (See "Redemption")

TAL-SHAYA: The Vulcan word for a technique of killing a humanoid painlessly and efficiently. When

Sarek is believed to have killed the Tellarite Gav, his accusers trot out this technique as the one he is alleged to have used. (See "Journey To Babel")

TAL SHIAR: The Imperial Intelligence force; a type of Romulan secret police. They even have authority over starship commanders and their orders are not to be questioned. (See "Face Of The Enemy")

TANTALUS FIELD: A monitoring/control device invented by aliens in the mirror universe. Kirk-Two steals it, and uses it to keep close personal watch on his underlings, as well as to kill anyone within its range. (See "Mirror, Mirror")

TAO CLASSICAL MUSIC: A type of music which Rishon Uxbridge composed. (See "The Survivors")

TARSIAN WAR: A war which the Angosians fought. In order to win they created super soldiers which the Angosians now feel are too dangerous to live in normal post-war society. (See "The Hunted")

TEACHER, GREAT: One of the lasting vestiges of the ancient technology of Sigma Draconis VI, a teaching device that can transfer temporary information into the brains of the Eymorgs; this learning is not permanent but is used only for immediate purposes. When the Teacher begins to wear down, the Eymorgs steal Spock's brain to power it. The Great Teacher of the Ancient Knowledge provides Dr. McCoy with the temporary knowledge needed to surgically re-attach the Vulcan's brain — including the speech centers. (See "Spock's Brain")

TEARS, ELASIAN: While the tears of Elasian males have no effect known to the galaxy at large, those of Elasian women like Elaan produce an aphrodisiac effect in males, not only of their own species, but of other humanoids as well — such as James T. Kirk. His devotion to the *Enterprise* helps him overcome the effect of the tears, although McCoy also appears to have synthesized a chemical cure. (See "Elaan Of Troyius")

TELEVISION: An outmoded form of communication and entertainment on Earth, television still flourishes on Planet 892-IV, where gladiatorial game shows lead in the ratings. (See "Bread And Circuses")

TELLURIAN SPICES: Fajo Kivas has these precious items and Andorians are bidding for them. (See "The Most Toys")

"TEMARC! THE RIVER TEMARC IN WINTER!": This phrase is one of the metaphors used by the Children of Tama to communicate. (See "Darmok")

"TEMBA — HIS ARMS WIDE.": Picard denotes this as a signal of friendship. It is a phrase used by the Children of Tama. (See "Darmok")

TEMPORAL RIFT: A time portal which exists without a detectable event horizon. (See "Yesterday's Enterprise" and "Cause And Effect")

TEN FORWARD: A non-alcoholic bar aboard the *Enterprise*. A spacious, relaxing lounge, it's a little unclear if access is limited to those of a certain rank, or open to the entire crew. It seems to be run by the mysterious but agreeable alien Guinan, who serves synthehol, food and the occasional shot or two of real liquor. (First seen in "The Child")

TERELLIAN SHIP: A ship containing the sole survivors of a world ravaged by an incurable plague. No planet will allow the ship to land and the people aboard must live out their lives on this vessel. (See "Haven")

TEST 24: After 23 attempts to find a cure for the aphrodisiac effect of Elasian tears, McCoy probably succeeds with this batch but is never required to use it on James Kirk. (See "Elaan Of Troyius")

TETRALUBISOL: Used to lubricate mechanical devices on board the *Enterprise*, this substance is highly toxic and blends easily with milk–which is how Lenore Karidian tries to murder Kevin Riley. (See "The Conscience Of The King")

TETRYON PARTICLES: When these particles are discovered in cargo bay four, this is an indication of an opening between subspace and normal space.

THALIAN CHOCOLATE MOUSSE: An excellent dessert originating on Thalos Seven. Available in Ten Forward. (See "The Dauphin")

THALIUM COMPOUND: Found in the rock strata on Mintaka. This substance interferes with sensor probes. (See "Who Watches The Watchers?")

THELASIAN FLU: The relatively harmless flu that triggers the aggressive immune system of the mutant children of Darwin, and leads to an accelerated aging disease in those affected — including Pulaski. (See "Unnatural Selection")

THERAGEN: A Klingon neurotoxin with interesting properties. At full strength, it kills, but McCoy discovers that when small quantities are mixed with alchohol, theragen serves as cure for the mental problems induced by prolonged exposure to the space warp encountered by the *Enterprise* in the Tholian region of space. (See "The Tholian Web")

THERMAL DEFLECTOR UNITS: These are used to create a protective shield against the raging firestorms on Bersallis Three to enable the *Enterprise* to evacuate all of the personnel from the surface. (See "Lessons")

THETA-BAND WAVES: These are being broadcast from Celtris Three, seemingly indicating the presence of metagenic weapons. (See "Chain Of Command")

THIRD SHAP, ALLAMARINE: One of the moves made in the Wadi game Chula. (See "Move Alone Home")

THOLIAN WEB: An enclosure technique used by the Tholians, a force-field grid of some sort, woven by at least two Tholian ships, that can keep a starship from moving past its barrier. (See "The Tholian Web")

THONGS: Throwing weapons employed by the miners on and under the surface of Ardana. (See "The Cloud Minders")

THORON FIELD: This can keep the defensive systems of Deep Space Nine from being scanned. (See "Emissary")

THRUSTERS: An engine mechanism on a starship which functions independently of the warp and impulse engines.

T'HY'LA: The Vulcan term which roughly translates as "friend". (See "Star Trek: The Motion Picture")

TIME LOOP: The *Enterprise* gets caught in this when they enter the Typhon Expanse and find themselves repeating the same day over and over, but with slight variations. The loop climaxes with the destruction of the *Enterprise* and then starts over again as they approach the Typhon Expanse. (See "Cause And Effect")

TIME SHIFT DETECTOR: A device constructed by Data in order to detect the presence of the time trav-

THE TREK UNIVERSAL INDEX

eling Devidians. When Samuel Clemens removes a transceiver from the device it stops functioning. (See "Time's Arrow")

T-K-L RATIONS: Standard rations used on the *Enterprise* when the food replicators are not functioning at peak performance. (See "Yesterday's Enterprise")

T-NEGATIVE: An uncommon blood type among Vulcans, but one which is shared by Sarek and Spock. (See "Journey To Babel")

T-9 ENERGY CONVERTER: A device stolen by the Ferengi which leads them into a confrontation with the *Enterprise* on a dead world once part of the T'Kon Empire. (See "The Last Outpost")

TOMID INCIDENT: The last Federation contact with the Romulans until Picard's encounter in the Neutral Zone. Presumably a hostile encounter, although the details are not recounted. (See "The Neutral Zone")

TOX-UTHAT: A small crystal cube invented by 27th Century scientist Kal Dano. The device is a Quantum Phase inhibitor which is very dangerous because it can cause the nuclear reactions in a star to halt, thereby effectively destroying the star. When Kal Dano realized that unscrupulous people were after it the scientist hid the device on Risa in the 22nd Century. It is found by Jean-Luc Picard in the 24th Century and he destroys it to keep it out of the hands of criminals known as the Vorgons. Why Kal Dano didn't just destroy it himself is unknown. (See "Captain's Holiday")

TRACTOR BEAM: A force beam that attracts rather than repels, useful in towing, creating navigational stability, and capturing other space vessels. The range of the *Enterprise*'s tractor beams is an amazing hundred thousand miles, although of course its effect is greater at close range.

TRANSCEIVER: A hidden communications tool used by Thelev, the Orion agent posing as an Andorian diplomat. (See "Journey To Babel") A device which Samuel Clemens removes from Data's Time Shift Detector. (See "Time's Arrow")

TRANSPORTER: A device which transforms matter into energy, and then transmits it to another location where a similar or identical device reassembles the energy patterns in (it is hoped) their original physical form. Statistically, the transporter is very

safe, but mishaps — some of them fairly unusual — have been known to occur. Perhaps the strangest was the magnetic disturbance which caused James Kirk to beam up as two separate versions of himself, one aggressive, one passive. One can hardly blame old-fashioned types like Leonard McCoy who distrust the transporters. The *Enterprise*'s transporters have a range which exceeds fifteen thousand miles. While one can beam from place to place on a ship it is rarely done for safety reasons; Kirk resorts to this desperate measure during the Organian crisis.

TRANSPORTER CODE 14: When Picard wants the Tox-Uthat destroyed, he signals "Transporter Code Fourteen" to Riker which causes the device to be beamed into space. (See "Captain's Holiday")

TRANSPORTER PAD: The point in the transporter room where a person stands in order to be beamed out.

TRANSPORTER PATTERN BUFFER: A device used to keep a transporter signal from degrading and thereby save the life of the person suspended in the transport beam. (See "Relics")

TRANSPORTER PSYCHOSIS: A serious disease caused when a body has a physiological reaction to the transporter beam. There is no cure for this. (See "Realm Of Fear")

TRANSPORTER ROOM: The rooms, located at key points on the *Enterprise*, where transporter pads are located.

TRANSPORT PASS: While travel to Stratos is restricted for Troglytes, some of them can obtain cards which allow them limited access to the floating city. (See "The Cloud Minders")

TRANSPORT PLATFORM: A platform with antigravity generators which serves as an elevator between the surface of Ardana and its cloudborne capital, Stratos. (See "The Cloud Minders")

TREATY OF ALGERON: To enter the Neutral Zone is a violation of this treaty, which originally established the Neutral Zone two hundred years before the time of the *Enterprise-D*. (See "The Defector")

TREATY OF ARMENS: The treaty between the Sheliak Corporate and the Federation. Section 133, paragraph 7 states that Tau Cygna V is a Sheliak planet and humans present on it are in violation of that treaty. Section 502, paragraph 716, subparagraph

5 reads, "Unwanted humans on H Class planets may be removed at the discretion of the Sheliak Corporate." Paragraph 1290, subsection D3 allows for arbitration by a third party in treaty disputes. The treaty is five hundred thousand words long and required 372 legal experts to negotiate it. (See "The Ensigns Of Command")

TRICORDER: A basic recording and sensor device, the tricorder may very well be the great-grandchild of today's laptop computers. They certainly pack a great deal of informational power in their easily-carried frames. Chemical composition, life form readings, geological data, radiation levels, medical data — all these, and more.

TRICORDRAZINE: Dr. Crusher uses this drug to treat Liko. (See "Who Watches The Watchers?") It is also used on Rachel Garrett in "Yesterday's Enterprise and is the medicine Pulaski utilizes to retard the progress of Riker's disease. (See "Shades of Gray")

TRICYANATE: A substance used on Beta Agni to contaminate the water supply and lure the *Enterprise* there so that Kivas Fajo can effect a flawless kidnapping of Commander Data when he arrives to deliver hytritium to neutralize the contamination. (See "The Most Toys")

TRILITHIUM RESIN: A toxic waste material produced by warp engines which can be used to manufacture a powerful explosive. It is a very unstable substance and must be transported with great care. (See "Starship Mine")

TRILLIUM 323: A mineral found on the planet Caldonia. (See "The Price")

TRI-OX COMPOUND: A powerful tranquilizer that affects the central nervous system. When Kirk is losing his fight with the *pon farr*-enraged Spock, McCoy claims to be giving Kirk an injection to help him cope with the atmosphere of the planet Vulcan. But the injection is really tri-ox. Moments later, it knocks Kirk into an unconscious state so deep that Spock thinks he has killed him. Tri-ox is also administered to Kirk after he is rescued from a space warp in the Tholian region. (See "Amok Time")

TRIPOLYMER COMPOSITES: The substance which Data is largely composed of. (See "The Most Toys")

TRISEC: Standard unit of time measurement on the planet Triskelion; as the name suggests, a trisec is approximately three Terran seconds in duration. (See "The Gamesters Of Triskelion")

TRITANIUM: Located only on the planet Argus X, this substance is over twenty times harder than the strongest diamond. (See "Obsession") A fairly reliable metal, but no match for the Echo Papa 607. (See "The Arsenal Of Freedom")

TRITITANIUM: This alloy is a primary component in starship construction. (See "Journey To Babel")

TRIXIAN BUBBLE JUICE: An exotic drink which Quark gets thrown in his face when he manages to insult the Tetrarch of the Paqu. (See "The Storyteller")

TUNNELING NEUTRINO BEAM: The beam used to destroy the metal-eating microbes that attack the *Enterprise* and the *Pagh*. (See "A Matter Of Honor")

TURBOLIFT: In function, the elevators on board the *Enterprise* and other similarly outfitted ships. Turbolifts operate in both horizontal and vertical directions. One can choose a destination merely by speaking, except in the case of malfunction or systems failure; in such instances, manual controls are available.

TYAN PARTICLE FOUNTAIN: A new type of mining technology being supervised by a Dr. Farallon. (See "Quality Of Life")

ULTRITIUM: An explosive. Traces of it are found on a destroyed Romulan vessel. (See "The Enemy")

UNITED EARTH SPACE PROBE AGENCY: An apparently imaginary agency invented on the spur of the moment by Kirk when Captain Christopher, a 20th Century jet pilot, is beamed aboard the *Enterprise*. This way, Christopher knows nothing about the future but is left with the impression that he has been told something about it. (See "Tomorrow Is Yesterday")

UNITED FEDERATION OF PLANETS: An interstellar alliance comprising Earth and various other peoples from across the galaxy: Coridians, Rigellians, Andorians, Tellarians and Vulcans. The

Romulans and Klingons are both opposed to Federation interests at the time of James T. Kirk but the Klingons eventually agree to sign a peace accord with the Federation. The Romulans remain uninterested in coming under the Federation's sphere of influence.

UNIT XY-75847: a squadron of Starfleet vessels on alert for Klingons during the Organian crisis. (See "Errand Of Mercy")

UNIVERSAL GRAVITATIONAL CONSTANT: A universal physical law which cannot be changed, except by someone in the Q Continuum. Altering it is apparently the only way Bre'el Four will be able to deal with the crisis caused by the decaying orbit of its moon. (See "Deja Q")

UTTABERRIES: Mr. Homn is sent by Lwaxana Troi to pick some of these, but when he's gone she, Troi and Riker are kidnapped by the Ferengi, Tog. (See "Menage A Troi")

VARON-T DISRUPTOR: A forbidden weapon, only five of which are still known to exist. Four of them are owned by the mad collector Kivas Fajo. This weapon tears a body from the inside out slowly, torturingly and painfully. Kivas Fako sleeps with one under his pillow and Data almost shoot Kivas with one. (See "The Most Toys")

VEGAN CHORIOMENINGITIS: A deadly brain disease. Kirk had it once, years before visiting the planet Gideon; although he was treated and recovered, the disease cells remain harmlessly in his blood. This is no problem for Federation citizens who have been immunized, but once Kirk is lured to Gideon and kisses Odona (who is later treated), the disease is destined to provide a drastic solution to the overpopulation on Gideon. (See "Mark Of Gideon")

VEGA NINE PROBE: This probe sent to the Beta Stromgren system discovers the existence of the strange creature dubbed Tin Man. (See "Tin Man")

VELTAN SEX IDOL: A rare item, but Kivas Fako has four of them in his collection. (See "The Most Toys")

VENTURI CHAMBER: Part of the power system for the engines of the Pakled's vessel, the *Mondor*. (See "Samaritan Snare")

VENUS DRUG: An outlawed drug, peddled by Harcourt Fenton Mudd, that enhances the sexual attractiveness of both genders. Unfortunately for Mudd, it works so well that he falls for the three women he's trying to pass off as beauties himself. (See "Mudd's Women")

VERUSTIN INFECTION: The disease which killed Jeremy Aster's father. (See "The Bonding")

VIEWSCREENS: Devices whose function is fairly self-evident from their name. There are many viewscreens on the *Enterprise*, from the small screens on desktop intercom devices to the large forward viewscreen in the main bridge, which generally shows the view ahead of the ship (from outside sensors) but can also show other angles and receive audio/video transmissions from other ships, bases and planets.

VILMORAN SYSTEM: The final link in the genetic program Prof. Galen was searching to complete when he died. (See "The Chase")

VIROTHERAPY: This is used as a cure for hyperonic radiation and was discovered by the scientist Minan. (See "The Ensigns Of Command")

VISOR: The device which enables Geordi LaForge to see, although the wavelength he sees on is greater than normal human vision.

VULCAN DEATH GRIP: There is no Vulcan death grip. However, Spock fakes one admirably well, putting Kirk out well enough to dupe the Romulans into thinking Kirk is dead. Although it doesn't kill Kirk, it does leave him feeling a bit worse for wear. (See "The Enterprise Incident")

VULCAN MIND FUSION: A complete merging of minds, difficult and hazardous even for advanced Vulcans.

VULCAN MIND MELD: A complete and unimpeded, directly mind-to-mind communication which can also be used to control another mind. Also difficult and dangerous, but not so much as mind fusion.

VULCAN MIND TOUCH: The most common variety of Vulcan telepathy, usually involving, but not always requiring, direct physical contact or proximity, practiced on numerous occasions by Spock: with the Horta on Janus IV, to search Van Gelder's memories, and to wipe Kirk's memories of Reena, among other occasions.

VULCAN NERVE PINCH: A very precise method of rendering a foe unconscious, far preferable to crude human fisticuffs to the more refined Vulcans.

WARP DRIVE: Achieved through a combination of matter and anti-matter, warp drive allows starships to achieve speeds in excess of light speed. The *Enterprise* is the first ship of its size to have warp drive.

WARP FACTOR: Standard measurements of warp speed. Warp 1 is the basic speed of light, 186 thousand miles per second. Increasing warp speeds are geometric in progression: Warp 2 is eight times Warp 1. Thus, each succeeding warp factor is a drastic increase over the previous level. Maximum warp (within safety limits) for the *Enterprise* is Warp 6, although it can be pushed beyond that. Warp 9 in particular is bad news, for the ship will definitely rip itself to pieces at such a high factor. Warp over 9.5 has unusual effects if the ship survives it.

WAVE FRONT FEEDBACK: Graviton waves generated inside a black cluster in response to the presence of the shields on a starship. If shields are dropped, the waves disperse harmlessly. If the shields are strengthened the waves increase in strength geometrically until they smash the vessel. (See "Hero Worship")

WORMHOLE: A dimensional gate through which a vessel can instantly travel from one point in the galaxy to another. The only existing stable wormhole exists near Bajor.

XENOPOLYCYTHEMIA: A blood disease that threatens McCoy's life until he is saved by a cure uncovered on the asteroid/spaceship of *Yonada*. (See "For The World Is Hollow And I Have Touched The Sky")

YELLOW ALERT: Code for a starship crew to prepare for any dangerous eventuality.

ZIENITE: Useful for curing some diseases, zienite gas in its unprocessed form has a debilitating effect on the Troglyte miners who harvest it for the unaffected cloud dwellers in Stratos. This gives rise to unfounded social distinctions based on nonexistent evolutionary differences: the miners are every bit as evolved as the cloud dwellers but seem underdeveloped when exposed to the gas. Taken away from its effects, they recover quickly. (See "The Cloud Minders")

INDEX

145

Also available from B🌲XTREE

• • • •

THESE WERE THE VOYAGES....

CAPTAINS' LOGS
THE COMPLETE TREK GUIDEBOOK

If you haven't picked up a copy of the indispensable TREK reference book, CAPTAINS' LOGS, you don't have the first — and last — word on the history of the future.

The Original CAPTAINS' LOGS features:

COMPLETE EPISODES GUIDES and OVERVIEWS w / credits and commentary from the actors, writers, producers and executives behind the entire TREK saga, including:

✧ TREK CLASSIC (Seasons 1 - 3, 79 Episodes)

✧ TREK: ANIMATED (Seasons 1 - 2, 22 Episodes)

✧ TREK: THE LOST YEARS
(The Unproduced '70s TREK SERIES)

✧ THE TREK FILMS
(from STAR TREK: THE MOTION PICTURE to THE UNDISCOVERED COUNTRY)

✧ THE NEXT GENERATION
(Seasons1- 5, 126 Episodes)

✧ DEEP SPACE NINE (The Pilot)

£13.99
ISBN 1 85283 899 X

• • • •

WELCOME TO THE EDGE OF THE FINAL FRONTIER...

EXPLORING DEEP SPACE & BEYOND
The First Comprehensive Guide to the New Wave in Science-Fiction Television

This book chronicles the making of television's most important genre shows located on the outskirts of explored space. EXPLORING DEEP SPACE begins by looking at the history of space stations in science fact and fiction, followed by an indepth analysis of the creation of DEEP SPACE NINE.

Also lying on the fringes of the final frontier are Warner Bros'. BABYLON 5, a space station on which the five warring intergalactic federations come together in search of peace; and SPACE RANGERS, an ambitious action / adventure set in the cosmos from the creative team behind BACKDRAFT and ROBIN HOOD:PRINCE OF THIEVES.

Featured in this volume are:

✧ DEEP SPACE creators
Rick Berman and Michael Piller

✧ The cast of DEEP SPACE NINE
including Avery Brooks, Rene Auberjonois and Terry Farrell

✧ BABYLON 5 creator J. Michael Straczynski

✧ SPACE RANGERS creator Pen Densham

£6.99
ISBN 1 85283 571 0

CAPTAIN'S LOGS

THE COMPLETE TREK VOYAGES

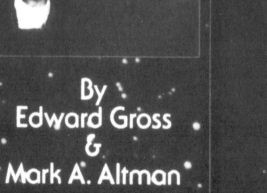

By
Edward Gross
&
Mark A. Altman

EXPLORING DEEP SPACE

AND BEYOND

By Mark A. Altman and David Ian Solter

B⬛XTREE

Excellence in Word Problems

Year 4

By Karen Hamilton

RISING STARS

Rising Stars UK Ltd., 76 Farnaby Road, Bromley,
BR1 4BH

Website: **www.risingstars-uk.com**

All facts are correct at time of going to press.

Published 2003
Reprinted 2004
Text, design and layout ©Rising Stars UK Ltd.
Editorial: Tanya Solomons
Concept design: Burville Riley
Design: Ken Vail Graphic Design, Cambridge
Illustration copyright ©Louisa Burville-Riley
Cover photo ©Guy Edwards/Getty Images

British Library Cataloguing in Publication Data

A CIP record for this book is available from the
British Library.

ISBN 1-904591-20-5

Printed by Wyndeham Gait, Grimsby, UK

Contents

How to use this book

The *Excellence in Word Problems* series is designed to help you use your mathematical skills to solve a range a problems, many of which are written in words rather than figures.

Rather than giving a sum like:

4 × 6 = ☐

a word problem might be along the lines of:

"If I have 4 six-packs of cola, how many cans of cola do I have in total?"

The answer is the same, but you need to think about it a bit more and remember to answer by writing or saying: **"I have 24 cans of cola in total."**

The introduction

This section of each page gives you an idea of the sort of problems you are likely to see and helps you to understand what maths you need to use.

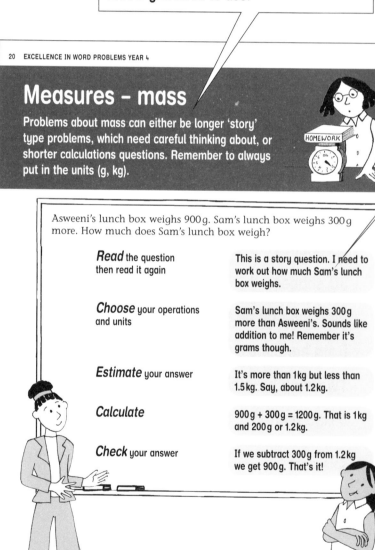

Measures – mass

Problems about mass can either be longer 'story' type problems, which need careful thinking about, or shorter calculations questions. Remember to always put in the units (g, kg).

Asweeni's lunch box weighs 900 g. Sam's lunch box weighs 300 g more. How much does Sam's lunch box weigh?

Read the question then read it again	This is a story question. I need to work out how much Sam's lunch box weighs.
Choose your operations and units	Sam's lunch box weighs 300 g more than Asweeni's. Sounds like addition to me! Remember it's grams though.
Estimate your answer	It's more than 1 kg but less than 1.5 kg. Say, about 1.2 kg.
Calculate	900 g + 300 g = 1200 g. That is 1 kg and 200 g or 1.2 kg.
Check your answer	If we subtract 300 g from 1.2 kg we get 900 g. That's it!

Hints and tips

Remember the following facts:
★ kilo = 1000   ★ centi = 0.01   ★ milli = 0.001

Hints and tips

The hints and tips section gives you useful ideas for completing the problems on the other page. These are the things you need to remember if you are doing a quiz or test!

The example problem

The flow chart takes you through an example problem *step-by-step*. This is important when answering word problems as it helps you to order your thoughts, do each part of the problem in the right order and *check your work!*

Every problem has the same five steps.
READ the question then read it again
CHOOSE your operations and units
ESTIMATE your answer
CALCULATE
CHECK your answer

We remember this by using this mnemonic:
RED
CLOWNS
ENTER
CAVES
CAREFULLY

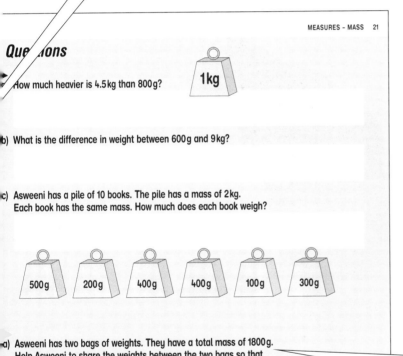

MEASURES – MASS 21

Que ons

a) How much heavier is 4.5 kg than 800 g?

1 kg

b) What is the difference in weight between 600 g and 9 kg?

c) Asweeni has a pile of 10 books. The pile has a mass of 2 kg.
Each book has the same mass. How much does each book weigh?

| 500 g | 200 g | 400 g | 400 g | 100 g | 300 g |

a) Asweeni has two bags of weights. They have a total mass of 1800 g.
Help Asweeni to share the weights between the two bags so that
the mass of one bag is twice that of the other.

b) Now share the weights between the two bags so that there
is a difference of just 200 g.

Challenge
'The total is 1000.'
Find 10 pairs of numbers that have a total of 1000 g.
They must not be multiples of 2 or 5.

The questions

The questions get harder as you go down the page.

● Section 1 questions are fairly straightforward and help you to practise your skills.
● Section 2 questions are a bit harder but will help you to remember all the key points.
● The Challenge sections are really tough and sometimes mean that you can make up games and your own questions! They can be great fun!

All about word problems

Ten top tips for working with word problems

1 *Work step-by-step.* Follow the flow chart.

Red
Clowns
Enter
Caves
Carefully

Read the question then read it again
Choose your operations and units
Estimate your answer
Calculate
Check your answer

2   Always *show your working* or 'method'. This will help
you to keep track of what you have done and may
help you to get extra marks.

3   Always *include your units* in the answer.
If you don't, you won't get full marks.

4 When you first read through a question, *underline important words and numbers*. This will help you to remember the important bits!

5 *Draw a picture* to help you. Sometimes a question is easier if you can 'see' it. Drawing 6 apples can help you if you need to divide them!

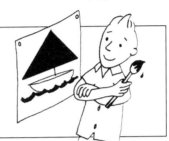

6 If the problem has a number of steps, break it down and do *one step at a time*.

7 When *checking your answers*, look at the inverse operation.

8 Sometimes an answer will 'sound right'. Read it out (quietly) and listen. *Does it make sense?*

9 If you are using measurements (grams, litres, cm), make sure that the *units are the same* before you calculate.

10 Once again! *Read the question then read it again.*

Place value

Place value questions will often ask you to estimate a total
or to complete an operation with a number such as 10 or 100.

Thomas had to estimate TV viewing figures to the nearest 100.
Here are the actual viewing figures:

Cartoon   7,670   Film   10,097   Soap opera   23,956

Read the question
then read it again

This is complicated. I have to
estimate three different figures.
It's best to work systematically.

Choose your operations
and units

I am rounding here. Rounding up
or down to the nearest 100. That
means looking at the 2nd and 3rd
digits from the right.

Estimate your answer

It's to the nearest hundred. That
means there are two '0's.

Calculate

Cartoon: 7,670 up to 7,700
Film: 10,097 up to 10,100
Soap opera: 23,956 up
to 24,000

Check your answer

I have rounded the numbers
to the nearest hundred.

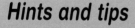

Hints and tips

★ Some place value questions have numbers written in different ways,
   e.g. 'What is the difference between 235 and two hundred and thirty-six?'
   It makes the question easier if you write the numbers out in the same way,
   e.g. 235 and 236.

Questions

a) If Hannah takes 354 away from 1250, will the answer be closer to 1300, 900 or 1000?

b) Hannah travels 589 km on Monday and 802 km on Tuesday. Is her total journey closer to 300 km, 1400 km or 1200 km

c) How many hundreds are there in

2300?   1500?   4000?

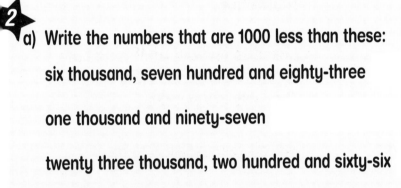

a) Write the numbers that are 1000 less than these:

six thousand, seven hundred and eighty-three

one thousand and ninety-seven

twenty three thousand, two hundred and sixty-six

b) Which is larger?
  i)   500 multiplied by 100   or 5 × 1000
  ii) 600 × 10   or 6 groups of 10 000
  iii) 5 × 1000   or 2 times 500

Challenge

What is the largest number you can make with these digits?
Now write the number in words.

What is the smallest number you can make with these digits?
Now write the number in words.

Fractions

Problems about fractions usually ask you to find a fraction of a number or to work out what fraction a smaller number is of a bigger number.

Stephanie has 16 pencils. She gives half of them away. How many does she have left?

Read the question then read it again

Read slowly and carefully. This one is fractions... but also subtraction.

Choose your operations and units

I need to find out what is half of 16, and then take it away from 16. The units are pencils.

Estimate your answer

Half 16 sounds like 8 to me.

Calculate

$\frac{1}{2}$ of 16 is 8. 16 – 8 = 8. Stephanie has 8 pencils left.

Check your answer

I can check by dividing 16 by 2 as well. Yes, it's 8 as well!

Hints and tips

Equivalent fractions can really help with these word problems:

$\frac{1}{2} = \frac{2}{4} = \frac{3}{6} = \frac{4}{8} = \frac{5}{10}$ $\frac{1}{5} = \frac{2}{10} = \frac{3}{15} = \frac{4}{20} = \frac{5}{25}$

$\frac{1}{4} = \frac{2}{8} = \frac{3}{12} = \frac{4}{16} = \frac{5}{20}$ $\frac{1}{10} = \frac{2}{20} = \frac{3}{30} = \frac{5}{50} = \frac{10}{100}$

$\frac{1}{3} = \frac{2}{6} = \frac{3}{9} = \frac{4}{12} = \frac{5}{15}$

Questions

1

a) Stephanie walks $\frac{1}{2}$ a kilometre. How far is this in metres?

b) $\frac{1}{5}$ of the children in Stephanie's class go home for lunch. There are 30 children in the class. How many go home for lunch?

c) What fraction of £4 is 50p?

2

a) There are 12 sweets in a packet. Stephanie gives a quarter of them to Christine and eats $\frac{1}{3}$ of the remaining sweets. How many sweets are left?

b) Stephanie walks $\frac{2}{5}$ of a kilometre. Christine walks $\frac{3}{10}$ of a kilometre. Who has walked furthest, Stephanie or Christine? Show your working.

Challenge

Stephanie walks 2 kilometres on Monday. The next day she walks half that distance. Each day she walks half the distance of the previous day. How far will she have walked in total by Friday?

Decimals

Problems about decimals are usually word stories. Many are about money and sometimes you will have to convert between pounds and pence. Remember to always put the decimal point in!

Daniel has 1.5 m of string. He cuts off 75 cm. How much string is left?

Read the question then read it again

Read slowly and carefully. The measurements are different units. I will need to convert one.

Choose your operations and units

How much string is left? That's subtraction. Let's keep the units as cm. 1.5 m = 150 cm.

Estimate your answer

It should be between 70 and 80 cm.

Calculate

150 cm – 75 cm = 75 cm
There is 75 cm of string left.

Check your answer

Let's check by adding.
75 + 75 = 150. Yes, it's right.

Hints and tips

★ Always look at the units first with decimal word problems, e.g. cm, m.

★ If they are different, convert one to make them the same.

★ Remember to put the decimal point back in at the end!

Questions

1

a) Daniel spent half of his £23.40 savings. How much did he spend?

b) What is the difference between 500 ml and 2.7 l?

c) Daniel has circled the decimal that he thinks is closest to each
whole number. Check his work. Tick the right answer and circle
the correct answer if Daniel got the answer wrong.

12	12.3	11.1	11.7	11.9
5	5.6	7.8	4.7	5.7
34	34.76	33.95	33.09	34.67

2

a) Daniel saves for four days. He is given £10 on Monday. He gets half the amount of the
previous day for the next three days. How much has he saved in four days?

b) Daniel now saves for another four days. On Monday he gets £1.13 and then
gets double the amount of the previous day for the next 3 days. How much
has he saved this time?

★ Challenge

You will need one set of digit cards 1–9. Shuffle the cards and choose four digits.
Work SYSTEMATICALLY to make as many decimal numbers that have *two* digits
after the decimal point.

Example:

| 2 | 9 | 7 | 3 |

37.92
37.29
39.72
39.27
32.93
32.39

Then place the numbers in each
set in numerical order, starting
with the smallest number.

Addition and subtraction

Addition and subtraction questions can be about anything, so remember to put in the unit or label next to each answer. This can be metres, litres or conkers!

Julia has 132 marbles. She drops her jar and loses 87. How many marbles does she have now?

Read the question then read it again

Read slowly and carefully. This is about rounding up and down.

Choose your operations and units

This is subtraction as she 'loses' 87 marbles.

Estimate your answer

Julia has about 130 marbles and loses about 90. The answer should be about 40.

Calculate

132 – 87 = 45
Julia now has 45 marbles.

Check your answer

Check by adding: 45 + 87 = 132. Yes, I'm right!

Hints and tips

★ Remember these facts:

When you add	the answer is always
two even numbers	EVEN
two odd numbers	EVEN
an even number and an odd number	ODD

When you subtract	the answer is always
an even number from an even number	EVEN
an odd number from an odd number	EVEN
an even number from an odd number	ODD
an odd number from an even number	ODD

Questions

1

a) Julia has 43 conkers. Tamara has 58 more. How many conkers does Julia have?

b) Julia had 62 stickers. She swapped 35 for a comic. How many stickers does she have now?

c) Julia scored 138 on level one of her computer game. She scored 297 on level two. What is her total score?

2

a) 603 spectators attended a football match this week. That is 263 fewer people than attended last week. How many spectators were there last week?

b) One length of the swimming pool is 25 m. Julia has swum three lengths so far. She is trying to swim 500 m. How many more lengths does she need to swim?

Challenge

Julia buys sheets of 5p and 7p stamps. What totals less than, but close to 100 can she make? She can use as many of each stamp as she needs to.

Money

Money questions can be adding, subtracting, multiplying or dividing. They also can be about giving or getting change for something.

Solkan spent quarter of his pocket money on a present for his mum. He had £10. How much did his mum's present cost?

Read the question then read it again

Read slowly and carefully.
A quarter is the same as dividing by 4.

Choose your operations and units

This is a division sum. I must remember to put in the £ sign or p if it's pence.

Estimate your answer

$\frac{1}{4}$ of 10 is between 2 and 3.

Calculate

$\frac{1}{4}$ of £10 = 10 ÷ 4 = £2.50. Solkan's mum's present cost £2.50.

Check your answer

Four lots of £2.50 = £10.

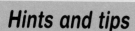
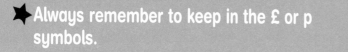

Hints and tips

★ Always remember to keep in the £ or p symbols.

★ There are 100 pence (p) in one pound (£).

Questions

£3.45

£1.99

£1.29

£5.63

£2.20

£1.10

1

a) What is the total cost of the least and most expensive items?

b) Solkan wants to buy two skateboards. How much will they cost?

c) Solkan has £5. He wants to spend as close to this as possible.
Which two items should he buy? How much change would he get?

2

a) These are tickets to a theme park.
What would be the cheapest price for a
family of two adults and four children?

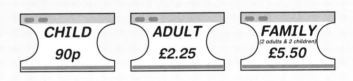

CHILD	ADULT	FAMILY
		(2 adults & 2 children)
90p	£2.25	£5.50

b) How much would a family of four save if they bought a family ticket
rather than individual tickets?

Challenge

Use the items from question 1.
Solkan has £10 to spend. How many different combinations of three items
could he buy and still have change?

Time

Time questions will have a start time and a finish time. You will need to work out either one or how long it is between the two different times.

Will is 10 minutes late for his dentist appointment. He arrives at 10:05. What time should he have arrived?

Read the question then read it again	Read slowly and carefully. Tricky one here. It goes across two hours.
Choose your operations and units	Subtract 10 minutes from the start time to give me the finish time.
Estimate your answer	It will be nearly 10:00 but the time will start with 9:??
Calculate	10:05 minus 10 minutes = 9:55 am. That sounds about right. Will should have arrived at 9:55 am.
Check your answer	Start at 9:55, add on 10 minutes and I get to 10:05. Correct!

Hints and tips

★ Watch out for questions about days, weeks, months and years. Remember these facts:
- 60 seconds in a minute
- 60 minutes in an hour
- 24 hours in a day
- 7 days in a week
- 52 weeks in a year
- 12 months in a year

Questions

a) Will arrived 25 minutes late for the start of a pop concert.
He arrived at 10 past 8. What time did the concert start?

b) Will arrives 15 minutes early for the bus. The bus is due to arrive
at 9:07. What time was Will at the bus stop?

c) A film starts at 3:05. It last for 85 minutes. What time does it finish?

a) It takes Keith twice as long as Will to run 6 kilometres. Will starts at
8:30 and finishes at 9:15. How long does it take Keith to run 6 kilometres?

b) Will plays in a five-a-side football tournament. Four matches were
played. Each game should have lasted half an hour. Unfortunately,
the tournament overran by 25 minutes. The tournament started at
11:30. What time did it finish?

Challenge

Will and Keith's school closes for six weeks on Friday 18th July for the
summer holidays. If the school opens on the nearest Monday,
when does school re-start for the new school year?
Show your working.

Measures – mass

Problems about mass can either be longer 'story' type problems, which need careful thinking about, or shorter calculations questions. Remember to always put in the units (g, kg).

Asweeni's lunch box weighs 900g. Sam's lunch box weighs 300g more. How much does Sam's lunch box weigh?

Read the question then read it again	This is a story question. I need to work out how much Sam's lunch box weighs.
Choose your operations and units	Sam's lunch box weighs 300g more than Asweeni's. Sounds like addition to me! Remember it's grams though.
Estimate your answer	It's more than 1kg but less than 1.5kg. Say, about 1.2kg.
Calculate	900g + 300g = 1200g. That is 1kg and 200g or 1.2kg.
Check your answer	If we subtract 300g from 1.2kg we get 900g. That's it!

Hints and tips

Remember the following facts:
★ kilo = 1000   ★ centi = 0.01   ★ milli = 0.001

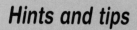
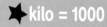

Questions

1kg

a) How much heavier is 4.5 kg than 800 g?

b) What is the difference in weight between 600 g and 9 kg?

c) Asweeni has a pile of 10 books. The pile has a mass of 2 kg.
Each book has the same mass. How much does each book weigh?

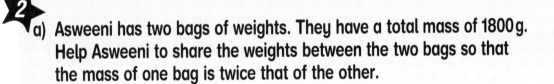

500 g   200 g   400 g   400 g   100 g   300 g

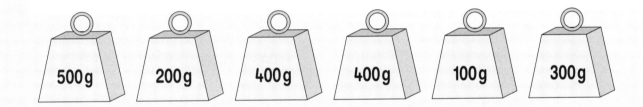

2

a) Asweeni has two bags of weights. They have a total mass of 1800 g.
Help Asweeni to share the weights between the two bags so that
the mass of one bag is twice that of the other.

b) Now share the weights between the two bags so that there
is a difference of just 200 g.

★*Challenge*

'The total is 1000.'
Find 10 pairs of numbers that have a total of 1000 g.
They must not be multiples of 2 or 5.

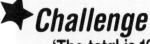

Measures – capacity

Capacity problems might ask you to work out how many spoons or cups it would take to fill a large bottle or barrel. These are about dividing. You might also need to find out the difference between two capacities.

Selcuk buys a 1 litre bottle of lemonade. He fills a glass and has a drink. There is 700 ml of lemonade left in the bottle. What is the capacity of the glass?

Read the question then read it again	Read slowly and carefully. I need to find out how much lemonade is in the glass.
Choose your operations and units	I think this is about subtraction. Let's keep the units the same. 1 litre is 1000 ml.
Estimate your answer	10 – 7 = 3
Calculate	1000 ml – 700 ml = 300 ml. The capacity of the glass is 300 ml.
Check your answer	I can check by adding. 300 ml + 700 ml = 1000 ml or 1 litre.

Hints and tips

★ If you have millilitres, centilitres and litres in a question, it helps if you make them all the same unit by multiplying or dividing by 10 or 1000.

millilitres ÷ 1000 = litres   centilitres ÷ 100 = litres
litres × 1000 = millilitres   litres × 100 = centilitres

Questions

1

a) Selcuk uses 4 buckets of water to wash a car. Each bucket has a capacity of 4 l. How many litres does he use in total?

b) Seluck's watering can holds 2 litres of water. He uses about 200 ml to water one plant. How many plants can he water if he fills the can?

c) A tin of paint holds 2.5 litres of paint. Selcuk needs 10 litres of paint. How many tins of paint does he need?

2

a) Selcuk needs 240 ml of water to make a cup of tea. His kettle has a capacity of 1.5 l. How many cups of tea could he make if he fills and boils the kettle twice?

b) Selcuk wants to make enough fruit punch to serve 5 people. How much of each ingredient would he need?

Fruit Punch
(serves 3)

1.5 l lemonade
210 ml fruit concentrate
75 ml lemon juice

⭐ Challenge

Selcuk has two jugs. One has a capacity of 3 l and the other has a capacity of 7 l. Explain how he could use the jugs to measure out 1 litre of liquid.

Measures – length

Length questions can be about very short lengths (mm) or huge lengths (miles or km). The problems may be about a journey or measuring something in your home.

On Sports Day Crystal throws the tennis ball 15 m. Jamie throws it 9.5 m. How much further does Crystal throw the ball?

Read the question then read it again

Read slowly and carefully. I need to find how much further Crystal threw the ball than Jamie.

Choose your operations and units

This is a subtraction question. 'Further than' tells me this. The units are metres.

Estimate your answer

15 – 10 = 5. That should be about right.

Calculate

15 m – 9.5 m = 5.5 m
Crystal throws the ball 5.5 m further.

Check your answer

I should check by adding and remember to include my units!

Hints and tips

★ Remember the multiples and the different units for length:
1000 mm = 1 metre = 100 cm
10 mm = 1 centimetre = $\frac{1}{100}$ metre

Questions

1

a) Crystal cuts 75 cm off a 4 m roll of ribbon. How much ribbon is left on the roll?

b) Crystal is 1.25 m tall. Pete is 20 cm taller. How tall is Pete?

c) Crystal jumped 1 m 90 cm in the sand pit. The winning jump was 2.5 m. How much further did Crystal need to jump to have equalled the winning jump?

2

a) Crystal's dad drives from London to Wolverhampton. The journey from London to Wolverhampton is 215 km. How far does he travel if he makes three return trips?

b) A rectangular playground has a perimeter of 71 m. The length of one side is 15.5 m. What are the lengths of the other sides?

⭐Challenge

I have 3.5 m of rope. It is cut into 3 pieces. Two pieces are the same length and the third piece is 1.5 m. What is the length of each of the two identical pieces of rope?

Puzzles

Number puzzles sometimes ask you to look for patterns. They also ask you to find numbers when you know something about each one, e.g. the sum when they are added and the product when they are multiplied.

Two numbers have a product of 12 and a difference of 1.
What are the two numbers?

Read the question then read it again

This needs careful thought. I am looking for two numbers that are pretty close together.

Choose your operations and units

I will need to test my ideas by multiplying and subtracting.

Estimate your answer

This one is too difficult to estimate.

Calculate

Work systematically.
What two numbers make 12 when I multiply them?
1 and 12
2 and 6
3 and 4
Now which of those have a difference of one?
Easy! 3 and 4.

Check your answer

3 × 4 = 12
4 – 3 = 1
Yes, 3 and 4 satisfy all the rules!

Hints and tips

★ With puzzles, it is important to think logically so make notes in the margin if you want to and use as much paper as you like!

Questions

a) I am a square number less than 100. I am divisible by 6.
What number am I?

b) I am the sum of the factors of 12. What am I?

c) We are multiples of 3. We are more than 10, but less than 50.
We are also multiples of 4. What numbers are we?

a) Which three consecutive numbers have a sum of 39? Is it possible for
four consecutive numbers to total 39?

b) The total of two numbers is 18. One number is twice the value of the other. What are the
two numbers?

★ Challenge

MULTIPLE   FACTOR   PRODUCT   SUM   DIFFERENCE
CONSECUTIVE   MORE THAN   LESS THAN

Use these words to make up two word puzzles for a friend.

Patterns and sequences

Problems involving patterns and sequences usually need you to work out the differences between the numbers.

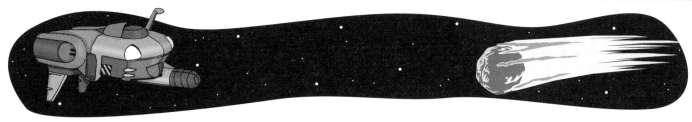

Special Agent Nigel needs to work out the next three numbers in this sequence to shoot down the giant asteroid that's heading towards us! He's stuck. Can you help him? 39, 48, 57, 66, ___, ___, ___

Read the question then read it again

'Next three numbers...'

Choose your operations and units

Find the difference between the numbers. That's subtraction.

Estimate your answer

48 – 39 = 9, 57 – 48 = 9, 66 – 57 = 9
The difference is 9.

Calculate

I need to add 9 to find the next three numbers.
66 + 9 = 75, 75 + 9 = 84, 84 + 9 = 93

Check your answer

Double check my answer. Yes, 75, 84 and 93 are the next three numbers in the sequence. Nigel can save the world!

Hints and tips

★ Practise counting on or back from any number in steps of any single-digit number.

★ When you've mastered that, try counting on or back in steps of any 2-digit number.

Questions

1

a) Oh dear, there is more than one asteroid! Nigel needs to guide the missile that will shoot down the second asteroid. Can you help him by working out the next three numbers in this sequence? 46, 39, 32, 25, ___, ___, ___

b) Here comes the next one! Nigel's in trouble again, can you help him? What are the next three numbers? 146, 150, 154, 158, ___, ___, ___

c) That was close! Now Nigel needs you to help him shoot the last asteroid down. Can you work out the next three numbers on his computer display? 247, 244, 241, 238, ___, ___, ___

2

a) Here are two control panels in Nigel's spaceship. Nigel has pressed all the buttons on the first control panel but you need to press all the correct buttons on the next one or the ship will crash! Shade them in on the control panel. Can you do it?

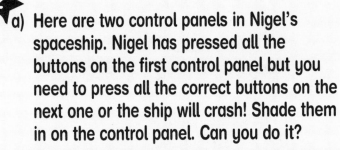

b) Nigel says that if he presses button number 110 on a third control panel then the ship will not crash. Should he press it or should you stop him? Explain your answer.

★Challenge

Patterns might not always be shown in numbers. What is the missing letter in this sequence?
J F M A M J ___ A S O N D

Multiplication and division

Multiplication and division problems are often set in the kitchen where you have to divide or multiply ingredients. Remember your times tables here!

Remelle buys 4 packs of bread rolls. Each pack contains 6 rolls. How many rolls has he bought?

Read the question then read it again

Read this carefully. What are you being asked to find out?

Choose your operations and units

This is multiplication. 4 packs times 6 rolls.

Estimate your answer

I think it should be 24.

Calculate

$4 \times 6 = 24$ rolls.
Remelle has bought 24 rolls.

Check your answer

Check by adding.
$6 + 6 + 6 + 6 = 24$.
Yes, I'm right!

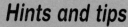

Hints and tips

★ Remember your written methods for multiplication and division. These can really help!

Questions

a) Remelle buys three dozen eggs. How many eggs does he buy altogether?

b) Remelle buys 5 bunches of flowers for his mum. There are 9 flowers in each bunch. What is the total number of flowers?

c) Remelle has 20 marbles. He shares them equally between 3 friends. How many marbles does each friend get?

a) A pack of 10 batteries costs £3. How much do two batteries cost?

b) There are 8 pencils in a complete set. How many sets can I make using 58 pencils?

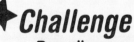 **Challenge**

Remelle exercises every second day. His best friend Selcuk exercises every fifth day. Start on day 1. When will be the first time that they exercise together? Work out the second, third and fourth times that they will exercise together. What pattern do you notice?

2D shapes

Questions about 2D shapes often ask you to talk about their properties (number of sides, whether sides are equal or parallel). Some problems will need you to draw shapes as well.

Draw a polygon with 4 sides, 4 right angles and 2 lines of symmetry.

Read the question then read it again	Read slowly and carefully. Do I need to draw a picture?
Choose your operations and units	List out the properties: 4 sides, 4 right angles, 2 lines of symmetry.
Estimate your answer	I think it's a rectangle because a square has 4 lines of symmetry.
Calculate	
Check your answer	Yes, my shape has 4 sides, 4 right angles and 2 lines of symmetry. It's a rectangle!

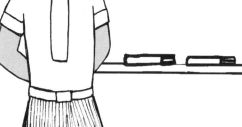

Hints and tips

★ Shape work is often about language. Learn the words to describe shapes, such as: line, side, edge, vertex, face, base, point, angle, centre and so on. This will help you to answer questions about all kinds of shapes.

Questions

1

a) Tamara has a bag full of polygons. She takes out three.
The sum of their sides is 12. What could the three shapes be?

b) Tamara has 4 polygons. The sum of all their sides is 16. What could the
4 shapes be? What do you notice about the total number of vertices
and the total number of angles?

c) Tamara cuts a shape in half. The sum of the sides of the two new
shapes is 6. What was the original shape? What are the new shapes?

2

a) Sketch the reflection of this shape.

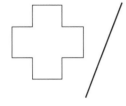

b) Draw a polygon that has one right angle and at least one line of symmetry.

 **Challenge**

Are there a maximum number of right angles that a polygon can have? Investigate.

3D shapes

Problems about 3D shapes will often ask you to work out how many faces, edges and vertices there are. You might also be asked how many smaller shapes fit into a bigger one.

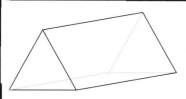

Name this shape. Then write the names of the shapes of the faces, the number of faces, edges and vertices in the shape.

Read the question then read it again

This question has many parts and lots of information is needed. Put the information in a table.

Choose your operations and units

I need to remember some facts about this shape and count all the different parts of the shape.

Estimate your answer

I think that this is a triangular prism, not a pyramid.

Calculate

Shape	Faces	Edges	Vertices
triangular prism	5	9	6

Tick off each face, edge and vertex as you count it. Don't forget the faces you can't see! The shapes of the faces are rectangles and triangles.

Check your answer

Check you have been right round the shape.

Hints and tips

★ Keep a note of all the shape names you know with the numbers of faces, edges and vertices next to each shape name.

e.g.

Shape	Faces	Edges	Vertices
cube	6	12	8

Questions

Complete this table about polyhedrons.

Name of polyhedron	Shape of faces	Number of faces	Number of edges	Number of vertices
cube				
	square and triangles	5		5
	squares and rectangles	6		
hexagonal prism				

a) Christine has a bag full of different polyhedrons... She takes out two shapes.
   Can you work out what the shapes could be? Here are some clues.
   They have: A total of 11 faces
                 A total of 20 edges
                 A total of 13 vertices

b) Christine's baby brother has a toy box.
   Its dimensions are: 20 cm by 50 cm by 1 m
   How many 10 cm cubes would he need to fill it?

Challenge

Which of these nets will NOT make a 3D shape? Explain why.

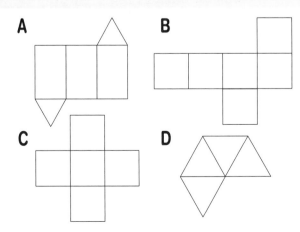

Position and direction

Position and direction questions can be about compass directions or finding a point on a grid. The problems can also be about horizontal or vertical lines.

Shanice programs her toy robot Robbie. He starts facing SE then makes a quarter turn clockwise. Which direction is Robbie facing now?

Read the question then read it again	Read slowly and carefully. Do I need to draw a picture?
Choose your operations and units	The answer is a direction so it should be one of the compass points.
Estimate your answer	A quarter turn to the right should make it SW I think.
Calculate	Using a drawn compass, move $\frac{1}{4}$ of a turn or 90 degrees from SE to... SW! Robbie is now facing SW.
Check your answer	A half turn would be NW so, looking back at my answer, SW looks right.

Hints and tips

★ Sketching a compass with the points labelled or a grid with the points plotted on are good ways of answering these problems systematically.

Questions

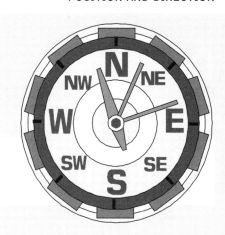

1

a) Robbie the robot is facing NW. He moves anti-clockwise through $\frac{1}{4}$ of a turn. Which direction is he facing now?

b) Robbie is facing south. He turns clockwise through 45°. Which direction is he facing now?

c) Robbie is facing east. He turns clockwise through 135°. Which direction is he facing now?

2

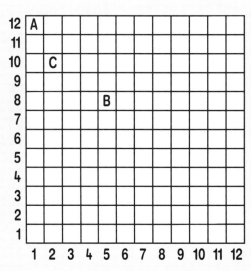

a) Without travelling north, use compass directions to describe the route from A to B to C.

b) Use coordinates to write instructions to draw a triangle. Ask a friend to follow your instructions to draw the shape.

Challenge

Use squared paper. Draw a plan of a garden. Include a path around a fountain in the middle.

Give instructions to a friend for moving around the garden from a starting point that you choose. You can use all 8 compass directions. Remember to tell your friend how many squares to move in each direction.

Data handling

Problems involving data handling often mean you
have to accurately read graphs, charts and tables.

Trevor was doing a survey on the number of passengers using his local station. He counted 25 people on the platform at the time of the 1:00 train. Can you draw the bar on the chart for him?

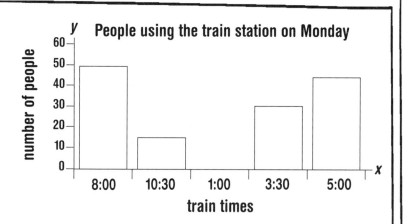

Read the question then read it again

Read the chart... 25 people... 1:00 train.

Choose your operations and units

I've got to draw a bar on the chart to show 25.

Estimate your answer

The top of the bar mustn't go over 30.

Calculate

Carefully mark the top of the bar, halfway between 20 and 30. Draw in the bar.

Check your answer

Read the completed graph. Yes, my graph is correct.

Hints and tips

★ Read the title of the graph, chart or table. What is it trying to tell you?   ★ Be careful when reading scales on graphs. Do they go up in 1s, 2s, 5s, 10s or 20s?

Questions

★**1**

a) How many people did Trevor count at the time of the 5:00 train?

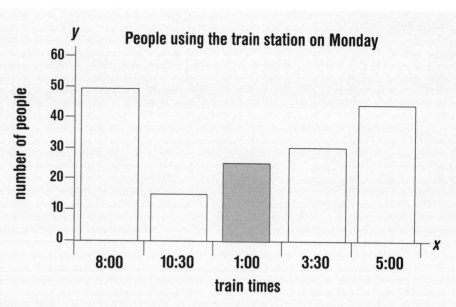

People using the train station on Monday

b) How many people did Trevor count at the time of the 10:30 train?

c) On a Monday, which train is most likely to be full?

★**2**

a) Trevor's results were very similar for Tuesday through to Friday. At what times of day do most people use the train from Trevor's local station? Why do you think this is?

b) How many people did Trevor count in total using the station on Monday?

★ # Challenge

Use squared paper. Can you draw the graph that Trevor might have drawn for people using the station on Sunday?

Two-step problems

Two-step problems have two steps! It is important to work out what each step is asking you to do before you complete it.

Ella counts 100 cars in a survey. Half are red, one quarter are blue, and the rest are white. How many cars were white?

Read the question then read it again

First find out how many cars are red and blue. Then subtract from 100.

Choose your operations and units

The units are cars. Add red and blue cars together then subtract from 100.

Estimate your answer

It is about $\frac{1}{4}$ of 100, so 25.

Calculate

$\frac{1}{2}$ of 100 = 50, $\frac{1}{4}$ of 100 = 25.
50 + 25 = 75
100 – 75 = 25
25 cars were white.

Check your answer

$\frac{1}{4}$ of 100 = 25. That is right!

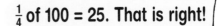

Hints and tips

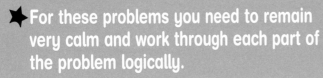 ★ For these problems you need to remain very calm and work through each part of the problem logically.

★ It is useful to number each step. That will help you.

Questions

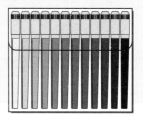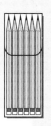

a) Ella buys 6 packets of pencils and 5 packets of felt-tipped pens. How many pencils and felt-tipped pens does she have altogether?

b) There are 153 books in the class book corner. If 30 children each take home two books, how many books are left in the book corner?

c) If four cakes cost £2.60, how much would three cakes cost?

2

a) Ella helps her mum to make coffee for her guests. They need to make 18 cups of coffee. Each cup has a capacity of 250 ml. How many times will they need to fill their kettle, which holds 1.5 l of water?

b) What is better value, one bottle or eight cans of Cola?

£1.29

17p

2 litre

Challenge

Two boys get 2 toys every day for a week.
Three girls get 3 toys every day for 3 days.
Who has the most toys, girls or boys?
Explain your working.

Mixed bag

These questions could be about anything! Read them carefully so you understand what you are being asked to do.

Marlon has 8 pet spiders. A spider has eight legs. How many spider legs does Marlon have altogether?

Read the question then read it again

8 spiders... each spider has 8 legs... how many legs?

Choose your operations and units

8 lots of 8. That's multiplication.

Estimate your answer

I know my 8 times table...

Calculate

$8 \times 8 = 64$
Marlon has 64 spider legs.

Check your answer

Have I answered the question? Yes, 64 is correct.

Hints and tips

★ When you have an answer to a problem, re-read the problem to check you have a sensible answer. Does it look correct?

Questions

1

a) Ebony thinks of a number. She subtracts 24 and she is left with 18.
What was Ebony's number?

b) Ricky is giving away his collection of 60 comics to 5 of his best friends.
How many comics does each lucky friend receive?

c) Max has 46 action figures. Josh has half as many again. How many
action figures does Josh have?

2

a) Can you change this recipe for trifle for
6 people to a recipe for 8 people?

Trifle
(serves 6)
330 ml cream
600 ml custard
540 g fruit
360 g of sponge
3 teaspoons of vanilla essence

b) The Shoemaker family are off on holiday in their camper van. They
drive for 862 miles. Ralph drives for 247 miles and Michael drives for
178 miles. How much further do they have to go?

Challenge

A street that's 30 m long has a horse chestnut tree every 6 m on both sides.
How many horse chestnut trees are on the entire street?

Answers

Place value

a) 900

b) 1400 km

c) 23, 15, 40

a) 5783, 97, 22266

b) i) Tick 500 multiplied by 100

   ii) Tick 6 groups of 10 000

   iii) Tick 5 × 1000

Challenge

98 631 or ninety-eight thousand, six hundred and thirty-one

12 589 or twelve thousand, five hundred and eighty-nine

Fractions

a) 500 m

b) 6 children

c) $\frac{1}{8}$

a) 6 sweets

b) $\frac{2}{5}$ is equivalent to $\frac{4}{10}$, which is more than $\frac{3}{10}$, so Stephanie has walked furthest.

Challenge

$3\frac{7}{8}$ kilometres or 3875 metres

Decimals

a) £11.70

b) 2.2 l

c) Tick and circle 11.9, Tick and circle 4.7, Tick 33.95

a) £18.75

b) £16.95

Challenge

Answers will vary.

Addition and subtraction

a) 101

b) 27

c) 435

a) 866

b) 425 m which is 17 lengths.

Challenge

Answers will vary but could include:

18 × 5p and 1 × 7p = 97

10 × 5p and 7 × 7p = 99

3 × 5p and 12 × 7p = 99

Money

a) £6.73

b) £11.26

c) The book and pack of pencils. He will get 26p change.

a) £7.30. £5.50 + 90p + 90p

b) 80p

Challenge

Answers will vary.

Time

a) 7:45
b) 8:52
c) 4:30

a) 1 and $\frac{1}{2}$ hours.
b) 13:55

Challenge
1ˢᵗ September.

Measures – mass

a) 3.7 kg
b) 8.4 kg
c) 200 g

a) Totals of 600 g in one bag and 1200 g in another.
b) Totals of 1000 g in one bag and 800 g in another.

Challenge
Answers will vary.

Measures – capacity

a) 16 l
b) 10 plants
c) 4 tins

a) 12 cups of tea.
b) 2.5 l lemonade, 350 ml fruit concentrate, 125 ml lemon juice.

Challenge
Selcuk should fill the 7 l jug first. He should then fill up the 3 l jug and pour that into the sink. He should then fill up the 3 l jug again. What is left in the 7 l jug is 1 l of liquid.

Measures – length

a) 325 cm or 3.25 m
b) 1.45 m
c) 60 cm

a) 1290 km
b) 15.5 m, 20 m, 20 m

Challenge
1 m

Puzzles

a) 36
b) 28. 1 + 2 + 3 + 4 + 6 + 12 = 28
c) 12, 24, 36, 48

a) 12, 13, 14. There aren't four consecutive numbers that total 39. The closest we can get to it is 38 (8, 9, 10, 11) or 42 (9, 10, 11, 12).
b) 6 and 12

Challenge
Answers will vary.

Patterns and sequences

a) 18, 11, 4
b) 162, 166, 170
c) 235, 232, 229

a) Shade in 40, 44, 48, 52, 56, 60, 64, 68, 72
b) Stop Nigel! The answer does not divide equally by 4, which is the pattern here.

Challenge
J for July. They are the first letters of the months of the year.

Multiplication and division

a) 36 eggs

b) 45 flowers

c) 6 marbles (with 2 left over)

a) 60p

b) 7 full sets of pencils

Challenge

They will first exercise together on day 10. They will then exercise together on days 20, 30 and 40. They exercise together every 10 days.

2D shapes

a) Answers will vary but could be square, triangle and pentagon or two rectangles and a square.

b) Answers will vary but could be two pentagons and two triangles or four rectangles. The total number of vertices is 16 and the total number of angles is 16. 16 is also the total number of sides.

c) The original shape is a triangle. The new shapes are triangles. Alternative answer: The original shape is a square (cut diagonally). The new shapes are triangles.

a)

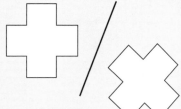

b) Answers will vary.

Challenge

The answer is 4. This is because there are only 360 degrees in any polygon.

3D shapes

Name of polyhedron	Shape of faces	Number of faces	Number of edges	Number of vertices
cube	square	6	12	8
square-based pyramid	square and triangles	5	8	5
cuboid	squares and rectangles	6	12	8
hexagonal prism	hexagons and rectangles	8	18	12

a) A square-based pyramid and a cube or cuboid

b) 100 cubes

Challenge

C and D will not make a 3D shape. C needs another square to make a cube. D needs a square to make a square-based pyramid.

Position and direction

a) South west

b) South west

c) South west

a) Go east 4 squares to (5, 12), then south 4 squares to (5, 8), then north west 2 squares to (3, 10), then west 1 square to (2, 10).

b) Answers will vary.

Challenge

Answers will vary.

Data handling

a) 45

b) 15

c) The 8 o'clock train.

a) Most people use the train in the mornings (8:00) and evenings (5:00) when they are going to and coming back from work.

b) 165

Challenge

Answers will vary but the graph should show fewer people using the train in the morning and evening than on week days.

Two-step problems

a) 36 pencils and 60 pens = 96

b) 93 books

c) £1.95

a) 3 times

b) One bottle

Challenge

The boys

Mixed bag

a) 42

b) 12 comics each

c) 69 action figures

a) 440ml cream, 800ml custard, 720g fruit, 480g of sponge, 4 teaspoons of vanilla essence.

b) 437 miles

Challenge

12 horse chestnut trees

Your notes